FRIENDS OF THE SUPREME COURT

INTEREST GROUPS AND JUDICIAL DECISION MAKING

FRIENDS OF THE SUPREME COURT

INTEREST GROUPS AND JUDICIAL DECISION MAKING

PAUL M. COLLINS, JR.

OXFORD
UNIVERSITY PRESS

Oxford University Press, Inc., publishes works that further Oxford University's objective of excellence in research, scholarship, and education.

Oxford New York
Auckland   Cape Town   Dar es Salaam   Hong Kong   Karachi   Kuala Lumpur   Madrid   Melbourne
Mexico City   Nairobi   New Delhi   Shanghai   Taipei   Toronto

With offices in
Argentina   Austria   Brazil   Chile   Czech Republic   France   Greece   Guatemala   Hungary   Italy
Japan   Poland   Portugal   Singapore   South Korea   Switzerland   Thailand   Turkey   Ukraine
Vietnam

Published by Oxford University Press, Inc. 198 Madison Avenue, New York, New York 10016
www.oup.com

Library of Congress Cataloging-in-Publication Data
Collins, Paul M., Jr.
    Friends of the Supreme Court : interest groups and judicial decision making / Paul M. Collins, Jr.
    p. cm.
        Includes bibliographical references and index.
        ISBN 978-0-19-537214-4 (alk. paper)
1. United States. Supreme Court. 2. Pressure groups—United States.
3. Constitutional law—United States—Decision making. 4. Political questions and
    judicial power—United States. I. Title.
    KF8742.C62 2008
    347.73'26—dc22
                                                                                2008021582

1 2 3 4 5 6 7 8 9

Printed in the United States of America
on acid-free paper

Note to Readers
This publication is designed to provide accurate and authoritative information in regard to the subject matter covered. It is based upon sources believed to be accurate and reliable and is intended to be current as of the time it was written. It is sold with the understanding that the publisher is not engaged in rendering legal, accounting, or other professional services. If legal advice or other expert assistance is required, the services of a competent professional person should be sought. Also, to confirm that the information has not been affected or changed by recent developments, traditional legal research techniques should be used, including checking primary sources where appropriate.

*(Based on the Declaration of Principles jointly adopted by a Committee of the
American Bar Association and a Committee of Publishers and Associations.)*

You may order this or any other Oxford University Press publication by
visiting the Oxford University Press website at www.oup.com

For Lisa and Wendy

CONTENTS

ACKNOWLEDGMENTS

If there ever was a time when a researcher worked alone in the pursuit of advancing knowledge, it was never known to me. Rather, in completing this work, I have benefitted from innumerable interactions with my colleagues, family, and friends. These ranged from quick chats in the hallway to informal barroom discussions over a Guinness at McCaffrey's Irish Pub to extended communications via email over the course of several years. While I bear all responsibility for any errors in fact or judgment contained in this work, I would be sinfully remiss to fail to acknowledge the assistance of a host of individuals and institutions whose support made this project possible.

The earliest incarnations of my work on amici curiae began at the University of Scranton, where I studied political science as an undergraduate. I entered "Da U" with an interest in the law that the faculty in the Departments of Political Science and Criminal Justice turned into an obsession. Indeed, it was at Scranton where I first came across the fact that interest groups use the judiciary, reading Walker and Epstein's (1993) introductory treatment of the Supreme Court (one of the few undergraduate texts I held onto). Confounded by what I viewed as an outlandish reality, I was intrigued. For encouraging an often bleary eyed undergraduate to pursue his passion, I thank Leonard Champney, Joseph Cimini, Jean Harris, Robert Kocis, William Parente, and Gretchen Van Dyke.

My education continued at Binghamton University, where I received my graduate degrees. The Political Science Department at Binghamton is an unbelievable place to study as it fosters both intellectual curiosity and collegiality. I am certain that my understanding of political science and law would not be the same without the solid theoretical and methodological training Binghamton provides. I am especially grateful to members of my dissertation committee. Tom Brunell went above and beyond the call of duty teaching me the ins-and-outs of Stata. Dave Clark was more than willing to provide methodological and theoretical assistance at a moment's notice. Dave Hacker, a quantitative historian, brought a unique perspective to bear that solidified for me the importance of interdisciplinary communication. Michael McDonald provided his patently sage advice throughout graduate school.

I am indebted to a number of scholars who offered their insights into previous iterations of this work and encouragement throughout the publication process. They remind me, time and time again, what a pleasure it is to be a social scientist. I am particularly grateful to Vanessa Baird, Sara Benesh, Eileen Braman, Bob Carp, Sue Collins, Pam Corley, Jolly Emrey, Lee Epstein, Matt Eshbaugh-Soha, Tom Hansford, Stefanie Lindquist, Chris Nemacheck, Jeff Segal, Harold Spaeth, Amy Steigerwalt, Rich Vining, Art Ward, Steve Wasby, and Chris Zorn. For his intrepid research assistance, I thank Chris Nicholson. For their unparalleled generosity, I am indebted to Joe Kearney, Thomas Merrill, and Harold Spaeth for sharing their data with me. I also thank my friends and colleagues at the University of Houston and the University of North Texas for putting up with my sometimes overzealous interest in friends of the Court.

I am grateful to the National Science Foundation for providing me with a research grant that enabled me to collect the data used in this analysis. The Department of Political Science at the University of North Texas afforded me course reductions and a collegial working environment for which I am extremely thankful. The dissertation on which portions of this book are based received the 2006 Council of Graduate Schools/University Microfilm International Distinguished Dissertation Award, recognizing it as the most distinguished dissertation in the social sciences defended between July 2004 and June 2006. My thanks go to the Council of Graduate Schools and the members of the award committee for their feedback and encouragement.

Although this book represents an original effort at untangling the influence of amici curiae on the Supreme Court, it has many antecedents. Portions of it previously appeared as "Lobbyists before the U.S. Supreme Court: Investigating the Influence of Amicus Curiae Briefs" in *Political Research Quarterly* (Volume 60, pp. 55–70) and "Amici Curiae and Dissensus on the U.S. Supreme Court" in the *Journal of Empirical Legal*

Studies (Volume 5, pp. 143–170). In addition, early versions of this research were presented at the annual meetings of the American Political Science Association (2005), New York State Political Science Association (2005), and Southern Political Science Association (2004, 2006). Special thanks go to the many colleagues who offered comments and critiques of those incarnations of this work.

I am particularly grateful to the team at Oxford University Press. Chris Collins took a chance on a young scholar, as well as the accompanying burden of guiding a novice through the publication process. I hope to have done him proud. I thank Isel Pizarro and Mark LaFlaur who were always quick to respond to any detail, no matter how mundane, relating to the publication process. I am additionally grateful to the three reviewers for providing outstanding feedback and encouragement.

The creative juices need to flow beyond the confines of one's formal education and professional employment, and I am eternally grateful to have a wonderful network of family and friends who allow my creativity to gush. Far too many to list here, they know who they are. I am especially thankful to my mother, the teacher, and my father, the attorney, for their encouragement and support on this endeavor. Perhaps it was destined that their son would grow up to teach (and write about) law. I also wish to extend my thanks to my brother, Pat, and sisters, Kelly and Katie. Their sharp wits and down-to-earth personalities make me proud to be their older brother.

It is not unfair to say that I have two women in my life: my wife (and sometimes collaborator) Lisa Solowiej and my mentor (and sometimes collaborator) Wendy Martinek. Through thick and thin, both Lisa and Wendy have always been by my side. They have helped me grow, both personally and professionally, into the person and scholar I am today. For their unending support and inspiration, I dedicate this book to Lisa and Wendy.

CHAPTER 1

Introduction

E. Schattschneider (1960) begins his celebrated treatise on the interest group system in American politics by discussing a fight that broke out in Harlem between a police officer and a soldier that inadvertently resulted in a riot, injuring some four hundred individuals and causing millions of dollars in property damage. Schattschneider's purpose in recounting the story was to highlight the fact that every conflict has two parts: "(1) the few individuals who are actively engaged at the center and (2) the audience that is irresistibly attracted to the scene" (1960: 2). Though those who are at the center of conflict no doubt play an important role in shaping its course, it is the audience who, according to Schattschneider, "do the kinds of things that determine the outcome of the fight" (2).

While Schattschneider's analogy was principally intended to underscore the significant role that interest groups perform in defining the scope of the conflict in the electoral arena, a more apt analogy regarding interest groups in the courts was perhaps never written. Each case presented to the U.S. Supreme Court involves at least two entities that have been involved in the dispute since its inception. For the most part, these litigants have defined the scope of the conflict in the trial and intermediate appellate courts. Discontented with the outcome in the appellate court, one of these litigants appeals to the Supreme Court, which agrees to hear the case. At this point, the audience becomes irresistibly attracted to the scene.

That audience—organized interests—becomes directly involved in the conflict through the filing of amicus curiae ("friend of the court") briefs: legal briefs submitted by entities other than the parties to litigation that aim to persuade the justices to rule in the manner advocated in the briefs. Once this audience becomes involved, the scope of the conflict grows. The amici provide the justices with myriad information regarding their perceptions of the correct application of the law in the case, at the same time highlighting diverse perspectives on the broader policy concerns implicated by the dispute.

This adversarial role of amicus briefs in American jurisprudence comports with the fact that the courts serve as battlegrounds for social and economic policy (Jhering 1913). In this mode, rather than merely deciding narrow legal controversies with little societal importance, courts, and the Supreme Court in particular, act as policy makers (e.g., Casper 1976; Dahl 1957; Segal and Spaeth 1993, 2002). On a regular basis, the Court grapples with a host of issues that have profound significance for the American polity. In recent years, the justices have adjudicated cases involving the rights of enemy combatants detained in connection with the war on terror (e.g., *Hamdan v. Rumsfeld* 2006), the ability of homosexuals to engage in intimate sexual conduct free from governmental interference (*Lawrence v. Texas* 2003), as well as the authority of local governments to transfer private property from one private owner to another in the name of economic development (*Kelo v. City of New London* 2005). And, of course, one would be remiss to ignore the fact that the Court effectively decided the outcome of the 2000 presidential election between George W. Bush and Al Gore (*Bush v. Gore* 2000).

It is precisely the Court's policy-making role that motivates organized interests to attempt to shape its legal and policy outputs by filing amicus briefs. In this sense, interest groups subscribe to an instrumentalist view of the law—using the law as a means to achieve their varied ends (e.g., Dewey 1916; Jhering 1913). In a recent treatment of legal instrumentalism, Tamanaha describes the willingness of organizations to use the judicial arena to etch their policy preferences into law:

> In situations of sharp disagreement over the social good, when law is perceived as a powerful instrument, individuals and groups within society will endeavor to seize or co-opt the law in every way possible; to fill in, interpret, manipulate, and utilize the law to serve their own ends. . . . Even those groups that might prefer to

abstain from these battles over law will nonetheless be forced to engage in the contest, if only defensively to keep their less restrained opponents from using the law as hammer against them. (2006: 1–2)

That groups exploit the legal arena to pursue their policy preferences presents an interesting conundrum to our understanding of judicial decision making. On the one hand, organized interests' use of the judiciary to further their economic, political, and social agendas acts as a challenge to the idealistic view of judges as almost omniscient decision makers who are so well versed in the corpus of law that the very idea of needing outside assistance to render their decisions is anathema. On the other hand, by informing jurists of the broader legal and policy ramifications of their decision making, interest group amicus activity fosters democratic input into the judicial area, potentially improving the quality of judicial decision making. Notwithstanding one's position on the normative debate surrounding the appropriateness of organizational activity in the Supreme Court, the potential influence of these groups on the justices is clearly an area of essential scholarly importance.

The purpose of this book is to scientifically analyze and explain the influence of interest group amicus curiae activity on Supreme Court decision making. To do this, I examine three avenues of influence. First, consistent with the dominant empirical approach to understanding the choices justices make (e.g., Pritchett 1948; Rohde and Spaeth 1976; Schubert 1974; Segal and Spaeth 1993, 2002; Sunstein, Schkade, Ellman, and Sawicki 2006), I explore the influence of amicus briefs on the ideological direction of the individual justices' votes. In developing two alternative informational theories for the influence of amicus briefs, this analysis provides the opportunity to engage the debate as to whether the justices' decision making is best explained as a function of their policy preferences or whether the justices are receptive to instruments of legal persuasion. Second, I analyze the effect of amicus briefs on variability in the justices' decision making (i.e., the error variance associated with the justices' choices). A novel perspective for understanding the influence of legal considerations, my approach sheds light on how legal influences— by undermining the justices' policy preferences and creating uncertainty with respect to the correct application of the law—are capable of reducing consistency in judicial decision making. Finally, I explore the relationship between amicus briefs and separate opinion writing, building on the notion that amicus briefs increase the ambiguity in the justices' already uncertain decision making. In so doing, I illustrate how organized interests who are unsuccessful at influencing the Court's majority can achieve a partial victory by contributing to a justice's decision to write or join a separate opinion. Taken as a whole, by investigating the influence of amicus briefs on three separate aspects of Supreme Court decision making, my goal is to provide a theoretically rich and empirically rigorous treatment of the relationship between organized interests and decision making on the nation's highest court.

I. An Area of Confusion

Although the justices seldom discuss the factors that influence their decision making outside the context of the opinions that accompany their decisions, several justices have nonetheless provided their perspectives as to the utility of amicus curiae briefs. Considered collectively, these statements reveal that the justices both value the informational content of amicus briefs and believe the briefs influence their decision making. Justice Breyer describes amicus briefs as follows:

> [amicus] briefs play an important role in educating the judges on potentially relevant technical matters, helping make us not experts, but moderately educated lay persons, and that education helps to improve the quality of our decisions. (1998: 26)

Justice O'Connor corroborates Breyer's perspective in noting that:

> The "friends" who appear today usually file briefs calling our attention to points of law, policy considerations, or other points of view that the parties themselves have not discussed. These amicus briefs invaluably aid our decision-making process and often influence either the result or the reasoning of our opinions. (1996: 9)

Similarly, Justice Douglas recognizes the value of amicus briefs in the following sentiment:

> In more recent years, the Court has been quite liberal about granting [amicus] briefs and I think that on the whole they serve a very useful purpose. We had some extraordinarily fine briefs by certain groups in the field of civil liberties. We've had some very fine amicus briefs on economic matters pertaining to Interstate Commerce by interested companies who would be affected

perhaps in another state by the ruling in a case where the state was before us. They have been, I think, very helpful and I think that even though they, the Court[,] denies them the permission to file, that they are always read. (1962: 1)[1]

Considering the above quotations from Justices Breyer, O'Connor, and Douglas, one might suspect that it is the conventional wisdom that amicus curiae briefs influence the decision making of Supreme Court justices. Interestingly, however, this is far from the case. Rather, scholars have reached the general consensus that amicus briefs, with the exception of those briefs filed by Solicitors General,[2] have little measurable influence on the justices' decision making on the merits (e.g., McGuire 2002: 156; Segal and Spaeth 1993: 241; Segal, Spaeth, and Benesh 2005: 329; Stumpf 1998: 401; Walker and Epstein 1993: 139). This state of affairs presents an interesting puzzle. If amicus briefs fail to influence the decision making of Supreme Court justices, why are the justices so willing to publicly speak to their influence; do they know something that judicial scholars do not? To put it another way, who is right, the justices or the academics? In an attempt to answer this question, I consider the strengths and weaknesses of the research designs employed in the more than fifty published studies dealing with amicus influence in the Court.[3] My conclusions about the extant literature are two-fold. First, past research only contributes to the confusion surrounding the issue. Second, rigorous and systematic analysis is needed to determine if amicus briefs influence the justices' decision making and, if so, how and under what circumstances.

No influence [handwritten margin note]

---

1 The phenomenon that Douglas highlights regarding denying amici permission to file is discussed in Chapter 3.
2 The Office of Solicitor General consists of the team of attorneys that represents the executive branch in the Supreme Court.
3 See Acker (1990, 1993); Alger and Krislov (2004); Barker (1967); Behuniak-Long (1991); Bersoff and Ogden (1991); Chauncey (2004); Chen (2007); Colker (2007); Collins (2004a, 2007); Day (2001); Ennis (1984); Epstein (1985, 1993); Epstein and Kobylka (1992); Eskridge (2002); Goodman, Levine, Melton, and Ogden (1991); Harper and Etherington (1953); Hassler and O'Connor (1986); Heberlig and Spill (2000); Hedman (1991); Ivers and O'Connor (1987); Kearney and Merrill (2000); Kobylka (1987); Kolbert (1989); Krislov (1963); Lawrence (1989); Manz (2002); McGuire (1990, 1995); McLauchlan (2005); Moorman and Masteralexis (2001); Morris (1987); Morriss (1999); Nicholson-Crotty (2007); O'Connor (1980); O'Connor and Epstein (1982a, 1983a); O'Neill (1985); Parker (1999); Pfeffer (1981); Puro (1971); Roesch, Golding, Hans, and Reppucci (1991); Ross and Catalano (1988); Rushin and O'Connor (1987); Samuels (1995, 2004); Schwartz and Boland (1995); Songer and Sheehan (1993); Spriggs and Wahlbeck (1997); Sungaila (1999); Tai (2000); Tremper (1987); Vose (1955, 1959); Wasby (1995); Wohl (1996); and Wrightsman (1999).

Although the first amicus curiae appeared before the Supreme Court in the early 1800s (Banner 2003; Covey 1959; Harris 2000), it took academics almost a full century to recognize that interest groups play an active role in lobbying the courts (Bentley 1908). While Truman's (1951) study of interest groups in the United States provided further evidence to corroborate Bentley's (1908) assertions regarding interest group participation in the judiciary, scholars as late as the 1960s dismissed this notion as little more than "political science folklore" (Hakman 1966; but see Harper and Etherington 1953; Krislov 1963; Vose 1955, 1958, 1959). However, in one of the first large-scale analyses of amicus participation in the Court, Puro (1971) demonstrated perhaps the only area on which legal scholars would reach consensus involving pressure group activity in the judiciary: interest group amicus participation in the Court is now the norm, not the exception (Bradley and Gardner 1985; Caldeira and Wright 1990; Kearney and Merrill 2000; Wohl 1996). While this has reached the status of conventional wisdom, much disagreement exists regarding whether amicus briefs influence the decision making of the justices; below, I address how this dissensus came to fruition.

Baumgartner and Leech (1998) posit that the academic literature on interest groups can be divided into areas of advance and areas of confusion, a differentiation directly applicable to the study of amici curiae. Areas of advance, they argue, exist because scholars have worked within a similar theoretical framework, such studies have adopted a relatively large empirical scope, and these studies pay attention to the import of the context of group participation. Literature falling into the area of advance is said to contribute to our accumulation of knowledge. Contrary to this, areas of confusion occur when there is a growth of research within an area but little or no accumulation of knowledge. I propose that research on amicus participation falls into the latter category. As evidence, I submit the following examples of research on amicus briefs that relate to Baumgartner and Leech's (1998) arguments.

Baumgartner and Leech (1998) contend that areas of confusion amass largely because scholars examine only a few groups,[4] study a limited

---

4 See, e.g., Harper and Etherington (1953), examining primarily the American Jewish Congress; Ivers and O'Connor (1987), analyzing the American Civil Liberties Union and Americans for Effective Law Enforcement; and Vose (1955, 1959), focusing on the National Association for the Advancement of Colored People.

number of issue areas[5] or cases,[6] and analyze group influence over a relatively short period.[7] With regard to studying only a few groups, issue
areas, or cases, while these studies may provide valuable theoretical
insight(s) into interest group impact on the Court, such studies are limited in terms of generalizability beyond the foci of their attention. For
example, although Hassler and O'Connor (1986) provide evidence that
specific groups' amicus briefs play an important role in environmental
litigation, it is unclear whether this group influence is limited to environmental law, a function of the groups being studied, or is more generally
applicable to Supreme Court litigation as a whole. Moreover, scholars
studying particular groups or issue areas may select these groups and
issue areas precisely because they expect to find evidence of interest group
influence. As Segal and Spaeth (1993: 241) note, "Few people want to
spend a year or two studying losing litigators." With regard to examining
group influence over a relatively short period of time, an obvious criticism
presents itself: these studies' findings may be an artifact of the time period
under analysis and therefore limited in terms of applicability beyond the
period under investigation.

Further, confusion has manifested itself regarding this topic because
scholars have used imprecise or incomplete measures to gauge the influence of amicus briefs on Supreme Court decision making. The most
common method used to measure the influence of amicus briefs on the
Court is to calculate the proportion of winning litigants with amicus
briefs supporting their position.[8] Typically speaking, this is simply
the number of times the litigant with amicus support prevailed divided
by the total number of times that litigant participated in the Court.[9]

# of briefs

---

5 See, e.g., McGuire (1990), exploring obscenity law; O'Connor and Epstein (1982a),
   analyzing employment discrimination litigation; Samuels (2004) investigating privacy
   litigation; Vose (1959), examining restrictive covenant cases; and Wasby (1995), focusing
   on race relations law.
6 See, e.g., Samuels (1995), examining *U.A.W. v. Johnson Controls* (1991); Parker (1999),
   investigating *Washington v. Glucksberg* (1997) and *Vacco v. Quill* (1997); and Moorman
   and Masteralexis (2001), analyzing *PGA Tour, Inc. v. Martin* (2001).
7 See, e.g., McGuire (1995), analyzing a six-year sample of the Court's docket and Epstein
   (1993), examining interest group litigation during the Rehnquist Court era.
8 See, e.g., Epstein (1993), Hassler and O'Connor (1986), Ivers and O'Connor (1987),
   Kearney and Merrill (2000), Kobylka (1987), Morris (1987), O'Connor and Epstein
   (1982a), Puro (1971), Rushin and O'Connor (1987), and Songer and Sheehan (1993).
9 Other variations of this approach exist. E.g., Ivers and O'Connor (1987) measure the
   amicus' winning percentage by dividing the number of times that the litigant the amicus
   supported prevailed over the total number of times the amicus filed a brief (see also Segal
   1988). Kearney and Merrill (2000) calculate the litigant's winning percentage when

Though this measure may appear intuitively appealing, in fact, it is quite problematic. Specifically, scholars using this measure to gauge the influence of amicus briefs on the Court fail to control for more established influences on judicial decision making, such as the justices' ideologies (but see Songer and Sheehan 1993).

> For instance, it may be possible to show that the Warren Court supported the position taken by the NAACP Legal Defense Fund, Inc. (LDF) in every desegregation case before it. But this does not necessarily mean that the Court was *influenced* by the LDF. The liberal Warren Court most likely would have supported desegregation with or without the support of the LDF. Before influence can be inferred, we must show that an actor in the Court's environment had an independent impact after controlling for other factors. (Segal and Spaeth 1993: 237)

A second measure of amicus influence on the Court consists of tallying citations to amicus briefs found in the justices' opinions.[10] However, this "blunt indicator" is not without its own problems. For example, justices may adopt arguments or respond to amicus briefs without making a direct reference to the briefs (O'Connor and Epstein 1983a; Samuels 2004). Further, Roesch, Golding, Hans, and Reppucci (1991) argue that the justices, because they are not trained in the sciences, may be reluctant to cite empirical research even when it influences their decision making. This is a particularly devastating contention for studies that rely on citation counts because "The most common method of introducing social science evidence to the Court is through 'non-record evidence' in amicus curiae briefs" (Rustad and Koenig 1993: 94). Thus, although studies that rely on tallying citations to amicus briefs may provide some leverage over whether the briefs are read,[11] these analyses offer little assistance in determining whether amicus briefs genuinely influence the behavior of the justices.[12]

---

it has one more amicus brief than its opponent, when the same number of briefs are filed for both sides, when it has one less amicus brief filed than its opponent, and so on.

10 See, e.g., Behuniak-Long (1991), Epstein (1993), Harper and Etherington (1953), Hedman (1991), Kearney and Merrill (2000), Kolbert (1989), Parker (1999), and Tai (2000).

11 Of course, using citation counts to determine if the briefs are read is similarly problematic to using such counts to evaluate if the briefs influence the justices' decision making. The justices no doubt read many briefs without referring to them in their opinions.

12 The most common variation of tallying citations in the justices' opinions is to determine whether the justices adopted arguments made by the amici in their opinions,

�️ "most useful"

Finally, perhaps the most useful studies on the influence of amicus briefs come from the controlled analyses of Collins (2004a), Kearney and Merrill (2000), McGuire (1990, 1995), and Songer and Sheehan (1993). However, all these studies examine the influence of amicus briefs using litigation success as the dependent variable (i.e., win or lose) and treat the Court as a unitary actor.[13] That is, rather than attempting to determine whether amicus briefs influence the directionality of the *votes* of the justices (i.e., liberal or conservative), these studies examine whether amicus briefs influence the *outcome* of the case. While not without merit, these studies provide little insight as to *why* amicus briefs might influence the decision making of the justices because "the model that best explains the Court's decisions may not fit the behavior of the individual justices" (Hagle and Spaeth 1993: 493). Indeed, judicial scholars have compellingly demonstrated that the justice-vote may be the most useful unit of analysis when attempting to explain influences on judicial decision making (Gibson 1983; Giles and Zorn 2000; Segal 1986). Perhaps more important, however, is the fact that these studies offer little to no theoretical guidance as to why amicus briefs should influence litigant success (McGuire 1995; Songer and Sheehan 1993; but see Collins 2004a; Kearney and Merrill 2000; McGuire 1990).[14]

✦ outcome v. votes

---

with or without citations to the briefs (e.g., Day 2001; Samuels 2004; Spriggs and Wahlbeck 1997; Sungaila 1999; Tai 2000; Wohl 1996). Similar to citation tallies, this method is problematic because the justices may adopt arguments made by amici merely as *post hoc* rationalizations for decisions influenced by other factors, such as their personal policy preferences.

13 Specifically, Collins (2004a), Kearney and Merrill (2000), McGuire (1995), and Songer and Sheehan (1993) use a dichotomous dependent variable measuring the success of the petitioning party. McGuire (1990) uses an alternative approach that captures the number of justices voting in favor of the libertarian position in obscenity cases. For an exception to focusing on litigation success, see Collins (2007), analyzing the influence of amicus briefs on the ideological direction of the Court's decisions.

14 Though McGuire (1995) and Songer and Sheehan (1993) fail to provide a compelling theory as to why amicus briefs might influence judicial decision making, McGuire (1990) makes the argument that, because the litigants in obscenity cases may be viewed by the justices as "scurvey little creatures" (56), amicus support may enable the justices to distinguish between claims that appear to be plainly prurient versus those that raise legitimate constitutional concerns. Clearly, however, such an assertion has little application beyond obscenity law because the lascivious nature of pornography is rarely implicated in cases falling outside of this issue area. In addition, Collins (2004a, 2007) and Kearney and Merrill (2000) argue that the influence of amicus briefs is best explained by the fact that amicus briefs present the justices with arguments that might not otherwise be available to them, packaging amicus influence in a legal persuasion framework. However, these studies fail to consider the possible interplay between the justices' ideologies and amicus briefs.

✦

There is little doubt that previous attempts to understand the possible influence of amici curiae in the Supreme Court have resulted in an area of confusion. Given this, it should hardly be surprising that judicial scholars have generally rejected the notion that amicus briefs influence the justices' decision making. By examining only a few groups or issue areas, a relatively short time frame, or proceeding without well developed theory, previous work has clearly resulted in a literature that grows but does not accumulate. Simply put, there is not enough research to date that establishes whether amicus briefs influence the justices' decision making. Thus, the currently available evidence allows me to neither accept nor deny the justices' claims that amicus briefs genuinely shape their decision calculi.

A. Moving Forward

With the goal of providing a richer and more rigorous treatment of the influence of amicus participation on the Court than currently exists, this book moves beyond past studies in a variety of ways. First, and most significantly, I develop a theoretical framework to understand why amicus briefs might influence the decision making of the justices. Incorporating theories developed in law, political science, social psychology, and a variety of other disciplines, I present informational theories of amici curiae that are attentive to both the goals of the amici and the justices. Importantly, while empirical tests of the theories focus on investigating the influence of amicus curiae briefs, this research provides a novel perspective on judicial decision making that is applicable to other aspects of judicial choice.

In addition, unlike past studies that focus on only one potential avenue for amicus influence, I explore the influence of amicus curiae briefs on three aspects of the choices justices make. First, I examine how amicus briefs might shape the ideological direction of the individual justices' votes. Distinct from previous studies that examine amicus influence on, for example, litigation success, this research strategy offers leverage over whether the justices are uniformly affected by amicus briefs or whether the influence of the briefs is contingent on the justices' policy preferences. Second, I explore the influence of amicus briefs on variability in the justices' voting behavior. Building on interdisciplinary theories of information overload, this allows me to explore how amicus briefs can create uncertainty for the justices as to the correct application of the law

in the case. Third, I investigate the influence of amicus briefs on the decision to author or join a separate opinion. In so doing, I illustrate how
the primary means for democratic input into the judiciary (amicus
briefs) relates to the central mechanism of democratic output (judicial
opinions) (Bennett 2001).

Moreover, distinct from the majority of extant examinations, I do
not focus on only a few groups or issue areas, nor do I analyze an abbreviated time frame. Instead, this book investigates the influence of amicus
activity in cases disposed of by the Court during the 1946–2001 terms.
While this forces me to forgo the detail that accompanies the study of a
single issue area (e.g., Epstein and Kobylka 1992; Samuels 2004), I believe
this sacrifice is more than compensated for by the generalizability this
study provides.

By embarking on this task, I hope to contribute to a better understanding of the influence of amicus curiae briefs on Supreme Court
justices. Above, I have presented evidence that scholars have failed—both
empirically and theoretically—to reach consensus as to whether amicus
briefs influence the justices' decision making. The research contained in
this book will offer both theoretical and empirical clarity on this issue.
Beyond answering this fundamental puzzle, this book aims to further our
understanding of interest group politics and judicial decision making, as
well as the decision making of political actors more generally.

It adds to the interest group literature by providing additional
insights into both group strategies and effectiveness. Though there is a
reasonably large body of research devoted to both of these issues, only
dissensus exists regarding the effectiveness of amicus briefs in the Supreme
Court. Further, by exploring organized interests' goals and motivations
for participating in the court system, this research will increase our knowledge as to the all-too-often overlooked (in the interest group literature)
litigation strategies of organized interests.[15]

This book also aspires to further our comprehension of the applications and limitations of the legal and attitudinal models of judicial decision making. By considering the influence of amicus briefs in light of
these two important theories of judicial choice, this research offers leverage over the robustness of these models, highlighting both their strengths

---

15 Consider, e.g., that a discussion of organized interests' use of the courts receives less
than ten pages of cumulative treatment in two of the most widely used texts on organized interests (Berry 1997; Cigler and Loomis 2002).

and weaknesses. In so doing, I hope to provide a more comprehensive understanding of the many factors that shape judicial decision making than currently exists.

Finally, a central contribution of this research lies in the information theory that I develop. Briefly, the theory that I formulate endeavors to explain how political actors with ideological goals respond to persuasive communication that sometimes supports and sometimes is contrary to these goals. Because this theory is general in its nature—in the sense that it is applicable to any political actor—it will be of use not only to legal scholars but also to those interested in the determinants of decision making more broadly.

II. Plan of the Book

Prior to presenting a chapter overview, it is useful to discuss the theoretical and methodological approaches taken in this book. Students of the Supreme Court generally work within one of three theoretical perspectives to explain the choices justices make: the legal, attitudinal, or strategic models. Proponents of the legal model focus primarily on how legal influences—framers' intent, the meaning of words, precedent, and persuasion—influence the justices' decision making. Under the legal model, the justices are viewed as neutral decision makers who set their personal preferences aside when rendering their decisions. That is, the justices are expected to rule consistent with their legal training by attempting to discover correct legal answers (e.g., Dworkin 1978, 1991). Conversely, advocates of the attitudinal model assert that the justices' decision making is primarily a function of their policy preferences. Lacking ambition for higher office, political accountability, and constituting a court of last resort that controls its own jurisdiction, the justices are argued to operate within an institutional setting that frees them to vote in accordance with their attitudinal predilections (e.g., Segal and Spaeth 2002). Finally, advocates of strategic models propose that while the justices' decisions are primarily motivated by policy concerns (thus accepting the attitudinal model), institutional constraints exist that limit the ability of the justices to vote in a manner that is compatible with their attitudes and values in every case. Instead, proponents of strategic models note that the justices might also consider the preferences of Congress, the president, and other justices when rendering their decisions and crafting opinions (e.g., Epstein and Knight 1998; Maltzman, Spriggs, and Wahlbeck 2000).

Throughout this volume, I work primarily within the two dominant approaches to judicial decision making—the legal and attitudinal models (although I do discuss and incorporate aspects of strategic models when appropriate). However, unlike previous studies that operate wholly within the confines of these paradigms, I incorporate a wide range of theoretical perspectives to expand on our conceptions of these models of judicial choice. In this sense, the perspective taken in this volume is diverse in its disciplinary nature. My motivation for adopting this modus operandi is a function of the recognition that the study of the law is inherently interdisciplinary: anthropologists, economists, historians, law professors, linguists, philosophers, political scientists, psychologists, sociologists, and the like all inform our understanding of the law. By assimilating these perspectives to offer leverage over Supreme Court decision making, I am confident that a more complete picture of how the justices render their decisions will be offered. Thus, the reader will regularly come across theories developed in other disciplines incorporated with theoretical perspectives that are familiar to political scientists and legal scholars. It will be fairly common to observe references to a wide array of literatures— history, law, political science, social psychology, and even marketing research—throughout this volume. In applying these varying perspectives on human decision making to explain the behavior of Supreme Court justices, I hope to reduce the communication barriers that too often exist between social scientists and legal scholars across varying disciplines (Cross 1997; Rosenberg 2000).

Just as there are a host of theoretical approaches relevant to the study of judicial behavior, there also exists a wide array of research strategies (i.e., methodologies). The traditional approach to understanding judicial decisions focuses on the analysis of legal doctrine (e.g., court opinions, executive orders, and legislative statutes; often in relation to one another). In its most basic form, this type of doctrinal analysis involves investigating what judges say they do. This is the approach most common to law schools, familiarly known as the case study method, which was originally advocated by Christopher Columbus Langdell at Harvard Law School in the 1870s. Although it is not necessarily associated with a theoretical perspective on judicial choice, this methodology is, nonetheless, commonly implemented to support legal versions of judicial decision making and for good reason. It is undeniable that one is hard pressed to find *any* Supreme Court decisions that lack consistency with at least one of the tenets of the legal model in its justification (Segal and Spaeth 1993, 2002).

While this methodological perspective dominated the analysis of judicial decision making in its formative years, beginning at the turn of the twentieth century a group of scholars known as the legal realists pushed to move the study of judicial choice away from using purely doctrinal analysis to incorporate techniques used in the social sciences, including economics, psychology, and sociology (e.g., Cohen 1935; Frank 1930; Holmes 1897; Llewellyn 1931; Yntema 1934). In part, this movement was a reaction to formalistic versions of judicial decision making that focused on what judges said they did, rather than how judges responded to particular stimuli (Tamanaha 2006).[16] Thus, for the legal realists, the scientific study of the law was a necessary condition to accurately understand the determinants of judicial decision making.

Despite their commitment to the scientific understanding of judicial choice, few realists actively practiced scientific inquiry (Leiter 2005). Rather, the scientific approach to judicial choice saw its genesis in the post–World War II behavioral revolution in political science (Segal and Spaeth 1993: 67). In pioneering work, Pritchett (1948) systematically analyzed voting blocs on the Roosevelt Court, while Schubert (1965) applied Guttman scales to describe the ideological nature of Supreme Court decision making. With these seminal studies, the realist call for the scientific study of judicial decision making had finally come to fruition. The current research follows this methodological tradition. That is, consistent with a voluminous body of work in political science and an increasingly large corpus of research in empirical legal studies, I use the tools of statistical inference to investigate the influence of amicus briefs on the Supreme Court. Though the statistical techniques employed here are somewhat sophisticated, the reader should take heart that I have endeavored to translate the core findings in as straightforward a manner as possible by interpreting the results in substantively meaningful ways, often relying on graphs to facilitate understanding.

Having laid out the theoretical and methodological perspectives used in this book, I will now turn to providing a chapter overview. In Chapter 2, I explore why interest groups use the judicial arena, the methods available to them in pursuing litigation, and the goals of organized interests in the courts. Chapter 3 provides a detailed treatment of the role of friends of the court, beginning with the historical origins of amici curiae and

---

16 See Tamanaha (2007) for an enlightening treatment of prelegal realist critiques of formalism.

culminating with a discussion of amici curiae in the contemporary Supreme Court. The remainder of this book is dedicated to theory development, as well as the formulation and empirical testing of my hypotheses. Chapter 4 examines the influence of amicus briefs on the ideological direction of the justices' voting behavior. In Chapter 5, I analyze the potential for amicus briefs to influence the consistency of judicial choice. Chapter 6 builds on these previous chapters by investigating whether amicus curiae briefs contribute to a justice's decision to write or join a separate opinion. Chapter 7 discusses the implications of this book for the scientific study of judicial decision making and pressure group activity in the Court, as well as that of the information processing theory that I develop. It closes with a discussion as to where future research in this area might head.

Two final thoughts are in order. First, the focus of this book is on the primary method of interest group participation in the Supreme Court: amicus curiae briefs filed in the Court's decisions on the merits. As such, I do not provide a treatment of amicus activity during the certiorari stage, nor do I cover the role of amici in oral arguments. These two important avenues for amicus participation have been rigorously covered by other scholars (e.g., Caldeira and Wright 1988; Johnson 2004; Johnson and Roberts 2004). To give them the attention they deserve would extend the length of this volume to mammoth proportions. Second, to maintain the substantive focus of this research, I do not rehash previously covered methodological issues implicated in the study of amicus briefs. Elsewhere (Collins 2004a, 2007), I have examined a variety of factors that might confound the influence of amicus briefs. These findings can be summarized as follows: (1) the impact of amicus briefs has not been attenuated over time (Collins 2007); (2) the influence of amicus briefs is not contingent on the salience or complexity of a case (2007); and (3) organized interests do not file amicus briefs for the sole purpose of appearing efficacious (i.e., in cases they are predisposed to win) (Collins 2004a, 2007).

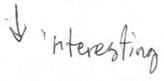 'nteresting

CHAPTER 2

Interest Group Litigation

Interest groups play a role in virtually every aspect of American national politics (Bentley 1908). In their most exalted form, representatives from pressure groups filled the smoky hallways of the House and Senate, patiently waiting for Representatives and Senators to emerge and willingly hear from the voices of the citizenry. While pressure politics have lost much of this sense of romanticism, due in part to allegations of scandal and corruption, interest groups nonetheless remain a mainstay in Washington politics. And, despite the fact that groups are most commonly associated with the elected branches of government—be it through the financing of political campaigns, the dissemination of information to executive agencies, or the everyday lobbying of members of the House and Senate— organizations nevertheless play a major role in judicial politics as well, particularly at the Supreme Court. To be sure, however, the lobbying of Supreme Court justices looks very different than the interactions between interest groups and elected officials. In fact, one attempt to personally lobby the justices resulted in a disastrous state of affairs, ultimately backfiring on the lobbyist.[17] Rather, interest group participation in the

---

17 Woodward and Armstrong (1979: 79–85) report that when Thomas G. "Tommy the Cork" Corcoran, a gas lobbyist, attempted to persuade Justices Black and Brennan to grant a rehearing of *Utah Public Service Commission v. El Paso Natural Gas Co.* (1969), what resulted was an extremely unusual set of circumstances. While both Black and

judiciary is very transparent, no doubt a result of the highly regulated and standardized procedures that are the hallmarks of American jurisprudence.

The purpose of this chapter is to provide a foundation for understanding why interest groups, given a wide selection of venues available in which to exercise their influence, opt to turn to the courts. Though the central focus of this book is on interest group participation as it relates to judicial decision making, the present discussion provides insight into interest groups' decisions to use the courts. Because organizations' choices to participate in the Supreme Court directly relate to the types of information and, more important, the wide variety of information available to the justices in the form of amicus briefs, an appreciation of organizations' motives for turning to litigation is essential as a backdrop for investigating the potential influence of amicus briefs on the justices' decision making. Accordingly, this chapter analyzes group decisions to, first, turn to the judicial arena, and, second, once that decision is made, to file amicus briefs.

I begin with a discussion of what constitutes an interest group. Such deliberation is necessary because the term will be used throughout the remainder of this analysis. Following this, I examine interest groups' decisions to litigate. Though early explanations focused on the lack of access to alternative venues as the primary explanation for this decision, I will instead show that a variety of factors affect this choice. Next, I discuss the three main methods interest groups use to lobby the Court, highlighting why amicus curiae participation has become the predominant method for group influence. Finally, I evaluate the goal(s) of interest group amicus curiae briefs, concluding that the primary goal of interest group amicus participation is to influence the justices' decision making in hopes of obtaining a policy congruent with the groups' preferences.

Brennan immediately threw Corcoran out of their chambers once they realized he was there to lobby them, the appearance of impropriety made Brennan so uncomfortable that he was willing to recuse himself from considering the rehearing petition. This was problematic because Brennan was the only member of the original majority who believed the Court should rehear the case. Further, because the Court's rules dictated that only a member of the original majority could bring up rehearing, and because Brennan was willing to remove himself due to Corcoran's visit, Chief Justice Burger (who also wanted to rehear the case) attempted to change the Court's rules to enable any justice present on the original case to bring up rehearing petitions. After a series of interchambers memorandum, including a threat by Justice Douglas to publish a ten-page dissent from the rehearing petition, Burger backed down and the rehearing petition was unceremoniously denied.

I. Interest Groups Defined

What is an interest group? Perhaps surprisingly, scholars have provided a wide variety of answers to this question (Petracca 1992: 5), some relating specifically to the tactics used by groups (e.g., Key 1958: 23) and others centering on groups' membership characteristics (e.g., MacIver 1937: 144). Still other scholars differentiate among organizational types in their choice of terms. For example, Schlozman and Tierney (1986: 10) reserve the terms "interest groups" and "pressure groups" for membership associations and classify "organized interests" as including, more broadly, associations with and without members in the ordinary sense.[18] While Schlozman and Tierney (1986) had their own reasons for these differentiations, I adopt their well-accepted definition of organized interests:[19] a "variety of organizations that seek joint ends through *political* action" (Schlozman and Tierney 1986: 11). As such, the terms "interest group," "organized interest," "pressure group," as well as "organization" and "group" will be used interchangeably throughout this book with the above definition in mind. Under this denotation, interest groups include corporations, governments, public interest law firms, trade associations, universities, and the like. Further, *ad hoc* organizations that pursue their goals in government fit nicely into this definition, such as the "167 Distinguished Scientists and Physicians" who filed an amicus brief in *Webster v. Reproductive Health Services* (1989). Finally, this definition encompasses the rare amicus curiae brief filed by a team of lawyers on behalf of a single individual. Simply put, because such a group of individuals is pursing political action, it can be thought of as an interest group under Schlozman and Tierney's broad definition.[20]

---

18 E.g., the American Bar Association would be considered both an "interest group" and a "pressure group" because its membership is made up of individuals. Conversely, the National League of Cities would be considered an "organized interest" because its membership is made up of cities that send representatives to the organization on their behalf.

19 See, e.g., Caldeira and Wright (1988, 1990), Hansford (2004a, 2004b), and Petracca (1992: 6).

20 On *extremely* rare occasions an individual may file an amicus brief *pro se* and without identifying the assistance of additional counsel, provided that the individual is a member of the Supreme Court bar (Caldeira and Wright 1988: 1123). See, e.g., the amicus curiae brief of Thurston Greene, *Arizonans for Official English v. Arizona* (1997). Such an amicus would not fall under any generally accepted definition of an interest group.

II. The Decision to Litigate

Interest groups turn to the courts for a variety of reasons. Early studies suggested that groups pursued litigation primarily as a result of political disadvantage. This view posits that groups litigate because they lack access to more traditional political forums, such as Congress and the executive (Barker 1967; Cortner 1968; Peltason 1955; Vose 1955, 1958). For example, in his groundbreaking study of the NAACP's successful campaign against housing segregation, Vose asserted, "In the face of failures to gain concessions from Congress, due in large part to the power wielded by the Southern delegation. . . . Negroes turned to the judiciary" (1955: 102). In a similar vein, Cortner, examining litigation in constitutional cases, found that minority groups

> are highly dependent upon the judicial process as a means of pursuing their policy interests, usually because they are temporarily, or even permanently, disadvantaged in terms of their abilities to attain successfully their goals in the electoral process, within the elected political institutions or in the bureaucracy. If they are to succeed at all in the pursuit of their goal, they are almost compelled to resort to litigation. (1968: 287)

In essence, political disadvantage theory asserts that groups found a type of safe haven in the courts. Absent access to more traditional means of policy influence, they turned to the judiciary, which welcomed them with open arms, providing an outlet for social change.[21] As evidence of this fact, scholars provided case studies of organizational participation in landmark Supreme Court decisions such as *Baker v. Carr* (1962), in which the Court authorized the federal judiciary to hear reapportionment claims (Cortner 1968), and *Brown v. Board of Education* (1954), where the Court desegregated the public schools (Barker 1967). More recently, scholars have pointed out that organizations representing the interests of gays, lesbians, bisexuals, and the transgendered, lacking widespread support in the elected branches of government, began staging litigation

---

21 One of the leading stimuli for the formation of this theory of interest group litigation came from Justice Stone's footnote 4 in *United States v. Carolene Products* (1938). In this famed footnote, Justice Stone explained that perceived governmental abuses against minorities would be subject to rigorous standards of judicial scrutiny, even when this forces the Court into a position that conflicts with the policies of the executive and legislative branches.

⟶ footnote 4 + majoritarianism

campaigns in an effort to obtain equal rights through favorable judicial precedents (e.g., Hilton 1995; Pinello 2006). One such campaign, orchestrated by Gay and Lesbian Advocates and Defenders and briefed by a number of other civil rights organizations, was extremely successful. In *Goodridge v. Department of Public Health* (2003), the Massachusetts Supreme Judicial Court ruled that a state law prohibiting same-sex marriage violated due process and equity provisions of that state's constitution, thus making Massachusetts the first state in the union to recognize same-sex marriage.

Political disadvantage theory, however, would not endure as the lone explanation for interest group involvement in the judiciary. Equipped with more persuasive theories and more rigorous methodologies, social scientists and legal scholars soon mounted a strong attack on political disadvantage theory, leading to its rejection as the sole account of interest group participation in the courts by the mid-1980s (Brodie 2002; Olson 1990). In its place, scholars turned to party capability theory. Beginning with Galanter's (1974) celebrated speculation that the judiciary privileges the "haves" versus the "have nots," researchers began to take a second look at interest group litigation in the courts. In the years following Galanter's (1974) conjectures, numerous studies accumulated confirming the ability of party capability theory to account for litigant success in state supreme courts (Wheeler, Cartwright, Kagan, and Friedman 1987), the federal courts of appeals (Songer and Sheehan 1992), and the U.S. Supreme Court (McGuire 1995; Sheehan, Mishler, and Songer 1992).

Applying this theory beyond an explanation for litigant success, scholars recognized that it was not just disadvantaged interest groups who found an outlet in the courts. Indeed, studies provided evidence that advantaged groups (upperdogs) outnumbered disadvantaged groups (underdogs) in the Court (Bradley and Gardner 1985) and that civil rights, the cornerstone of political disadvantage theory, was but one area of interest group participation in the judiciary (e.g., O'Connor and Epstein 1982b). In addition, Caldeira and Wright (1990) found that among interest groups using the amicus curiae brief in the Supreme Court, business, trade, and professional organizations filed the greatest number of briefs, with governments coming in a close second (see also Olson 1990). Clearly, organizations such as the American Bankers Association and the American Bar Association are a far cry from conventional definitions of disadvantaged groups.

In essence then, scholars soon recognized that no single rationale is capable of explaining why groups turn to litigation. Some groups use litigation because they do not find outlets in other institutional arenas, consistent with political disadvantage theory. Others litigate because they perceive the possibility of obtaining unique and long-lasting benefits from litigation; benefits perhaps unavailable to them in other political institutions. As Wasby (1995: 105) notes:

> Judicial decisions, particularly Supreme Court rulings on constitutional matters, are difficult to dislodge. Thus a victory there is more permanent, decreasing uncertainty and stabilizing the environment, than one in Congress or in presidential administrations, which will be affected by election shifts.

Yet another reason interest groups turn to the courts is to protect gains won in alternative venues. For this to occur, the group must foresee a real threat to its successes in more traditional avenues of influence (Olson 1990). Consider, for example, the efforts of Colorado for Family Values (CFV) in *Romer v. Evans* (1996). CFV successfully initiated the passage of Amendment 2 to the Colorado State Constitution,[22] which precluded Colorado state and local governments from enacting, adopting, or enforcing any statutes, regulations, or ordinances that would protect homosexuals, lesbians, and bisexuals from discrimination claims on the basis of such groups' minority status. When Amendment 2 was challenged in the Supreme Court as a violation of the Fourteenth Amendment's Equal Protection Clause, CFV filed an amicus brief in an attempt to defend Amendment 2 from judicial invalidation. Although they failed, CFV's efforts offer a concrete example of a group turning to the Court to protect gains won in alternative venues.

In addition, groups use the courts as a means of providing a counterbalance to their opposition's perceived dominance in the judiciary.[23] This differs from protecting prior successes in that groups need not have anything to protect. Instead, such groups turn to the courts to have their positions known. Indeed, this is the predominant explanation Epstein (1985) offers for the rise of conservative groups' use of litigation in

---

22 See amicus curiae brief of Colorado for Family Values, *Romer v. Evans* (1996).

23 This explanation might be particularly true for organizations with abundant resources (e.g., Olson 1990: 863). "If an organization has salaried attorneys on staff, even if they were not initially hired to litigate, 'start-up costs' of entering litigation are diminished" (Wasby 1995: 106).

the 1970s. Seeking to offer the justices alternative perspectives to counter those of liberal groups, conservative organizations such as Americans for Effective Law Enforcement (AELE) and the Pacific Legal Foundation turned to the Court. As one of the founders of the AELE put it, the group's purpose was "not to put the ACLU out of business (but) to make sure that the courts hear the law enforcement side of arguments."[24]

Finally, interest groups may become involved in litigation due to distinctive characteristics of the particular group. That is, some groups may be predisposed to litigation. The Product Liability Advisory Council (PLAC) provides a clear example of such a group.

> [The] Product Liability Advisory Council, Inc. is an association of industrial companies that was formed for the principal purpose of submitting amicus curiae briefs in appellate cases involving significant issues affecting the law of product liability. Its members, together with other corporations doing business in this country, have borne the brunt of the massive and discriminatory increase in punitive damages verdicts that has occurred in the last two decades and that this Court's decision in *Pacific Mutual Life Insurance Co. v. Haslip* [1991], has not succeeded in stemming [case citation and parentheses omitted].[25]

As is evident by the PLAC's amicus brief, the group turned to the Court in an attempt to persuade the justices to reconsider a prior ruling regarding the constitutionally permissible size of punitive damage awards. While the PLAC might also pursue this goal in legislative forums, for example lobbying Congress to enact statutes aimed at capping punitive product liability verdicts, they do not (Granger 2003). Rather, the group believes that its best venues for achieving its goals are the appellate courts.

As another example of a group that is predisposed to litigation, consider Americans for Effective Law Enforcement (AELE).[26] AELE was founded in 1966 by Fred E. Inbau, then a professor of criminal procedure at Northwestern University Law School. The group's purpose is to provide a voice for the law enforcement community in criminal procedure cases.

---

24 Quoted in Ivers and O'Connor (1987: 164).
25 Brief for the Product Liability Council as amicus curiae, *TXO Production Corporation v. Alliance Resources* (1993).
26 The information discussed below on AELE can be found on its webpage (www.aele.org, last accessed May 31, 2007).

Among its paramount goals is to overturn the Court's decision in *Mapp v. Ohio* (1961), which applied the exclusionary rule—the dictate that illegally obtained evidence is inadmissible in courts of law—to state prosecutions. In addition to this, the AELE seeks to establish good faith exceptions to the exclusionary rule, allowing for the admission of otherwise illegally obtained evidence when police officers believe they acted in a legal manner. To achieve this latter goal, AELE drafted a "Model Statute" and submitted it to all members of Congress and more than seven thousand state legislators. While the AELE is able to pursue good faith exceptions to the exclusionary rule through legislative bodies, it is unable to address the *Mapp* decision outside of the Court. Such is the case because the Court rested the *Mapp* decision on the Fourth Amendment's prohibition against unlawful search and seizures, as applied to the states via the Fourteenth Amendment. Because Congress cannot legislatively overturn a constitutional decision of the Court, absent a constitutional amendment, AELE is forced to look to the Court in hopes of achieving this goal. Within the Supreme Court, AELE does so by filing amicus briefs (Epstein 1985: 163).

As is clear from the above discussion, there is no single reason why interest groups use the courts. Rather, at least five, often interrelated, reasons exist. First, groups may turn to the courts due to their lack of access to alternative venues, such as Congress and the executive. Second, groups may use the courts because of the unique benefits that can be obtained from judicial decisions. In particular, because constitutional decisions are difficult to dislodge, this offers organizations the possibility of long-lasting influence. Third, interests may use litigation as a means to protect gains won in other venues. Fourth, pressure groups may seek out the judicial arena to counterbalance their oppositions' participation. Finally, some organizations may use the courts because their goals predispose them to litigate.[27]

III. Methods of Interest Group Litigation

Once groups have made the decision to litigate, they primarily have three outlets for participation in the courts other than as a direct party

---

27 See Scheppele and Walker (1991) for a superb treatment of these explanations that is subjected to rigorous empirical testing.

in litigation.[28] First, interest groups can participate by setting up test cases, which usually rest on constitutional issues (Wasby 1995). In setting up test cases, organized interests either provide for a statute/policy to be challenged (thus establishing the necessary standing for trial)[29] or are approached by an individual willing to challenge a statute/policy under the guidance of the interest group. *Boy Scouts of America v. Dale* (2000) provides an example of the latter scenario. James Dale, a homosexual Eagle Scout whose membership in the Boy Scouts had been revoked after the Scouts discovered his sexual preference, approached Lambda Legal, a public interest law firm committed to ensuring equal rights for homosexual, bisexual, and transgendered Americans. He sought to challenge the Boy Scouts' policy that forbids membership to homosexuals. After agreeing to argue his cause, Lambda Legal first sought his reinstatement within the Boy Scouts' internal organization. When this failed, Lambda Legal unsuccessfully filed a complaint in New Jersey Superior Court under the New Jersey Law Against Discrimination. Lambda Legal's next step was a successful appeal to the New Jersey Superior Court's Appellate Division, which was later upheld by the New Jersey Supreme Court. The last step for Dale and Lambda Legal was defending their claim before the United States Supreme Court, which ruled 5–4 that forcing the Boy Scouts to include homosexuals impaired the organization's First Amendment right of protected association (Ackerman and Grossman 2004).

Setting up test cases is arguably the rarest form of interest group participation because it is extremely time consuming and requires a great deal of resources. Interest groups participating in planned litigation require full time staffs and attorneys, the ability to generate publicity, the cooperation of other groups, and a narrow issue focus (Wasby 1995). Furthermore, the goals of planned litigation are long term and often carried out incrementally. In this sense, organized interests involved in setting up test cases are repeat players, playing for rules to "maximize gain

---

28 In addition to methods discussed here, interest groups may attempt to act as intervenors and do so on rare occasions. As prospective intervenors, interest groups must establish that the outcome of the case would substantially impair their interests or, alternatively, that they are allowed to intervene under statutory law. In practice, requests for intervenor status are often denied, primarily due to the adversarial nature of American jurisprudence (e.g., Lowman 1992). When intervenor status is denied, groups often participate as amici curiae (e.g., Goepp 2002).

29 In pertinent part, the doctrine of standing requires a litigant to demonstrate that an actual controversy exits involving a direct and significant injury to the litigant (e.g., Stern, Gressman, Shapiro, and Geller 2002: 810).

over a long series of cases, even where this involves the risk of maximum loss in some cases" (Galanter 1974: 100). In essence, the goal of organized interests in planned litigation "is not sought immediately; cases are brought and won; and then a goal that 'seems crazy one year is reached as intermediate points are filled in'" (Wasby 1995: 148). Given the long-term costs and resources necessary for planned litigation, it should be no surprise that this is the method that interest groups adopt least often for involvement in the courts.

As a second method of involvement in litigation, interest groups may choose to sponsor cases that others bring to the courts. In this role, organized interests assume the costs and provide resources for a party in exchange for using the case as a means of highlighting their policy goals. Sponsorship differs from setting up test cases primarily in that organized interests have the opportunity to sponsor cases once individuals have advanced them into the appellate stages. Thus, rather than active involvement from the initial point at which a law has been challenged, sponsorship involves targets of opportunity: taking over cases individuals have begun. However, this is also an extremely time consuming and costly effort as it requires resources very similar to those expended in planned litigation. In addition, it also gives groups less leeway in structuring the legal questions faced by the courts since the process has already begun. Thus, given the complexities involved in setting up test cases and sponsoring parties, interest groups choose these routes far less often than their most frequent means of participating in the courts, through the filing of amicus curiae briefs (Epstein 1991; Hansford 2004a).

The amicus curiae brief provides interest groups with a distinctive outlet for participating in the courts. Although it is much less costly than setting up test cases or sponsoring litigation,[30] it also has a downside. Namely, unlike planned litigation, it does not allow groups to control the

---

30 Although I am unaware of studies that have been undertaken examining the costs of amicus participation vis-à-vis case sponsorship or planned litigation, Caldeira and Wright (1988: 1112) uncover estimates ranging from $15,000 to $20,000 for an amicus brief filed by a "reputable law firm," while Smith and Terrell (1995) report that amicus briefs have been filed for less than $1,500. In addition, it is not uncommon for attorneys to author amicus briefs *gratis* to gain valuable experience that might attract future clients (e.g., Ward 2007). Similarly, law professors will occasionally write amicus briefs *pro bono*, requiring only that the organized interests identified on the briefs handle the costs of printing (e.g., Moorman and Masteralexis 2001: 293). In contrast, a local attorney and the NAACP Legal Defense Fund were awarded $1.7 million and $2.3 million, respectively, for fees and expenses that accrued during *Missouri v. Jenkins* (1989) (Wasby 1995: 97). Though the latter is clearly an extreme example, the point is that

course of the litigation (Epstein 1985: 148). Instead, groups participating as amici curiae are bound by the facts of the case and the lower court record, neither of which they necessarily had the opportunity to shape. Nonetheless, amicus participants may raise issues not addressed by the direct parties to litigation, and often do (Spriggs and Wahlbeck 1997). A classic example of this was the American and Ohio Civil Liberties Unions' amicus brief in *Mapp v. Ohio* (1961). In it, the amici argued for the application of the exclusionary rule to the states, a position that the Court subsequently adopted (Day 2001).[31]

In addition to introducing new or alternative legal positions, amicus participation also allows groups to present social scientific evidence to the Court because, unlike the direct parties to litigation, amicus participants may be policy specialists, equipped with an intimate knowledge of a particular policy area. For example, Stern, Gressman, Shapiro, and Geller (2002: 659–660) point out that "an association of psychologists might be better able to marshal facts pertaining to the general effects of severe criminal sentences or mandatory notice to the parents of a child attempting to obtain an abortion" than nonspecialists.

Finally, amicus briefs inform the courts of the broader policy implications of a decision (Caldeira and Wright 1988; Spriggs and Wahlbeck 1997). In this capacity, amicus briefs present the justices with information regarding the wide-ranging economic, social, and policy consequences of their decisions. In so doing, amici perform a function similar to that which lobbyists perform for legislations. That is, by informing the justices of the implications of their decisions, amici enable justices to render decisions that both maximize the application of their policy preferences and allow them to create efficacious law. Thus, just as material obtained from lobbyists enables legislators to make rational decisions, the information contained in amicus briefs permits justices to make choices that take into account the policy consequences of their decisions (Epstein and Knight 1999: 215). Given the low costs associated with amicus participation, coupled with the wide variety of uses for amicus briefs, it should be of little surprise that amicus briefs are currently

---

amicus participation is *much* less expensive than case sponsorship or planned litigation.

31 Interestingly, the ACLU's amicus brief almost did not include the suppression issue. In fact, it was at the insistence of "three able and respected young lawyers" that it was incorporated into the brief (Day 2001: 373).

present in more than 90% of the cases given full treatment by the Supreme Court (Kearney and Merrill 2000).

IV. The Goal(s) of Amicus Participation

Interest groups participating as amici curiae use the language of the law in the pursuit of their policy goals. This is the fundamental assumption underlying most analyses of amici participation in the Court, whether it is explicitly acknowledged (e.g., Collins 2004a, 2007; Epstein and Rowland 1991; Hansford 2004a, 2004b; Koshner 1998; Krislov 1963; Spriggs and Wahlbeck 1997) or simply implicit in a study's research design (e.g., Caldeira and Wright 1988; Kearney and Merrill 2000; Songer and Sheehan 1993).[32] Though there is a general consensus on this topic among judicial scholars, interest group scholars more generally note that an additional goal of membership-based interests is the pursuit of organizational maintenance (e.g., Moe 1980; Wasby 1995: 116). Contrary to these scholars' assertions, I adopt Hanford's (2004a, 2004b) premise that organizational maintenance represents a constraint on organized interests, rather than a goal. In other words, organizational maintenance is not ultimately an end, but a means to an end.

The notion that organizational maintenance constitutes a goal for membership-based interest groups stems from the reality that such organizations must consider the effect of their lobbying decisions on their ability to attract and maintain membership support. Contrary to this, institutional amici (e.g., corporations) do not face this constraint in their decisions to lobby because they do not make membership appeals (e.g., Salisbury 1984). When analyzed in more detail, it becomes clear that organizational maintenance represents a constraint on membership-based interests or, at best, a secondary goal (e.g., Caldeira, Hojnacki, and Wright 2000; Collins 2004a, 2007). Such is the case because membership-based

---

32 The studies that make policy goals implicit do so by using a dependent variable that measures the amici's influence on the Court's policy outputs. For example, Caldeira and Wright (1988) do not explicitly acknowledge that amici seek to influence the Supreme Court's selection process but then test to determine if they do, thereby implicitly assuming that amici seek to influence the Court's certiorari decisions. Similarly, Kearney and Merrill (2000) and Songer and Sheehan (1993) do not specifically state that amici seek to influence the Court's decisions on the merits but test for such influence. In so doing, these authors imply that amici pursue policy goals by attempting to etch their policy preferences into law.

interests, identically to institutional amici (e.g., corporations), pursue policy goals (e.g., Hansford 2004a, 2004b). However, unlike institutional amici, they must consider their ability to both maintain their current base of support and attract new members when making their lobbying decisions. Should the group fail to maintain a minimal level of support, it will cease to exist. Given this, attempts to maintain and attract membership support represent a constraint that only membership-based interests face. In other words, organizational maintenance is a necessary condition for the group's survival, but not in and of itself a goal.[33]

Having established that the goal of organized interests participating as amici curiae is the pursuit of favorable policies, it is necessary to consider how amici go about achieving this goal in the Supreme Court. This attempted influence occurs at two stages in the Court: the case selection stage and the merits stage. At the certiorari stage, the goal of amici is to encourage the justices to either grant or deny full review to a case (e.g., Wasby 1995: 221). Past research indicates that amicus briefs supporting a grant of review do indeed serve this function. In highlighting to the justices the potential policy significance of a case, organized interests provide the justices with reliable signals that the case warrants their attention (Caldeira and Wright 1988: 1112). For example, Caldeira and Wright (1998) find that the presence of amicus briefs in favor of a certiorari petition is one of the three most important influences on the justices' case selection decisions.[34]

At the merits stage, amici pursue their policy goals in at least two interrelated ways. First, interest groups seek to influence the outcome of the Court's decision as it immediately relates to the *parties* to litigation. In civil rights cases, this might mean attempting to secure relief for the immediate party to litigation or supporting the government's alleged

---

33 To draw an analogy familiar to scholars, consider the research scientist operating in a "publish or perish" environment whose primary goal is to obtain tenure. To do so, this scientist needs to secure adequate funding, whether from an employer or a grant agency, to maintain computer, lab, and other research equipment. Procuring and maintaining these research needs represents a constraint on the scientist in that they are necessary to conduct and publish research that will enable the scientist to achieve his or her primary goal—tenure. For an alternative perspective, viewing organizational maintenance as a goal, rather than a constraint, see Koshner (1998) and Lowery (2007).

34 While Caldeira and Wright's (1988) original analysis of the influence of amicus briefs on the probability of granting certiorari indicated that amicus briefs filed in *opposition* to the certiorari petition also increased the likelihood of a grant of certiorari, their subsequent and more rigorous analysis revealed that this finding failed to obtain statistical significance (1998: 33).

infringement of that litigant's rights. However, due to the very nature of the Court's jurisprudence, this goal is likely only an afterthought for most organizations. Because the Court's role is deciding primarily those cases that have substantial importance beyond the particular litigants involved—and because interest groups are surely aware of this fact (e.g., Wasby 1995; Vose 1958)—an amicus curiae is instead likely to argue a cause beyond the specific facts at hand. This is done in an attempt to influence the Court's decisions as they apply to other citizens who are, or will be, similarly situated as the amicus' supported litigant.

Griswold v. Connecticut (1965) provides an example of this. In that case, Estelle Griswold, the Executive Director of the Planned Parenthood League of Connecticut, was charged with violating a Connecticut statute that made it a crime to distribute contraceptives after she dispensed birth control measures to a married couple. When the case reached the Supreme Court, four amicus briefs were filed supporting a physician's right to give medical advice, instruction, and information regarding the use of contraceptives. The American Civil Liberties Union (ACLU) argued that the statute violated the right to privacy guaranteed by the Due Process Clause of the Constitution, while the Planned Parenthood Federation of America highlighted to the justices the fact that an overwhelming majority of physicians view contraceptive materials as essential tools of preventative medicine, the use of which safeguards the public welfare and is protected by both the right to privacy and patient-physician confidentiality. The brief of 141 physicians in the fields of gynecology, obstetrics, and pediatrics described how upholding the statute would result in the imposition of moral standards at the expense of best medical practices, in addition to arguing that the statute violated a physician's right to freedom of speech. Finally, the Catholic Council on Civil Liberties presented the justices with a Catholic perspective on the use of contraceptives, arguing that the privacy to engage in conjugal union as an expression of love is so core to the institution of marriage that the Connecticut law is troubling even to the conservative Catholic Church. In presenting their unique perspectives on the validity of the Connecticut law banning the allocation of contraceptives, none of the amici focused on relieving Griswold's conviction; instead, they sought to create the constitutionally permissible right of a physician to discuss and dispense birth control under the protection of the right to privacy.

Similarly, in State Farm v. Campbell (2003), which engaged the constitutionality of a Utah jury's punitive damage award of $145 million dollars to a policy holder whose insurance company refused to settle liability claims stemming from an auto accident, numerous amici participated for the purposes of demonstrating the broader policy ramifications of the decision. For example, the Product Liability Advisory Council provided the Court with an historical account of punitive damage awards in America, concluding that the failure to prohibit disproportionate damage awards has contributed to the apparent litigation crisis in the United States. Conversely, 21 social science and law professors presented the Court with an overview of statistical studies of punitive damage awards, concluding that juries behave especially rationally in determining the extent of such awards and therefore it is unnecessary to transfer the responsibility to set punitive damage awards away from juries by authorizing judges to perform such tasks. Further highlighting the fact that amici seek to shape the Court's policy outputs were the amicus briefs of the U.S. Chamber of Commerce and Ford Motor Company, both of which urged the Supreme Court to develop rigorous guidelines and more coherent jury instructions for the determination of punitive damage awards.[35] Thus, it should be clear that even though amici almost always support a particular litigant, they do not do this for the immediate purpose of relieving or ensuring that particular litigant's conviction (as in *Griswold*) or relieving or affirming punitive damage awards (as in *State Farm*). Instead, they argue their positions for the primary purpose of shaping the Court's policy output as it will affect others in similarly situated positions.

Thus, the paramount goal of amicus participation is to employ legal persuasion to influence the outcome of the Court's decision as it relates to the *policy* announced in the case (e.g., Epstein 1985; Epstein and Kobylka 1992; Wasby 1995). This differs from focusing on the outcome of a case as it relates to the litigants in that the group might attempt to

---

35 A total of 31 briefs were filed in *State Farm*, none of which focused on specifically alleviating or affirming the punitive damage award. For example, Abbot Laboratories et al. furnished the Court with their own overview of social scientific studies involving punitive damage awards (which was refuted by the brief of 21 social science and law professors); the Association of Trial Lawyers in America argued that the Supreme Court should not involve itself with setting limitations on punitive damage awards since to do otherwise interferes with the ability of states to operate as laboratories of democracy, free from federal interference; the Business Roundtable argued that allowing juries to set punitive damage awards on the basis of a corporate defendant's wealth violates due process; while Professor Keith Hylton provided a detailed overview of deterrence theory as the justification for punitive damage awards.

Goal of amici

establish new constitutional rights through precedential rulings or develop favorable guidelines through the Court's interpretation of statutes. *On a case-by-case basis, the goal of organized interests is to have the justices endorse policies favorable to those groups' interests.* This follows from the notion that the central significance of the Court in American government is not the Court's individual decisions but instead the general policies it announces through a series of decisions (e.g., Canon 1973). Through a sequence of such decisions, the Court is able to directly shape the decisions of lower courts, which dispose of the vast majority of legal controversies in the U.S. (e.g., Songer, Segal, and Cameron 1994; Songer and Sheehan 1990), as well as the policies of federal agencies charged with implementing the Court's decisions (e.g., Spriggs 1996). In influencing the ideological direction of the individual justice's votes on a case-by-case basis, interest groups, in turn, indirectly influence the ideological dispositions of lower court decisions and the policies of federal agencies, thus seeing their optimal policy preferences etched into law, first, by the Supreme Court, and later via responsive lower courts and government bureaucracies. In this sense, the influence of amicus participation follows the hierarchy of the justice system in that, if groups can shape the ideological directions of the Supreme Court's decisions, and if the ideological directions of the Supreme Court's decisions directly affect the ideological directions of lower court decisions, then interest groups are able to indirectly influence the entire justice system. This is likely one of primary reasons that amicus briefs are such an everyday occurrence in the Supreme Court but are rarely filed in lower courts (e.g., Epstein 1994; Martinek 2007).

In the analyses that follow, subjecting the influence of amici curiae to empirical scrutiny, I examine how amici can achieve their policy goals by focusing on two dependent variables. First, I investigate how amicus briefs shape the ideological direction of the individual justices' decision making and the consistency of that decision making. Although this dependent variable is a somewhat crude measure of amici influence on the Court's policies, it is entirely consistent with the principal goal of interest groups participating as amici curiae: to influence the Court's policy outputs. In this capacity, it is able to capture the fact that some amici advocate for conservative policies, while others lobby for liberal policies. As a result, it is a substantially more appropriate dependent variable to gauge the influence of amici than litigation success because it is congruous with interest groups' primary goal in the Court. Thus, its use has the potential to rectify the confusion surrounding the influence of amici in the Court stemming from previous studies' use of a dependent variable (litigant success) that is only of secondary import to pressure groups. Simply put, if amici are effective in shaping the justices' decision making, this influence should be especially evident through the use of a dependent variable that is compatible with the paramount goal of amici in the Court. Second, this dependent variable is an especially useful measure of the justices' policy positions in that it can distinguish votes based on the ideological direction of the policy, rather than on the basis of whether the justice voted in favor of the petitioner or respondent. Therefore, unlike a measure of litigation success, this dependent variable is able to recognize, for example, that the Court's majority in *Roe v. Wade* (1973) announced a liberal policy as that majority determined that a woman's discretion to have an abortion is encompassed by the right to privacy. As such, it provides information about the broader social impact of the decision (e.g., that the justices are favorable or unfavorable toward reproductive rights) that cannot be captured by knowing whether a justice voted to reverse or affirm the lower court's decision. Inasmuch as this information is important for lower courts and federal agencies that alter their behavior on the basis of the ideological direction(s) of the Court's decisions, this further makes the use of this dependent variable appropriate.[36]

Second, I analyze the influence of amici on a justice's decision to write or join a regular concurring, special concurring, or dissenting opinion.[37] In so doing, I shed light on an overlooked avenue of interest

---

36 It should be noted that I opt not to use the most obvious alternative—the ideological direction of the Court's decisions as the dependent variable—for three reasons. First, such a decision would treat the Court as a unitary actor, which is an unrealistic assumption. For example, if we accept that Justice O'Connor was the swing vote on the final Rehnquist Court (e.g., Byrne 1998; Martin, Quinn, and Epstein 2005), then treating the Court as a uniform actor is problematic because O'Connor occasionally defected from the conservative majority on the Court, forming a new liberal majority. Second, because one of the primary goals of this research is to determine if ideology acts as a mediating variable as to how the individual justices' respond to the influence of amicus briefs, it makes little sense to test such a theory by treating the Court as a unitary actor. This would presume a uniform ideology for the Court as a whole (e.g., Giles and Zorn 2000). Finally, because the Court's decisions are, of course, a function of the individual justices' votes, by using the ideological direction of the individual justices' votes as the dependent variable, I am able to capture the individual behavior that, in the aggregate, makes up the Court's decisions, while controlling for justice-specific attributes.

37 Regular concurring opinions reflect agreement with the majority's disposition of a case (e.g., reverse or affirm), but expand on the logic behind the majority's reasoning for

group effectiveness. Though an interest group would surely prefer that a unanimous Court endorse the positions it espouses, influencing a justice's decision to write separately is not without its own benefits. Although separate opinions are without precedential value, they nonetheless serve to highlight weaknesses in the majority opinion, present avenues to distinguish the majority opinion for future litigation, suggest alternative interpretations of the majority opinion, in addition to increasing the likelihood that the majority's precedent will be reversed (e.g., Spriggs and Hansford 2001). Moreover, separate opinions make compliance by lower courts more difficult by confounding the clarity of legal rule(s) established by the Supreme Court in the case (e.g., Corley 2005). As such, an interest group that is unsuccessful at persuading the majority to adopt its position can nonetheless achieve a partial victory by contributing to a justice's decision to write or join a separate opinion. This might be particularly beneficial if the group is involved in repeated litigation.

The reader should note that I do not focus my attention on exploring how interest groups influence the rule of law articulated in the Court's opinions, with the exception of a few case studies used for illustrative purposes. This was a very conscious decision. I have no doubt that amici attempt to persuade the justices to adopt, in their opinions, various interpretations of the Constitution or statutes for the purposes of establishing favorable precedents. However, comparing, for example, the arguments made in amicus briefs to the language used in the justices' opinions (e.g., Samuels 2004) is an unsatisfactory manner for detecting amici *influence* because the justices might use the arguments provided by amici merely as *post hoc* rationalizations for decisions made on the basis of other factors. As such, the research strategy employed in this book follows the imperative advocated by the legal realists. That is, I use statistical methods to evaluate whether, and to what extent, amicus briefs influence the justices' decision making, rather than relying on a purely doctrinal analysis that is arguably ill suited for explaining legal outcomes. To be clear, however, while I am of a firm mind that evidence illustrating that the justices' opinions reflect arguments of the amici does not necessarily provide evidence of amici influence, this fact should not diminish the import of

hole
in
language
study

---

that disposition. Special concurring opinions also reflect agreement with the majority's disposition of a case, but disagree as to the majority's reasoning for that decision. Dissenting opinions disagree with both the majority's disposition of a case and the majority's reasoning for reaching that outcome.

such research. After all, the language of opinions, while perhaps an inapposite source for determining the causes of judicial choice, does matter as an authority for the entire U.S. justice system and, as such, research along these lines surely contributes to our knowledge of the role of friends of the Court. Accordingly, I join contemporary behavioral scholars in recognizing the merit of qualitative analyses of the Court, but "believe that evidence as to the factors that affect Supreme Court decisions must be systematically demonstrated" through falsifiable inquiry (Segal and Spaeth 1994: 10).

V. Summary and Conclusions

The primary purpose of this chapter was threefold. First, I examined why, given a wide variety of venues to exercise their influence, interest groups turn to the courts. I argued that while lack of access to other venues still constitutes a motivation for litigation, several other explanations exist, including the protection of gains won in alternative forums and as a means to counterbalance their oppositions' use of the judiciary. This section was important because it highlighted the numerous reasons that contribute to groups' decisions to turn to the courts and, due to this, suggests that a wide variety of groups use litigation, each bringing with them unique perspectives for the justices to consider. Second, I discussed the three primary methods for interest group involvement in the Supreme Court, concluding that because amicus curiae participation allows groups to influence public policy while expending a minimal amount of resources, this method has become the primary technique used by interest groups. Finally, I offered a discussion of interest group goals as amici, deducing that the primary goal of amicus participation is to persuade the justices to endorse policies congruent with groups' varying preferences.

CHAPTER 3

Amicus Curiae Participation
in the Supreme Court

Having identified the various methods interest groups use to lobby the courts, as well as their goal(s) in doing so, it is now appropriate to discuss the amicus strategy in more detail. The purpose here is to provide an understanding of the context of interest group amicus curiae involvement in the Supreme Court. This is significant because, to investigate whether amicus briefs influence the justices' decision making, it is necessary to have a full comprehension of the role of amici in the Court. For example, it is important to offer insight into the barriers faced by organizations seeking to file amicus briefs because the rules and norms governing amicus activity have the potential to promote amicus activity by certain types of organizations at the expense of others. Likewise, it is vital to grasp what types of arguments amici supply to the justices as these are the mechanisms interests groups use to marshal their persuasion attempts.

I commence by presenting an overview of the history of amicus participation, beginning with its roots in Roman and English law and continuing up to its current incarnation in the U.S. Supreme Court. Next, I examine the regulations that govern amicus participation in the Court. Third, I investigate the frequency of amicus participation over time, in specific issue areas, and the ideological positions advocated by the amici. Following this, I analyze the class of organizations that participate as amici curiae, as well as the types of information amicus briefs supply the justices.

I. The History of Amici Curiae: From Friendship to Advocacy[38]

The origin of the amicus curiae can be traced to Roman law (e.g., Covey 1959; Harper and Etherington 1953; Krislov 1963). In the Roman system, amici provided the courts with information on areas of law beyond the expertise of judges. This typically took the form of either impromptu oral communication and/or nonbinding written opinions (Harris 2000: 4).[39] The role of the amicus was very much that of a neutral advisor: to educate the courts and assist judges in avoiding erroneous decisions. Thus, the amicus was not a party to litigation, "but served as an impartial assistant to the judiciary, providing advice and information to a mistaken or doubtful court" (Lowman 1992: 1244).

In English law, the traditional role of the amicus as a neutral advisor to the courts continued until the early eighteenth century (e.g., Krislov 1963: 696). However, it saw its first metamorphosis as early as 1736 in *Coxe v. Phillips* (Krislov 1963; Harris 2000). This case involved a relatively routine, but collusive, contract dispute over a promissory note.[40] Phillips used the suit to embarrass and attempt to invalidate the current marriage of her former husband, Muilman. Their marriage had been previously voided when it was discovered that she had a living husband at the time of that marriage. Subsequently, Muilman, to the annoyance of Phillips, married another woman. Phillips argued that she was still legally married to Muilman and presented this as evidence to prove that she was unable to enter into a contract with Coxe. If the English court adopted this position, Muilman's current marriage would be invalidated as a result. However, the court allowed Muilman to have an amicus participate on his behalf, informing the judges that his marriage to Phillips had already been declared void. Muilman's amicus was so successful that the

---

38 I borrow the subtitle of this section from Krislov (1963).

39 The function of amici in oral communication in Roman, English, and nineteenth century American law has been described as a type of oral "Shepardizing"—informing the courts of relevant precedents and statutes of which they may be unaware, usually in a spontaneous manner (Krislov 1963: 695). It should be noted, of course, that during these time periods the administration of justice was carried out primarily in an oral manner since the corpus of available statutes and precedents was minimal at best. In fact, it was not until 1849 that the Supreme Court announced that it would no longer hear oral arguments from litigants who failed to file written briefs (Banner 2003: 121). In the modern era, amici very rarely participate in the Court's oral arguments. For example, from 1953 to 1985, amici presented oral argumentation in less than 6% of orally argued cases (Gibson 1997).

40 This discussion of *Coxe* is adopted from Krislov (1963: 696–697).

court not only vacated the judgment but also held Phillips in contempt of court. The important point of this case is that it is one of the first times that any court, English or otherwise, authorized the participation of an amicus to both inform the court and protect its own interests, in that the court allowed Muilman the opportunity to prove the validity of his current marriage. "Thus, even in its native habitat, the amicus curiae brief early underwent changes that ultimately were to have profound repercussions. A step had been taken toward change from neutral friendship to positive advocacy and partisanship" (Krislov 1963: 697).

When the amicus arrived in America, the adversarial tradition continued and would proliferate. The first appearance of an adversarial amicus curiae in the United States Supreme Court came in the 1823 case of *Green v. Biddle* (Harris 2000; Krislov 1963; O'Connor 1996).[41] The case involved Green's attempt to remove Biddle, an alleged trespasser, from his lands. Biddle argued that because he made substantial renovations to the lands, Green should be forced to repay him for the improvements under two Kentucky land laws. Green's defense against this claim was that the Kentucky laws were invalid, citing an interstate compact between Kentucky and Virginia in which Kentucky agreed to follow Virginia land law, which contained no such provisions for the compensation of land improvements. When the case reached the U.S. Supreme Court, Biddle did not appear to argue his cause, and the Court ruled in Green's favor.

Upon hearing this, and being aware of the grave repercussions the Court's decision would have for individuals in similar situations as Biddle, Kentuckian Henry Clay appeared as amicus curiae. Clay, a celebrated orator, former Speaker of the House of Representatives, and a presidential candidate in the 1824 election, arguing for rehearing:

> upon the ground that it involved the rights and claims of numerous occupants of the land in Kentucky, who had been allowed by the laws of that State, in consequence of the confusion of the land titles, arising out of the vicious system of location under the land

---

41 Prior to this case, the Court did see amicus participation in two cases—*Beatty's Administrators v. Burnes's Administrators* (1814) and *Livingston v. Dorgenois* (1813). However, those amici performed a role different from that of the contemporary amicus. In both cases, the amici appeared at oral arguments in an unofficial and spontaneous manner, rather than representing a nonparty to the case, as in *Green v. Biddle* (Banner 2003).

law of Virginia, an indemnity for their expenses and labour bestowed upon lands of which they had been the bona fidei possessors and improvers, and which were reclaimed by the true owners. He stated, that the rights and interests of those claimants would be irrevocably determined by this decision of the Court, the tenant in the present cause having permitted it to be brought to a hearing without appearing by his counsel, and without any argument on that side of the question. (21 U.S. 1, at 17)

As amicus, Clay performed a dual role. First, he acted as an advisor to the Court, suggesting that because Biddle failed to appear before the Court, the lawsuit was likely collusive. Second, and more important, his appearance as amicus in the case was that of an advocate, rather than a neutral friend of the Court.[42]

This role of amicus as advocate continued, and it is now well accepted that amici curiae play almost entirely an adversarial role in American jurisprudence (e.g., Collins 2004a; Kearney and Merrill 2000; Krislov 1963; Spriggs and Wahlbeck 1997). Indeed, in his examination of amicus participation in the nineteenth century, Banner (2003: 113) concludes that there was never a time in American jurisprudence that amici acted as solely neutral bystanders; instead, the partisan role of the amicus has always been the norm. Following Clay's inaugural appearance as an amicus, the adversarial amicus brief flourished and was used most commonly to protect governmental interests. For example, in *Ball Engineering Company v. J.G. White* (1919), the U.S. Solicitor General successfully argued that the contractual seizure of a construction company's building materials did not constitute a seizure under the meaning of the Fifth Amendment and therefore fell under tort law, leaving the government free from fiscal liability claims resulting from the seizure. However, in the early twentieth century, private organizations soon recognized that the amicus brief might provide them with an outlet to influence social change in the Court.

Ah How (alias Louie Ah How) v. United States (1904) marked the first appearance of an amicus curiae brief filed by a nongovernmental interest group in the U.S. Supreme Court (Krislov 1963). In that case, the Chinese Charitable and Benevolent Association of New York filed an

---

42 Clay was only partially successful. Though he was able to convince the justices to rehear the case, when they did so his position was rejected: a split Court reaffirmed its previous ruling.

amicus brief bringing to the Court's attention the organization's perceived abuses of Chinese immigrants in the New York City area by the government. It suggested that the Court reverse the Eastern District Court of New York's decision that ordered the removal of the appellants from the United States to their homeland of China. While the Court affirmed the lower court ruling, in making its argument, the Benevolent Association was clearly playing an adversarial role. This tradition followed with the appearance of the National Association for the Advancement of Colored People in *Guinn v. United States* (1915), in which the Association argued that discrimination with regard to the right to vote is unconstitutional, and the American Civil Liberties Union in *Carlson v. California* (1940), in which the ACLU argued that boycotting is a constitutionally protected form of First Amendment expression.

Of course, it is important to note that not all amicus participation in the early twentieth century involved liberal organizations and civil rights and liberties cases. For example, in *United States v. Butler* (1936), a host of organizations squared off on opposing sides of a dispute involving the constitutionality of the Agricultural Adjustment Act as it related to the ability of Congress to institute processing taxes on agricultural goods for the purposes of decreasing agricultural production. Organizations supporting the validity of the Act included the American Farm Bureau Federation, the League for Economic Equality, and the National Beet Growers Association. Amici challenging the Act's validity included the Farmers' Independence Council of America, General Mills, and the National Association of Cotton Manufacturers. Similarly, in *Muller v. Oregon* (1908), Louis Brandeis submitted his now celebrated "Brandeis Brief" on behalf of the National Consumer's League, presenting the Court with statistical evidence regarding the detrimental mental and health effects that result from women working long hours.[43]

II. Rules and Norms

Modern Supreme Court rules and norms involving amicus filings allow for essentially unlimited participation. This, however, was not always

---

43 Although Brandeis's role in the case was not that of a traditional amicus curiae in that Brandeis insisted on appearing on behalf of the State of Oregon, for all intents and purposes his role was that of an amicus, as Justice Frankfurter acknowledged in 1916 (Krislov 1963: 708).

the case. This section explores the rules and norms regarding amicus participation and discusses the obstacles to the open door policy that has predominated more recently. The current state of affairs regarding virtually unlimited participation is very much a product of the justices' beliefs that amicus briefs aid in the quality of their decision making.

The Court's rules regarding amicus participation have remained essentially unchanged since they were first adopted in 1939 (Kearney and Merrill 2000: 762).[44] Supreme Court Rule 37 states that private amici, such as interest groups, must obtain permission from both of the parties to litigation to participate, which is often granted. If one or both of the parties refuse to grant such consent, the potential amici may petition the Court for leave to file and the Court almost always grants such petitions (Bradley and Gardner 1985; O'Connor and Epstein 1983a).[45] Unlike private amici, representatives of federal and state governments are not required to obtain permission from the litigating parties to file amicus briefs. On rare occasions, the Court may request the participation of an amicus, usually the Solicitor General or an administrative agency of the federal government. Such invitations are almost always accepted (Salokar 1992: 143). For example, in *Retail Clerk's International Association v. Schermerhorn* (1963), a case involving the question of whether nonunion employees were required to pay dues to their contracting union without being required to join said union, the Court invited the Solicitor General to participate to express the views of the National Labor Relations Board.[46]

As is clear, the Court's modern rules and norms are very open to amicus participation. However, the justices have not always allowed virtually limitless participation. Specifically, while the Court's rules have undergone little alteration, their implementation varied during the 1940s and 50s (Kearney and Merrill 2000: 763, Krislov 1963: 710). During this period, large numbers of amicus briefs were submitted in an assortment of cases involving the government's investigation of the Communist Party,

---

44 Prior to the codification of rules regarding amicus participation, the ability to file an amicus brief was left to the discretion of the justices.

45 For example, O'Connor and Epstein (1983a) report that, from 1969 to1981, the Court denied permission to file in only 11% of motions for leave, while Epstein and Knight (1999) reveal that, during the 1994 term, the Court denied only 1 of 111 motions for leave (0.9%). The vast majority of such denials are a result of the briefs being filed beyond the Court's very specific deadlines for the due dates of briefs (Stern, Gressman, Shapiro, and Geller 2002: 658).

46 For the Court's invitation see 373 U.S. 746, at 757.

most notably in *Lawson v. United States* (1949). Here, the "Hollywood Ten"—a group of screenwriters in the film industry—declined to testify before the House Un-American Activities Committee. During this period, the Court was flooded with so-called amicus briefs that were submitted without even the pretense of following the rather simple rules of the Court. Such "briefs" typically ignored the requirement of party consent and declined to petition the Court for leave to file, which is a requirement if the consent of the parties is withheld (Harper and Etherington 1953). Further, the justices viewed these briefs not as well-researched legal instruments, as was expected in an amicus filing, but instead as emotional appeals lacking in legal merit (Harper and Etherington 1953: 1173; Kearney and Merrill 2000: 763; Krislov 1963: 710; Puro 1971: 39–40). To avoid being viewed as a body susceptible to such meritless propaganda, the Court amended its formal rules in 1949 to emphasize that the consent of all parties was required for a nongovernmental amicus to file and stressed the procedures for filing a motion for leave to file if consent was denied (Kearney and Merrill 2000: 763).[47] Most important, however, was the unwritten policy that the Court adopted: to deny virtually all motions for leave to file when party consent was withheld (Harper and Etherington 1953: 1173–1176; O'Connor and Epstein 1983a: 37–38).

The Solicitor General (SG), the principal attorney for the executive branch in the Supreme Court, took the Court's unwritten policy—to deny virtually all motions for leave—as a signal that the Court wanted him to deny permission to file in all cases in which the government was a party, and the SG obliged (Krislov 1963: 714).[48] This was a particularly devastating position for potential amici because the SG participated as a party in approximately half of the Court's cases. Prior to the Court's informal rule, the SG granted consent to file almost automatically and amicus briefs proliferated. After the emergence of the Court's unwritten policy, the SG withheld his permission almost mechanically and these denials resulted in a drought of amicus participation. For example, during the 1949 term, 118 amicus briefs were filed with certiorari petitions and in cases on the merits. This number dropped to 70 during the 1950 term, and to 44 during the 1951 term, reaching an all-time low in 1953 when only 34 briefs were filed (Schubert 1959: 74).

---

47 It is important to note that the Court did not change its prior practice but instead clarified the practice for potential amici.

48 "Him" is used because presidents have yet to appoint a female Solicitor General.

Soon, however, both the Court and the SG would reverse their policies regarding amicus filings, due in large part to comments made by Justices Frankfurter and Black in *On Lee v. United States* (1952).[49] Justice Frankfurter argued:

> The rule governing the filing of amici briefs clearly implies that such briefs should be allowed to come before the Court not merely on the Court's exercise of judgment in each case. On the contrary, it presupposes that the Court may have the aid of such briefs if the parties consent. For the Solicitor General to withhold consent automatically in order to enable this Court to determine for itself the propriety of each application is to throw upon the Court a responsibility that the Court has put upon all litigants, including the Government, preserving to itself the right to accept an amicus brief in any case where it seems unreasonable for the litigants to have withheld consent. If all litigants were to take the position of the Solicitor General, either no amici briefs (other than those that fall within the exceptions of Rule 27) would be allowed, or a fair sifting process for dealing with such applications would be nullified and an undue burden cast upon the Court. Neither alternative is conducive to the wise disposition of the Court's business. (343 U.S. 924, at 924–925)

Justice Frankfurter's comments clearly reveal his unhappiness with the SG's policy to automatically deny leave to file amicus briefs. Further, his comments suggest that such amicus briefs benefit the justices' decision making (see also Breyer 1998; Douglas 1962; O'Connor 1996). Specifically, Frankfurter notes that amicus briefs aid the Court and that their demise would not be conducive to the justices' judicious disposition of cases. In his concurring opinion in the same case, Justice Black expressed the view that "the Court's rule regarding the filing of briefs amici curiae should be liberalized" (343 U.S. 924, at 925), thus challenging both the Court's and the SG's policy regarding amicus submissions.

These statements successfully caused a sea change in both policies. In 1957, the SG issued a "Statement of Policy and Practice Regarding Applications to the Solicitor General for Consent to File Amicus Curiae Briefs in the Supreme Court," which served to effectively liberalize the

---

49 See also Justice Frankfurter in *United States v. Lovknit Manufacturing Company* (1952).

SG's position towards amicus briefs (Krislov 1963: 715). Though the Court failed to issue an explicit policy statement on the state of amicus briefs, it was clear that when consent to file was refused, the Court was granting far more motions for leave to file than denying motions. For example, in 1954 the Court denied all motions for leave, while in 1961 it granted 93% (Krislov 1963: 716). By the early 1960s, the volume of amicus participation, for both the certiorari and merits stages, had rebounded to its pre-1949 levels.

Thus, the Court's modern rules and norms clearly allow for essentially unlimited amicus participation. For a Court facing an increasing workload, as evident in the rise of certiorari petitions that the justices must mull over each year, this suggests that the justices genuinely believe amicus briefs can aid in their decision-making process. If they did not view amicus briefs as useful tools—whether to assist them in making the correct legal decision or as a means to maximize their policy preferences—they likely would continue to use formal or informal policies that limit the participation of organized interests. Simply put, the Court would likely deny permission to file amicus briefs as a means to avoid, for example, the heavy amount of paper that accompanies such filings.[50] That the justices do not opt for such policies implies that they may legitimately benefit from the assistance of such friends of the Court.

III. Levels of Amicus Participation

In this section, I analyze the levels of amicus participation during the 1946–2001 terms of the Supreme Court, as well as the issue areas in which amicus briefs are most commonly filed and the positions advocated in the briefs. Such considerations are important for three reasons. First, by tracking the levels of amicus participation before the Court, a clearer picture of the context of amicus participation is provided. This investigation offers a snapshot of how many amicus briefs the justices saw at any given point in time. Second, by examining the issue areas in which amici participate most often, it will offer leverage over the question of whether

---

50 Under Supreme Court Rule 33, amici are required to submit 40 copies of the briefs to the Court, which are limited to 30 pages per brief (although the page limit is often extended by attaching appendixes to the briefs). Briefs supporting the petitioner are submitted with a light green cover, while a dark green cover is required for briefs supporting the respondent.

they are a common occurrence in all issue areas or whether their presence is more pronounced in civil rights and liberties law, the issue area on which most examinations of amicus influence focus (e.g., Acker 1990; Cortner 1968; Ivers and O'Connor 1987; Kobylka 1987; Wasby 1995). This is significant because, if amicus participation is limited to particular areas of the law, then an analysis of their influence might be best suited to these issue areas. For example, if amicus briefs are not present in federal taxation cases, including such cases in a statistical examination might call the validity of any results into question in that one would be looking for the influence of amicus briefs in an area in which no amicus briefs are present. Finally, by analyzing the positions advocated by the amici— liberal or conservative—intuitions can be gained as to whether liberal groups dominate amicus activity or whether conservative interests find equal representation in the Court (e.g., Epstein 1985).

Figure 3.1 identifies the percentage of Supreme Court cases, in all issue areas, with amicus participation during the 1946–2001 terms.[51] As is clear, the percentage of cases with at least one amicus brief increased rapidly during the period under investigation. For example, during the 1946–1955 terms, amicus briefs were present in an average of 23.3% of cases; this number increased to 34.1% during the 1956–1965 terms, and jumped even further to 52.2% during the 1966 to 1975 terms. The heaviest period of amicus participation occurred during the 1990–2001 terms, where at least one amicus brief was filed in almost 90% of cases before the Court. Given this, amicus participation is clearly now a staple of interest group activity in the Court.

A. Amicus Participation by Issue Area

Figure 3.2 presents information on amicus participation in the Court by analyzing the percentage of cases within five issue areas in which at least one amicus brief was filed during the Vinson, Warren, Burger, and Rehnquist Courts.[52] It is evident that amicus briefs are filed in each of

---

51 More specifically, Figure 3.1 indicates the percentage of orally argued cases decided on the merits, using the case citation as the unit of analysis. As such, the figure excludes briefs filed at the certiorari level. A full discussion of the data on amicus curiae briefs is provided in the Appendix.

52 The issue areas presented in Figure 3.2 are derived from the Spaeth (2002, 2003) databases. Civil rights and liberties issues include cases involving criminal procedure (e.g., search and seizure), civil rights (e.g., discrimination), the First Amendment

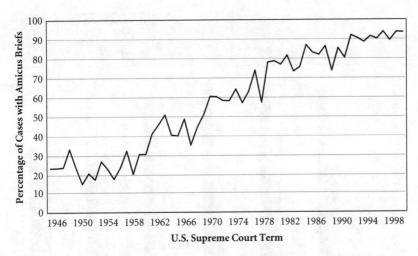

Figure 3.1. Percentage of U.S. Supreme Court Cases with Amicus Curiae Participation, 1946–2001 Terms

these five issue areas, although some issue areas have a higher percentage of amicus participation. Specifically, amicus briefs are filed most often in civil rights, economics, and federalism cases; but two of these issue areas, civil rights and economics, are also the areas in which most of the Court's cases are involved. Further, Figure 3.2 indicates that for all issue areas, amicus participation has been on the upswing; the greatest levels of participation occurred during the Rehnquist Court (1986–2001), consistent with Figure 3.1.

Table 3.1 offers an alternative examination of the levels of amicus participation in each issue area. The first row indicates the percentage of cases with at least one amicus brief for each issue area. These figures largely reflect those presented in Figure 3.2. During the 1946–2001 terms, at least one amicus brief was filed in more than 70% of federalism cases, more than 60% of civil rights and liberties cases, and almost 60% of economics cases. Considering all issues areas combined, amicus briefs were

---

(e.g., freedom of expression), due process (e.g., defendants' rights), privacy (e.g., abortion), and attorneys (e.g., attorneys' commercial speech). Economics includes cases involving economic activity (e.g., liability claims) and union activity (e.g., arbitration). Judicial power involves cases dealing with, e.g., federal court deference to state court proceedings. Federalism cases involve, e.g., federal preemption over state law. Federal taxation typically involves disputes dealing with the Internal Revenue Code. The small numbers of cases (less than 2%) regarding interstate boundary disputes and issues that do not easily lend themselves to categorization are excluded from consideration.

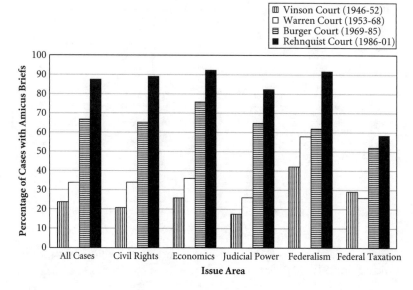

Figure 3.2. Amicus Curiae Participation by Issue Area and Chief Justice's Court, 1946–2001 Terms

Table 3.1. Amicus Curiae Participation by Issue Area, 1946–2001 Terms

	Civil Rights	Eco-nomics	Judicial Power	Federalism	Federal Taxation	Totals[a]
Percent of Cases with Amicus Briefs	60.2 (2,047)	57.3 (992)	51.3 (439)	70.7 (227)	38.4 (109)	57.5 (3,865)
Number of Briefs Filed	8,497	3,755	1,501	1,057	230	15,214
Mean Briefs per Case	2.50	2.17	1.75	3.29	.809	2.26
Maximum Number of Briefs in a Case	78	32	22	24	16	78
Percent of Amicus Participation	53.0	25.7	11.4	5.9	2.8	100
Percent of Cases Decided	50.5 (3,398)	25.8 (1,732)	12.7 (856)	4.8 (321)	4.2 (284)	100 (6,726)

[a] The total column includes 1.99 percent of cases that do not fit into the six issue areas listed here. Numbers in parentheses indicate the number of observations.

present in more than 57% of cases, revealing that during the time frame under analysis here, the justices regularly received persuasion attempts from organized interests.

Rows two and three of Table 3.1 present the number of amicus briefs filed in each issue area and the mean number of amicus briefs per case, respectively. For all issue areas, there is an average of two amicus briefs filed. This figure rises for civil rights and federalism issues as should be expected given the salient nature of civil rights cases for public advocacy groups and public interest law firms, and federalism cases for the American states. The lowest levels of amicus participation occur in federal taxation cases: on average we can expect less than one amicus brief per case in this area.

Row four of Table 3.1 specifies the maximum number of amicus briefs filed in a case for each issue area. The case attracting the most amicus attention, 78 briefs, was *Webster v. Reproductive Health Services* (1989), which involved the constitutionality of abortion.[53] In fact, civil rights and liberties issues produce the three cases with the highest number of amicus filings. *Webster* is followed by *Regents of the University of California v. Bakke* (1978), a high-profile affirmative action case in which 54 amicus briefs were filed, and *Cruzan v. Director, Missouri Department of Health* (1990), a case involving a dispute over whether the parents of a patient who is in a persistent vegetative state can refuse life-saving medical treatment on the patient's behalf. In that case, 39 amicus briefs were filed. Among economics cases, *Container Corporation of America v. Franchise Tax Board* (1983) attracted the most amicus participation with 32 briefs. That case, which dealt with the question of whether U.S. corporations can constitutionally be taxed for profits earned by their overseas subsidiaries, captivated organized interests both foreign and domestic: numerous U.S. corporations and states participated and a brief was filed on behalf of the Government of the Kingdom of the Netherlands. *Daubert v. Merrell Dow Pharmaceuticals* (1993), dealing with whether the general acceptance of scientific evidence is a necessary precondition for that evidence's admission at trial under the Federal Rules of Evidence, attracted 22 amicus briefs, the most among cases regarding judicial power. Among federalism cases, 24 amicus briefs were filed in *Federal Energy Regulatory Commission v. Mississippi* (1982). That case focused on the State of

---

53 This record has since been broken in the University of Michigan affirmative action cases, *Gratz v. Bollinger* (2003) and *Grutter v. Bollinger* (2003), in which more than 100 amicus briefs were filed.

Mississippi's allegation that provisions of the Public Utility Regulatory Policies Act were beyond the scope of congressional powers under the Commerce Clause. As these examples illustrate, it is fairly common for the justices to be the target of a great deal of advocacy efforts, highlighting points of law and policy that might not otherwise be available to them in such high profile cases.

Finally, row five of Table 3.1 indicates each issue area's percentage of all amicus participation. These findings reiterate those discussed above. As expected, civil rights and liberties cases make up the largest percentage of cases with amicus participation, more than 50%; this finding is not surprising given that scholars have long identified these cases as among the most salient to organized interests (e.g., Wasby 1995). Economic decisions make up the second largest category, followed by cases involving judicial power, federalism, and federal taxation, respectively.

B. Ideological Positions Advocated by the Amici

Early studies of interest group activity in the judicial arena found that liberal organizations dominate in the Supreme Court, with little evidence that the justices hear from the conservative side of the debate with any great frequency (e.g., Cortner 1968; Hakman 1966). The implication of this research is vital to understanding organizational participation in the legal system. If the Court hears primarily from liberal organizations, this suggests that the arguments presented to the justices are relatively homogenous, generally supporting, for example, the expansion of core civil rights and liberties. More recently, O'Connor and Epstein (1983b) reevaluated this research by classifying interest groups as either liberal or conservative. These authors uncovered strong evidence that these early studies underestimated the litigation activities of conservative interests: while liberal interests do engage in more case sponsorship, the levels of conservative and liberal amicus activity are, in fact, quite similar (see also Epstein 1985). Though this influential study of organizational participation in the Court revealed that the justices regularly hear from both liberal and conservative interests, it is limited because O'Connor and Epstein (1983b: 480) did not categorize the ideological orientations of the group's *positions* on a case by case basis but instead classified organizations "based on the socio-political status of their clientele group as well as on their professed ideological stance." Although this strategy is capable of capturing the overall sense of an organization's positions, it is imprecise for those occasions in which a traditionally liberal organization makes a conservative argument and vice versa. In other words, to capture the ideological orientation of the persuasion attempts made by organized interests, we are best served by considering the arguments advanced by the amici in each case, rather than their more general ideological proclivities.

Consider the American Civil Liberties Union (ACLU), a group classified as liberal by O'Connor and Epstein (1983b: 482). While the general ideological stance of the organization is liberal in nature, it has filed amicus briefs endorsing the conservative position in more than 50 cases. For example, in *Wisconsin v. Mitchell* (1993), the ACLU advanced the conservative position, arguing that a Wisconsin penalty-enhancement statute, allowing for longer maximum sentences for so-called hate crimes, was a constitutionally permissible use of state police powers, even though the statute conflicted with individuals' free speech rights under the First Amendment. The ACLU's conservative position in the case so frustrated one of its affiliate organizations that the ACLU of Ohio filed its own amicus brief, arguing to the justices that its parent organization accorded insufficient weight to First Amendment values. Similarly, in *Pittsburgh Press v. Pittsburgh Commission on Human Relations* (1973), the ACLU again found itself in conflict with one of its usual allies, the American Newspaper Publishers Association (ANPA). In that case, the ACLU argued that it was constitutionally permissible to compel a newspaper to cease publishing help-wanted advertisements that made a specific reference to the sex of prospective employees, despite the fact that—as argued by the ANPA and accepted by the four dissenting justices—this order constituted a prior restraint on expression in violation of the First Amendment.[54] Accordingly, it is clear that to understand the ideological orientation of amici, we must examine the specific ideological positions advanced in the briefs, and not the more general orientations of each organization. To do this, I investigate the liberal and conservative positions advocated by the amici during the 1946–2001 Supreme Court terms by coding the ideological direction of the briefs according to contemporary definitions of liberal and conservative, as identified in the Spaeth (2002, 2003) databases. Below, I offer examples from each issue area.[55]

---

54 In particular, the *Pittsburgh Press* classified help-wanted ads using the following categories: "Jobs-Male Interest," "Jobs-Female Interest," and "Male-Female."

55 A full discussion of how amicus briefs were coded as liberal and conservative is presented in the Appendix.

The liberal position in a First Amendment free expression case, falling under the broader category of civil liberties, advocates for the constitutionality of the expression, while a conservative position argues for its suppression. For example, in *Barnes v. Glenn Theatre* (1991), a case involving an Indiana law that prohibited nude dancing as a form of entertainment, the ACLU argued the liberal position: the ban was a form of censorship in violation of the First Amendment. The American Family Association took the conservative position in positing that nude dancing, because it is a form of commercial expression, deserves only minimal, if any, First Amendment protection.

hmm?   The liberal position in a religious exercise case supports the free exercise of religion, while a conservative position does the opposite. *Church of the Lukumi Babalu Aye v. City of Hialeah* (1993) provides an excellent example of this. The case involved the Santerian practice of animal sacrifice. When a Santerian church made its intention to move to the City of Hialeah known, the city council reacted by passing an ordinance regulating animal sacrifice. The Church argued that the regulation was not one of broad applicability but instead was intended solely to limit its free exercise of religion. Americans United for Separation of Church and State advocated the liberal position in its amicus brief by arguing that animal sacrifice, however repugnant, is a long-standing and sincere exercise of religion; thus any statute aimed specifically at limiting this form of religious expression violated the First Amendment. Conversely, the International Society for Animal Rights (ISAR) advocated the conservative position: that there is no constitutional right to animal sacrifice. In other words, ISAR sought to suppress the free exercise rights of the Santerians in question.

In economic cases, a liberal amicus brief takes, for example, a proliability position, while a conservative brief does the opposite, as *BMW of North America v. Gore* (1996) illustrates. This case involved the constitutionality of an Alabama punitive damage award of $2 million dollars to a customer who purchased a "new" car for $40,750.88, without knowing that the car had been repainted at the cost of $601.37. The Association of Trial Lawyers of America argued the liberal position, asserting that the award did not offend substantive due process. Conversely, the U.S. Chamber of Commerce took the conservative position, proposing that the award violated the Due Process Clause of the Fourteenth Amendment because of the manner in which the Alabama Supreme Court calculated the punitive damages.

In the context of issues involving judicial power, the liberal position is, for example, pro-exercise of judicial power, while the conservative position is pro-judicial restraint. This might mean that the amicus is asking the Court to expand its rule-making authority (or that of other courts) by taking the liberal position, or alternatively, asking the Court to decline to do so by advocating the conservative position. For example, in *Daubert v. Merrell Dow Pharmaceuticals* (1993), the American Association for the Advancement of Science (AAAS) advanced the conservative position, arguing that scientific evidence must meet the criteria of being generally accepted in the scientific community for it to be admitted in court. In so doing, AAAS sought to limit the ability of trial court judges to discern for themselves the admissibility of evidence. Conversely, the Association of Trial Lawyers in America (ATLA) argued the liberal position: that such a decision would tie the hands of trial court judges, limiting their discretion in determining which evidence is admissible in courts of law. Thus, the ATLA sought to expand the rule-making authority of trial court judges.

For federalism cases, the liberal position is pro-federal government/anti-state, while the conservative position is the reverse. For example, in *Barnett Bank v. Nelson* (1996), a case involving the question of whether a federal statute authorizing banks to sell insurance in small towns preempted a Florida regulation restricting bank insurance sales, the Florida Bankers Association took the liberal position, arguing that the federal statute superseded state authority. The National Conference of State Legislatures advocated the conservative position, maintaining that the authority to regulate the insurance business rests with the states.

In federal taxation cases, a liberal amicus might support the federal government at the expense of the taxpayer or alternatively support the federal government at the expense of a state government, depending on the particulars of the case. *United States v. American College of Physicians* (1986) provides a clear example of the former. The case centered on whether advertisements in the *Annals of Internal Medicine*, published by the tax-exempt American College of Physicians, were taxable on the grounds that they were unrelated to the College's tax-exempt purposes. The American Society of Association Executives filed an amicus brief in support of the conservative position, arguing that Congress did not intend to make all advertising appearing in journals published by tax-exempt organizations subject to taxation and, thus, the advertising content must be judged on a case-by-case basis, rather than by applying a blanket tax on all advertising in the journal. Conversely, the American Business Press argued the liberal position: that all profits gained from advertising must be taxed, regardless of their relationship to the tax-exempt status of the organization.

The small numbers of amicus briefs in cases involving interstate relations are not coded as advocating liberal or conservative positions because the very nature of this litigation makes it virtually impossible to do so because the majority of these cases implicate state boundary disputes. For example, *Georgia v. South Carolina* (1990) involved the boundary line between Georgia and South Carolina at the mouth of the Savannah River. Amicus briefs were filed by the Solicitor General and the State of Alaska, offering the Court suggestions as to the proper determination of the boundary. However, neither of these briefs advocated a particular disposition, nor did they make liberal or conservative arguments as understood by any coherent definitions of the terms.

Figure 3.3 presents the proportion of amicus briefs that advocated the liberal position during the 1946–2001 Supreme Court terms. As is clear, both liberal and conservative arguments found their way into the Court via amicus filings. While there was a relatively large amount of variability in the proportion of liberal briefs during the 1946–1970 terms (mean = .569, standard deviation = .113), this was substantially attenuated after the 1970 term (mean = .527, standard deviation = .041). Interestingly, prior to the boom in conservative interest group litigation

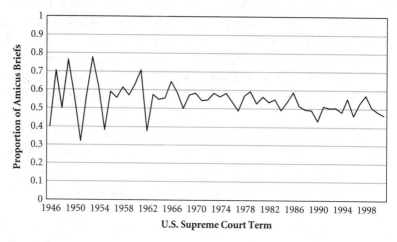

Figure 3.3. Proportion of Amicus Curiae Briefs Advocating the Liberal Position, 1946–2001 Terms

in the 1970s (e.g., Epstein 1985; O'Connor and Epstein 1983b), conservative amici often outnumbered liberal amici, particularly during the 1951
term in which conservative amicus briefs represented almost 70% of all
amicus filings. Thus, it appears that even during the heyday of liberal
group participation, conservative argumentation was equally represented
in the Court via amicus briefs.

Figure 3.4 offers an alternative look at the positions advocated by the
amici. This figure presents the average number of amicus briefs supporting the liberal and conservative positions. This figure makes it abundantly
clear that the levels of conservative and liberal amicus participation effectively matched one another for virtually all terms under analysis. In fact,
the overall correlation between the average number of liberal and conservative briefs is an astonishing 0.97. The largest discrepancies occurred
during the 1947 and 1949 terms, in which liberal amicus briefs outnumbered conservative ones more than twofold. However, it is important to
note that these terms represent some of the lowest levels of amicus participation under examination. Given the results reported in Figures 3.3
and 3.4, it should be quite obvious that neither liberal nor conservative
groups dominate amicus activity in the Supreme Court. Rather, both
ends of the ideological spectrum find a voice in the Court.

This is a noteworthy finding in light of the fact that it provides
evidence that amici do not overwhelmingly file briefs in cases they are

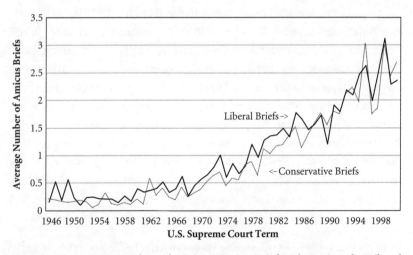

Figure 3.4. Average Number of Amicus Curiae Briefs Advocating the Liberal
and Conservative Positions, 1946–2001 Terms

predisposed towards winning. If this was the case, we would expect to observe the number of conservative amicus briefs outnumber liberal amicus briefs during the tenure of the conservative Vinson Court (1946–1952), while liberal briefs would outnumber conservative briefs in the Warren Court era (1953–1968). Immediately following Warren's tenure as Chief Justice, we would expect to see an increase in the number of conservative briefs (and a decrease in the number of liberal briefs) throughout the conservative Burger (1969–1985) and Rehnquist Courts (1986–2001) eras. That the levels of conservative and liberal amicus briefs effectively matched one another for virtually all terms under analysis provides compelling evidence that amici file briefs in cases that genuinely touch on their interests, rather than "cherry pick" cases for the purposes of appearing efficacious (i.e., file briefs primarily in those cases they are predisposed toward winning as a function of their ideological compatibility with the Court).[56]

IV. Who Participates?

In this section, I investigate the organizations that participate as amicus curiae in the Court's decisions on the merits. The purpose here is to provide insight into whether amicus participation is dominated by particular types of organizations at the expense of others. While an understanding of the Court's rules and norms governing amicus participation suggests that this should not be the case, as all nongovernmental organizations face the same procedural requirements to file amicus briefs, such a consideration is useful. It will establish if the interest group choir in the Court sings with a distinctly upper class accent (e.g., Schattschneider 1960) or, alternatively, that a wide variety of pressure groups attempt to exercise influence in the Court. This analysis is significant because, if the justices only hear from particular types of groups, this implies that the arguments presented to them are likely very homogenous. For example, if corporations dominate amicus activity in the Court, it is probable that the justices are rarely presented with statistical evidence as this information is generally espoused by trade associations and public advocacy groups (e.g., Rustad and Koenig 1993). If, however, the justices are

---

56 For more rigorous analyses examining whether amici file briefs in cases they are predisposed towards winning, which corroborate the above discussion, see Collins (2007) and Solowiej and Collins (2008).

hearing from a multitude of voices in the Court, this intimates that each organized interest offers the Court novel argumentation that might otherwise be unavailable to the justices. As such, a heterogeneous choir of interest group voices in the Court suggests that the justices receive a wide range of information that might aid them in maximizing the application of their policy preferences and/or creating efficacious law (e.g., Collins and Solowiej 2007).

To offer leverage over the types of interest groups who participate in the Court, I analyze amicus participation during the 1950, 1968, 1982, and 1995 terms; this represents a single term from each of the Vinson, Warren, Burger, and Rehnquist Courts.[57] To examine participating organizations, I adapt the classification scheme developed by Caldeira and Wright (1990) and Collins and Solowiej (2007). That is, I categorize all amici participating in these terms according to their membership characteristics. For example, I differentiate between membership organizations (e.g., public advocacy organizations) and staff organizations (e.g., public interest law firms). I also distinguish governmental amici (e.g., state and local governments) from business amici (e.g., corporations). These distinctions are useful for two reasons. First, they simplify the complex nature of amicus participation in the Court. To be sure, the number of organizations that file amicus briefs is nearly overwhelming. For example, during the 1995 term alone the Court had more than 1,600 friends. By reducing the types of amici into basic categories, much can learned about the characteristics of participating organizations. Second, by differentiating among groups on the basis of their basic unit of membership, intuitions can be gained regarding the interest group choir in the Court. For example, it can easily be discerned if amicus activity is dominated by corporations or whether public advocacy groups find an equal voice in the Court.

Table 3.2 presents the 11 categories of organizations and offers examples of each category. Amici were categorized using the amici's own statements contained in the "Interests of Amicus Curiae" section of each brief, which is required information under Supreme Court Rule 37.[58] Note that each organization present on the brief was coded separately, with no

---

57 The data on the 1950 and 1968 terms were collected by the author, data for the 1982 term were collected by Caldeira and Wright (1990), and the information on the 1995 term was collected by Collins and Solowiej (2007).

58 Information in this section of the briefs contains a description of the amicus and typically includes an overview of the group's history of involvement in the courts and a very brief discussion as to how the case at hand will affect the organization's interests.

Table 3.2. A Typology of Interest Group Amici Curiae

Type of Amicus	Examples
Individuals	academics, attorneys, legislators, scientists
Corporations	DiGiorgio Fruit Corporation, Mobil Oil, San Francisco Chronicle
United States	National Labor Relations Board, Solicitor General
State Governments	Commonwealth of Pennsylvania, State of New York
Local Governments	City of New York, Palo Verde Irrigation District
Public Advocacy	American Civil Liberties Union, Americans for Effective Law Enforcement
Public Interest Law Firms	Pacific Legal Foundation, Trial Lawyers for Public Justice
Trade Associations	American Bankers Association, American Sociological Association
Unions	American Federation of Teachers, Major League Baseball Players Association
Peak Associations	AFL-CIO, U.S. Chamber of Commerce, National League of Cities
Other	Hills College Baptist Church, Miccosukee Tribe of Indians of Florida

particular importance given to those amici who appear first on the brief because amici may list themselves alphabetically or randomly on the briefs (Behuniak-Long 1991).[59] Clearly, the classification of several categories is obvious (i.e., individuals, corporations, governments, and unions). However, a brief overview of other typologies is constructive to eliminate any confusion surrounding the classification of amici.

Organizations are classified as public advocacy groups whose membership is made up of individuals, regardless of their professional or occupational status and whose goals are political, rather than economic, in nature. For example, the American Jewish Congress is catalogued as a

---

59 Organized interests might choose to cosign an amicus brief, rather than file an individual brief, for a variety of reasons. For example, groups may do so to lighten the financial burden that accompanies filing an individual brief, to build relations with like-minded organizations, and/or as a low-cost means of pursuing organizational maintenance (provided the group is membership-based). For a more comprehensive discussion of the decision to cosign versus file an individual brief, see Collins (2004a).

public advocacy organization since it defines itself as "a national organization of American Jews founded in 1918 and committed by its constitution to the dual and inseparable purposes of defending and extending American democracy and preserving Jewish heritage and its values."[60]

Groups are classified as public interest law firms if they are nonprofit *legal* organizations that either provide counsel to individuals to further litigation consistent with the group's jurisprudential philosophies or initiate litigation themselves on behalf of their members' interests. Public interest law firms differ from public advocacy organizations because they focus primarily on providing individuals with attorneys. Perhaps not surprisingly, it was essentially effortless to locate such groups because they almost unvaryingly identify themselves as public interest law firms, nonprofit law firms, or some combination of the two. For example, the Lesbian Rights Project identifies itself as "a San Francisco-based nonprofit public interest law firm organized to protect and defend, through legal action and legal education, the rights of lesbians and gay men."[61]

Organizations whose distinguishing characteristic is that membership is based on occupational status are classified as trade associations. These groups differ from public advocacy organizations in that there are no professional barriers to joining public advocacy groups, while such barriers do exist with respect to membership in a trade association. Moreover, these organizations tend to provide benefits to their members that are primarily economic in nature. For example, the Retail Gasoline Dealers Association of Michigan identifies itself as "a Michigan nonprofit membership corporation serving the interests of the retail gasoline dealers of that State. The Association has more than 2,000 members in the State of Michigan, and more than 1,450 members in the Detroit Metropolitan Area. Its Detroit membership is fairly representative of all the retail gasoline dealers of that area."[62]

Peak associations are made up of organizations of organizations. That is, peak associations represent the interests of other institutions, such as labor unions and businesses. In this way, peak associations do not have members in the ordinary sense. Instead, their membership is made

---

60 See amicus curiae brief of the American Civil Liberties Union and the American Jewish Congress, *Epperson v. Arkansas* (1968).

61 See amicus curiae brief of Lambda Legal et al., *Board of Education v. National Gay Taskforce* (1985).

62 See amicus curiae brief of the Retail Gasoline Dealers Association of Michigan, *Standard Oil v. F.T.C.* (1951).

up of institutions. For example, the National Congress of Petroleum Retailers is a "trade congress of affiliated retail gasoline dealer associations throughout the nation, formed for the purpose of fostering and promoting the interests and welfare of the 275,000 gasoline retailers in the United States. It is the only trade association of retail dealers in petroleum products having a nation-wide representation."[63]

Finally, groups that do not conform to any of these categories are classified as "other" amici. These include the Hills College Baptist Church, the Miccosukee Tribe of Indians of Florida, as well as *ad hoc* organizations such as the Plaintiff's Committee In re Air Crash Disaster at Lockerbie, Scotland.

Table 3.3 reports participating amici in the terms under analysis.[64] As this table makes clear, a wide variety of organizations engage in amicus activity in the Supreme Court. The first column indicates the number of cases in which at least one of the organizations classified appeared on an amicus brief. The purpose here is to recognize how frequently the justices see each organizational type in cases with amicus participation. Note that the numbers in parentheses do not total 100 because different types of amici often participate in the same case. This column reveals that, for example, individuals appeared on amicus briefs in 21% of cases where an amicus brief was filed. The most common amici are trade associations, who appear in 63% of cases with amicus participation, followed by state governments (41.5%), public advocacy groups (38.7%), public interest law firms (37.2%), and the U.S. government (36.4%), respectively. Groups appearing somewhat infrequently include labor unions (14.2%) and local governments (19.0%).

Column two reports the number of briefs filed in which each of the organizational types participated, that is, how often each category of amici appears on the briefs. Again, note the percentages do not equal 100 because divergent amici often appear on the same briefs. The most frequent amici in terms of the number of briefs filed is again trade associations (38.3%), followed by public advocacy organizations (27.8%), state governments (16.7%), public interest law firms (16.6%), and corporations (11.5%). The least frequent amici with regard to the number

---

63 See amicus curiae brief of the Michigan Petroleum Association and the National Association of Petroleum Retailers, *Standard Oil v. F.T.C.* (1951).

64 Table 3.6 reports the same information, broken down by the terms under analysis.

Table 3.3. Amicus Curiae Participation in the Supreme Court

Amicus Type	Number of Cases	Number of Briefs	Number of Amici
Individuals	53 (20.9)	78 (7.4)	544 (12.1)
Corporations	69 (27.3)	120 (11.5)	376 (8.4)
United States	92 (36.4)	101 (9.6)	96 (2.1)
State Governments	105 (41.5)	175 (16.7)	1,139 (25.4)
Local Governments	48 (19.0)	64 (6.1)	160 (3.6)
Public Advocacy	98 (38.7)	291 (27.8)	700 (15.6)
Public Interest Law Firms	94 (37.2)	174 (16.6)	263 (5.9)
Trade Associations	160 (63.2)	401 (38.3)	761 (17.0)
Unions	36 (14.2)	50 (4.8)	90 (2.0)
Peak Associations	83 (32.8)	108 (10.3)	175 (3.9)
Other	61 (24.1)	92 (8.8)	177 (4.0)
Totals	253	1,048	4,481

Numbers in parentheses indicate within column percentages. These data represent amicus curiae participation in the 1950, 1968, 1982, and 1995 Supreme Court terms. The same information, broken down by term, is located in Table 3.6. Sources: 1950 and 1968 terms: collected by author; 1982 term: Caldeira and Wright (1990); 1995 term: Collins and Solowiej (2007).

of briefs filed are individuals (7.4%), local governments (6.1%), and unions (4.8%).

Column three identifies the percentage of total amici that each type of group represents. These figures offer leverage over how often the justices observe each type of amicus. In terms of the number of amici, the most common participants are state governments, who compose a quarter of amici, followed by trade associations (17.0%), public advocacy groups (15.6%), individuals (12.1%), and corporations (8.4%). These figures comport with the literature that demonstrates that the highest levels of coalitional activity occur among state amici and trade associations (e.g., Collins and Solowiej 2007). In other words, these figures reveal that, for example, state governments frequently cosign amicus briefs in an attempt to demonstrate broad support to the Court on matters that implicate state and local concerns (e.g., Collins 2004a).

Having examined the organizational typology of amici that participate in the Court, it is now appropriate to evaluate whether the interest group choir is most consistent with a pluralist or elitist perspective.

According to pluralist theories, organized interests represent a broad cross-section of society; competition among these divergent groups prevents one group type from dominating amicus activity in the Court, thus potentially moderating the Court's policy outputs (e.g., Dahl 1961; Truman 1951). Conversely, elitism is denoted by the dominance of particular types of organizations: corporate and institutional interests. Under this conception, the interest group choir is biased, reflecting inequalities in the American political system (e.g., Schattschneider 1960). As Baumgartner and Leech (1998: 117) note, one of the shortcomings of research that evaluates interest group activity in the federal government is that there is no single point of reference for determining whether organizational participation is most consistent with a pluralist or elitist viewpoint. Accordingly, to reach a conclusion supporting one perspective or the other, one is best served by comparing results to other studies of lobbying activity in Washington (e.g., Caldeira and Wright 1990; Collins and Solowiej 2007; Lowery and Gray 2004). To do this, I contrast these results with Schlozman and Tierney's (1986: 67) seminal study of interest group participation in Washington. Those authors found that corporations accounted for 52% of organizations, trade associations made up 25% of Washington lobbyists, and public advocacy organizations, including public interest law firms, composed only 7% of pressure groups. Schlozman and Tierney (1986: 87) used those figures to rightly conclude that "the number of organizations in the Washington pressure community is tilted heavily in favor of the advantaged, especially business, at the expense of the representation of broad publics and the disadvantaged."

Considering first the number of amici for comparison, interest group participation is starkly different in the Court. Corporations make up only 8% of amici, while trade associations account for 17% of friends. Public advocacy organizations, including public interest law firms, compose more than 21% of amici. It is therefore clear that both broad public interest organizations and corporate and professional interests participate in the Court in roughly equal numbers. Indeed, the same conclusion is reached by examining the number of cases or the number of briefs in which each category of amici appear. For example, corporations appear on 12% of briefs and trade associations are present on 38% of briefs, while public interest groups appear on 44% of amicus briefs. Similarly, while corporate interests participate in 27% of cases with an amicus brief, and trade associations participate in 63% of controversies, public advocacy organizations appear in 39% of disputes and public interest law firms are present in 37% of the Court's litigation. Thus, whether one examines the number of amici, the number of briefs on which the amici appear, or the number of cases, the pressure group system in the Supreme Court reflects a much more diverse set of interests than Washington lobbying activity more generally. This indicates that a pluralist account of pressure groups best comports with amicus participation in the Court. High resource groups (i.e., elitist organizations), such as corporations and professional associations, do not dominate amicus activity. Rather, a diverse spectrum of organized interests finds a voice in the Court, including *ad hoc* organizations of individuals. These results provide evidence that not only is amicus participation pluralistic in terms of the liberal and conservative positions advocated by the amici, but it is also pluralistic with regard to the organizations represented in the Court. This suggests that the justices are the recipients of diverse argumentation regarding their legal and policy decisions. To more clearly parse out the types of arguments presented to the justices, I now turn to the important task of analyzing the information contained in amicus filings.

V. Types of Information Supplied by Amicus Briefs

The primary purpose of this research is to investigate whether amicus briefs influence the decision making of the justices and, if so, how and under what circumstances. Above, I offered support for the premise that the justices genuinely believe that amicus briefs can influence their decision making, as illustrated by the development of the relatively lax rules and norms regarding amicus activity. In addition, I provided evidence that a wide variety of organizations participate as amici in the Court. Though it is reasonable to assume that because a broad range of interests file amicus briefs, each offer the justices their own unique perspectives on the issues before the Court, such an assumption is unnecessary. Rather, here I analyze the persuasion attempts contained in amicus filings to determine the types of information amici offer the justices.

To analyze the information amici supply the justices in their advocacy efforts, it is necessary to obtain data about the arguments contained in both the litigant and amicus briefs. By examining the information contained in petitioner, respondent, and amicus briefs, intuitions can be gained as to whether amicus briefs offer the justices new information or simply reiterate information found in the parties' briefs, as some suggest (e.g., Flaherty 1983; Vose 1955). Several options present themselves in pursuing this line of inquiry. For example, Comparato (2003: 74) posits that this information can be obtained simply by examining the main headings of the "Arguments" section in the "Index" of the briefs. This section generally outlines the arguments advanced by the amici and parties and identifies the legal authorities relied on to support those advocacy efforts. Similarly, Spriggs and Wahlbeck (1997) code the information contained in amicus briefs relying on the "Arguments" sections of the briefs. They argue that this is an appropriate way to code arguments because Supreme Court Rule 24.6 requires that briefs be "logically arranged with proper headings."

To determine what type of information amici offer the justices, I have opted for a hybrid approach. Specifically, I examine the "Arguments" section of the briefs to determine, first, what types of arguments amici advance and, second, whether the briefs reiterate the arguments made by the parties to litigation. Next, I examine the "Table of Authorities" section to inspect the authorities the amici use to justify their argumentation (e.g., cases, statutes, legal texts). This offers additional leverage as to whether amicus briefs reiterate the arguments of the parties. For example, it is plausible that an amicus brief might merely repeat the arguments of the party it supported in the "Arguments" section but rely on alternative authorities, such as novel precedents, statutes, or social scientific research, for its justification for doing so.

I have classified the information contained in amicus filings into four categories: legal, policy, separation of powers, and other.[65] Legal issues encompass state and federal statutory and constitutional issues, including the suggested application (or disregard) of precedent, proper procedure, or common law. Legal issues also include statements about threshold issues, such as whether the parties have standing or the Court has jurisdiction. Policy issues contain arguments about the course of action the Court should take and statements about public policy. For example, this includes information regarding the possible influence that the decision will have on society at large or on particular segments of society, including testimony about the economic and political repercussions of the decision. Separation of powers issues encompass arguments regarding the preferences of other actors in American government, such as Congress, the executive, and state

---

65 These categories are well recognized in the amicus literature as subsuming the persuasion attempts made by amici curiae in the courts (e.g., Collins 2004a; Comparato 2003; Epstein and Knight 1998, 1999; Kearney and Merrill 2000; Spriggs and Wahlbeck 1997).

officials. Finally, arguments that do not fit into any of these categories are coded as other. Note that for the purposes of this analysis, these categories are mutually exclusive (e.g., an argument fitting into the legal category does not also fit into the separation of powers category).

The purpose of this section is to illustrate the types of information contained in amicus filings in an effort to understand the context of amicus briefs as it relates to both the party briefs and legal persuasion more generally. Importantly, here I do not draw any inferences as to their influence on the justices' decisions making. To investigate the argumentation in the briefs, I analyze 121 arguments advanced in 52 amicus briefs filed in 12 cases. Two cases were decided under the Vinson Court, two cases were decided under the Warren Court, and I examine four cases from both the Burger and Rehnquist Courts. To gain insight over a range of cases common to the amicus environment, I have selected cases in which amicus briefs are both symmetrical and asymmetrical.[66] To reflect symmetrical participation, I selected four cases, decided under the Vinson, Warren, and Burger Courts, where a single brief was filed for each ideological position, and two cases, decided under Rehnquist Court, where there were two briefs filed for each ideological position. These numbers mesh roughly with the typical scenario for each chief justice's term in cases where an identical number of amicus briefs were submitted for each litigant. To reflect asymmetric amicus participation, I selected six cases in which the number of amicus briefs supporting the liberal and conservative positions were lopsided in one ideological direction. That is, I selected three cases where liberal amicus briefs outnumbered conservative briefs by a difference of two or more and three cases in which conservative amicus briefs outnumbered liberal briefs by a difference of two or more. Finally, to maximize variability among cases, I selected cases falling under diverse issue areas.

Table 3.4 identifies the cases, issues, briefly discusses the legal questions they involve, and reports the amici participating in each case. In general, the cases under consideration represent a heterogeneous set of issue areas. The cases involve civil liberties (e.g., *Robbins v. California*), civil rights (e.g., *Kadrmas v. Dickenson Public Schools*), economics (e.g., *E.P.A. v. National*

---

66 In the cases under analysis, the number of liberal and conservative briefs matched one another 21% of the time. In the remaining 79% of cases, briefs advocating for one ideological position outnumbered the other by an average of 2 briefs (standard deviation = 2).

Crushed Stone Association), judicial power (e.g., *Lujan v. National Wildlife Federation*), and taxation (e.g., *State Board of Insurance v. Todds Shipyards*). In addition, the amici constitute a very disparate group, representing eight of the nine primary organizational classifications as reported in Table 3.2. For example, the amici include individuals (e.g., Len Marek et al.), corporations (e.g., Capital Cities Communications), governments (e.g., North Dakota), public advocacy groups (e.g., ACLU), public interest law firms (e.g., Pacific Legal Foundation), trade organizations (e.g., National Cattlemen's Association), and peak associations (e.g., AFL-CIO).

Table 3.5 summarizes the information contained in the 52 amicus briefs under analysis. Several findings are of note. First, the vast majority of amicus briefs, more than 70%, offer the justices information that is not found in the party briefs. Frequently, these briefs provide the justices with treatments of precedents not addressed by the parties, point to alternative constitutional and statutory interpretations, and/or discuss a case's policy ramifications for society at large. Attesting to the diversity of the sample, this figure is effectively identical to that reported by Spriggs and Wahlbeck (1997), who found that amicus briefs offered the justices new information 67% of the time.[67] Second, it is clear that the justices are offered additional information even in cases with asymmetric participation. For example, in *O'Lone v. Estate of Shabazz*, every single amicus brief provided the justices with persuasion not found in the briefs of the parties. In that case, only the amicus brief of the Commonwealth of Pennsylvania repeated an argument made by one of the parties. In fact, new arguments are more likely to be found in asymmetric cases. Compared with cases with an identical number of liberal and conservative briefs, in cases where one ideological position outnumbers the other by two or more, novel information increased by 8%. This finding is of interest because it indicates that increases in the number of amicus briefs in a case do not necessarily lead to repetition in the information available to the justices.

Third, note that every single amicus brief supplied the justices with some new legal authorities. This makes clear that even when an amicus repeats the arguments made by the party it supports, it does so by

---

67 Spriggs and Wahlbeck (1997) examined all amicus briefs filed during the 1992 Supreme Court term. However, they did not code the individual arguments contained in the briefs, as in the present analysis, but instead coded briefs on the basis of whether they presented the justices with information not contained in the party briefs.

Table 3.4. Cases, Issues, and Amici Under Analysis

Schwegmann Brothers v. Calvert Distillers (1951)	**Antitrust:** Does the Miller-Tydings Act authorize wholesalers to prevent retailers from selling goods below fixed minimum prices?
	Conservative Amici: American Booksellers Association et al.; Louisiana State Pharmaceutical Association; National Association of Retail Druggists et al.; Pennsylvania **Liberal Amici:** U.S. Solicitor General
Adler v. Board of Education (1952)	**Security Risks:** Is a New York civil service law, declaring ineligible for employment any person advocating or belonging to an organization that advocates the overthrow of government by force or violence, consistent with the First Amendment's freedoms of speech and assembly?
	Conservative Amici: State of New York **Liberal Amici:** ACLU
State Board of Insurance v. Todd Shipyards (1962)	**State Tax:** Is a state tax on insurance premiums paid out-of-state on out-of-state insurance allowable under the Due Process Clause of the Fourteenth Amendment?
	Conservative Amici: Church Fire Insurance et al. **Liberal Amici:** Louisiana
Gideon v. Wainwright (1963)	**Right to Counsel:** Does the Sixth Amendment's right to assistance of counsel in criminal prosecutions apply to state court proceedings?
	Conservative Amici: Alabama **Liberal Amici:** ACLU et al.; Massachusetts et al.; Oregon
Robbins v. California (1981)	**Search and Seizure:** Is the warrantless opening of a closed container found in a lawfully searched vehicle a violation of the Fourth Amendment?
	Conservative Amici: U.S. Solicitor General **Liberal Amici:** State Public Defender of California

Continued

Table 3.4 (continued). Cases, Issues, and Amici Under Analysis

E.P.A. v. National Crushed Stone Association (1980)	**Environmental Protection:** Is the Environmental Protection Agency required to consider economic ability as a factor in granting variances from complying with pollution discharge limitations?
	Conservative Amici: New England Legal Foundation **Liberal Amici:** Natural Resources Defense Council
Philadelphia Newspapers v. Hepps (1986)	**Defamation:** Does a private figure plaintiff, alleging defamation, have the burden of proving falsity of speech on a matter of public concern?
	Conservative Amici: American Legal Foundation **Liberal Amici:** ACLU et al.; AFL-CIO; Capital Cities Communications; Print and Broadcast Media Organizations
Witters v. Washington Department of Services for the Blind (1986)	**Religious Establishment:** Are state rehabilitation aid payments to a blind student for education at a Christian college in violation of the Establishment Clause of the First Amendment?
	Conservative Amici: American Jewish Committee; American Jewish Congress; Christian Legal Society; National Legal Christian Foundation; Rutherford Institute; U.S. Solicitor General **Liberal Amici:** ACLU et al.; Americans United for Separation of Church and State; Anti-Defamation League of B'nai B'rith et al.
O'Lone v. Estate of Shabazz (1987)	**Free Exercise of Religion:** Do New Jersey prison regulations, preventing Muslim inmates from attending Friday afternoon congregational ceremonies, violate the Free Exercise Clause of the First Amendment?
	Conservative Amici: Pennsylvania; U.S. Solicitor General **Liberal Amici:** ACLU et al.; American Jewish Congress; Catholic League for Religious and Civil Rights et al.; Imam Jamh Abdullah Al-Amin et al.; Len Marek et al.

Table 3.4 (continued). Cases, Issues, and Amici Under Analysis

Kadrmas v. Dickenson Public Schools (1988)	**Poverty Law:** Does a North Dakota statute, authorizing certain public school districts to charge a busing fee, violate the Equal Protection Clause of the Fourteenth Amendment?
	Conservative Amici: North Dakota; U.S. Solicitor General **Liberal Amici:** ACLU et al.; Children's Defense Fund
Thornburgh v. Abbott (1989)	**First Amendment:** Are federal prison regulations, governing the receipt of subscription publications by federal inmates, in violation of the Free Speech and Press Clauses of the First Amendment?
	Conservative Amici: Missouri; Florida and Idaho **Liberal Amici:** American Publishers Association; Correctional Association of New York
Lujan v. National Wildlife Federation (1990)	**Standing to Sue:** Does the respondent meet the requirements for judicial review as a person adversely affected or aggrieved by the actions of the Interior Department?
	Conservative Amici: American Farm Bureau; National Cattlemen's Association et al.; Pacific Legal Foundation; Washington Legal Foundation **Liberal Amici:** California et al.; Wilderness Society

offering the justices new legal authorities to support those persuasion attempts. For example, in *Kadrmas v. Dickenson Public Schools*, the Solicitor General repeated the respondent's argument that a school bus fee does not violate the Equal Protection Clause of the Fourteenth Amendment simply because the fee produces greater hardship on those individuals with lesser financial resources. However, the SG justified this claim through the citation of no less than 15 United States Codes that were not referenced by the respondent. Thus, even when an amicus reiterates an argument already advanced by a party to litigation, it almost always does so through the introduction of fresh legal authorities.

Table 3.5. Information Contained in Amicus Curiae Briefs

	Symmetric Cases	Asymmetric Cases	All Cases
Number of Briefs	16 (100)	36 (100)	52 (100)
Briefs with New Authorities	16 (100)	36 (100)	52 (100)
Number of Arguments	38 (100)	83 (100)	121 (100)
Number of New Arguments	25 (65.8)	61 (73.5)	86 (71.1)
Number of Reiterated Arguments	13 (34.2)	22 (26.5)	35 (28.9)
Number of Legal Arguments	27 (71.1)	61 (73.5)	88 (72.7)
Number of Policy Arguments	8 (21.1)	15 (18.1)	23 (19.0)
Number of SOP Arguments	2 (5.3)	6 (7.2)	8 (6.6)
Number of Other Arguments	1 (2.6)	1 (1.2)	2 (1.7)

Numbers in parentheses indicate within column percentages.

Finally, the results indicate that amicus briefs most often offer the justices legal argumentation. Indeed, some 73% of arguments under analysis were legal in nature. This is followed by policy arguments (19.0%), separation of powers arguments (6.6%), and other arguments (1.7%). While the SG's brief in *Kadrmas* offers a clear example of legal argumentation, the other categories might be less obvious. Accordingly, examples of these arguments are offered below.

The Correctional Association of New York's amicus brief in *Thornburgh v. Abbott* offers an excellent illustration of a policy argument advanced by an amicus. In its brief, the Association argued that without rigorous judicial scrutiny, prison censorship inevitably expands beyond its legitimate boundaries. To support this claim, the amicus offered the Court a detailed discussion of the censorship policies in New York correctional facilities, suggesting that the justices adopt New York's four-part policy for prison censorship.

In its amicus brief in *Lujan v. National Wildlife Federation*, the Pacific Legal Foundation (PLF) offered the justices two related separation of powers arguments. First, the group argued that the framers of the Constitution envisioned a judiciary that while powerful, would not usurp the powers of the other branches of government. Second, the PLF argued that the Court should not expand on the doctrine of standing to sue because doing so would be an unwise expansion of judicial power. In making these arguments, the PLF was clearly offering the justices information regarding the proper role of the judiciary in a government of separated powers.

The amicus brief of Imam Jamh Abdullah Al-Amin et al., filed on behalf of several Arab-American civil rights organizations, offers an example of a nontraditional argument advanced by an amicus. In the brief, amici presented the justices with a detailed history of Islamic Friday prayer service, framing it for the justices as comparable to Saturday temple services for Jews and Sunday services for a variety of Christian denominations. As such, the amici offered the justices novel information regarding the religious services of Arab-Americans implicated by the case.

In sum, it is evident that amicus briefs often supply the justices with information that is otherwise unavailable to them. More than 70% of amicus briefs offer the justices new argumentation and every brief under analysis expanded on the legal authorities found in the party briefs. In addition, amicus briefs most often contain legal argumentation but additionally contain policy, separation of powers, and nontraditional argumentation.

VI. Summary and Conclusions

This chapter discussed and analyzed five central issues important for understanding the context of amicus activity in the Court. First, I explored the history of amicus participation from Roman law to its current incarnation in the U.S. Supreme Court. It was made abundantly clear that the amicus curiae has shifted in its primary function from a neutral legal advisor in Roman courts to very much an adversarial legal weapon in the U.S. system. Second, I discussed the rules and norms governing amicus activity in the Court. This section revealed that the justices welcome the participation of organized interests, presumably because they aid the justices in their decision making. Given that the Court is constantly facing an increasing workload, as evidenced by the growing number of certiorari petitions submitted to the Court, the open door policy toward amicus participation provides reasonably strong evidence that the justices look favorably on the information contained in amicus filings. Third, I examined the frequency of amicus participation in the Court and the positions advocated by the amici. The results indicated that though amicus briefs are most commonly filed in civil rights and liberties cases, their presence is well established across all issue areas and they are very much an everyday occurrence in the Court. In addition, the results revealed that amici advocate liberal and conservative positions with almost equal vigor. Fourth, I investigated the types of organizations who file amicus briefs in the Court. This analysis indicated that amicus participation in the Court is pluralistic in the sense that particular types of organizations do not dominate amicus activity. Instead, a wide array of organizations finds a voice in the Court. Finally, I discussed the types of information amicus briefs offer the justices. Here it was concluded that the vast majority— more than 70%—of amicus briefs offer the justices new argumentation and all amicus briefs under analysis supply the justices with alternative legal authorities. I now turn to the central importance of this book: establishing the theoretical foundations for the expected influence of amicus briefs on the individual justices' decision making and subjecting these accounts to empirical validation.

Table 3.6. Amicus Curiae Participation in the U.S. Supreme Court

Type of Amicus	Number of Cases				Number of Briefs				Number of Amici			
	1950	1968	1982	1995	1950	1968	1982	1995	1950	1968	1982	1995
Individuals	2	5	26	20	2	5	37	34	4	6	158	376
	(8.7)	(12.5)	(21.7)	(28.6)	(4.3)	(6.3)	(7.1)	(8.5)	(3.2)	(3.0)	(6.4)	(22.3)
Corporations	6	4	43	16	6	4	61	49	32	27	200	117
	(26.1)	(10.0)	(35.8)	(22.9)	(13.0)	(5.0)	(11.7)	(12.3)	(25.6)	(13.6)	(8.1)	(6.9)
United States	8	9	50	25	8	9	59	25	8	9	50	29
	(34.8)	(22.5)	(41.7)	(35.7)	(17.4)	(11.3)	(11.3)	(6.3)	(6.4)	(4.6)	(2.0)	(1.7)
State Governments	6	9	67	23	13	17	114	31	42	64	684	349
	(26.1)	(22.5)	(55.8)	(32.9)	(28.3)	(21.3)	(21.8)	(7.8)	(33.6)	(32.3)	(27.7)	(20.7)
Local Governments	0	3	38	7	0	3	51	10	0	3	102	55
	(0.0)	(7.5)	(31.7)	(10.0)	(0.0)	(3.8)	(9.8)	(2.5)	(0.0)	(1.5)	(4.1)	(3.3)
Public Advocacy	3	11	44	40	4	16	199	72	4	33	454	209
	(13.0)	(27.5)	(36.7)	(57.1)	(8.7)	(20.0)	(38.1)	(18.0)	(3.2)	(16.7)	(18.4)	(12.4)
Public Interest Law Firms	0	3	60	31	0	4	123	47	0	6	186	71
	(0.0)	(7.5)	(50.0)	(44.3)	(0.0)	(5.0)	(23.6)	(11.8)	(0.0)	(3.0)	(7.5)	(4.2)
Trade Associations	3	8	101	48	6	9	250	136	21	31	416	293
	(13.0)	(20.0)	(84.2)	(68.6)	(13.0)	(11.3)	(47.9)	(34.0)	(16.8)	(15.6)	(16.8)	(17.4)
Unions	4	1	24	7	4	2	33	11	7	2	50	31
	(17.4)	(2.5)	(20.0)	(10.0)	(8.7)	(2.5)	(6.3)	(2.8)	(5.6)	(1.0)	(2.0)	(1.8)

Continued

Table 3.6 (continued). Amicus Curiae Participation in the U.S. Supreme Court

Type of Amicus	Number of Cases				Number of Briefs				Number of Amici			
	1950	1968	1982	1995	1950	1968	1982	1995	1950	1968	1982	1995
Peak Associations	6	8	42	27	7	9	47	45	7	10	73	85
	(26.1)	(20.0)	(35.0)	(38.6)	(15.2)	(11.3)	(9.0)	(11.3)	(5.6)	(5.1)	(3.0)	(5.0)
Other	0	3	50	8	0	5	69	18	0	7	99	71
	(0.0)	(7.5)	(41.7)	(11.4)	(0.0)	(6.3)	(13.2)	(4.5)	(0.0)	(3.5)	(4.0)	(4.2)
All Amici	23	40	120	70	46	80	522	400	125	198	2,472	1,686

Numbers in parentheses indicate within column percentages. Number of orally argued cases decided each term: 1950–97; 1968–113; 1982–156; 1995–79.
Sources: 1950 and 1968 terms: collected by author; 1982 term: Caldeira and Wright (1990); 1995 term: Collins and Solowiej (2007).

CHAPTER 4

Amici Curiae and Judicial Decision Making

On October 14, 1980, the Supreme Court noted probable jurisdiction[68] in *Metromedia v. San Diego*. The case involved a City of San Diego ordinance that would serve to effectively eliminate the erection of outdoor advertising displays within the city.[69] San Diego argued that the ordinance was fully within its police powers because the ban on outdoor advertising both eliminated hazards to motorists brought about by distracting billboards and improved the appearance of the city. Metromedia, along with several other companies engaged in the outdoor advertising business, argued that the ban violated its First Amendment rights to freedom of speech and expression. For the Supreme Court, the case centered on the fact that the San Diego ordinance banned both commercial and noncommercial advertising, the latter including social and political messages

---

68 When the Supreme Court determines that a case "on appeal" should be fully briefed and argued, it does so with an order noting probable jurisdiction. This process is very similar to the more common certiorari procedure: both appellate routes require only a vote of four justices and the petitions are virtually identical in form (e.g., *Eaton v. Price* 1959; Stern, Gressman, Shapiro, and Geller 2002: 332–338).

69 The ban did, however, allow for the advertising of goods and services sold onsite, along with a small number of other exceptions.

that traditionally carry more substantial First Amendment protections than commercial speech.[70]

This fact was not lost on Metromedia and its fellow appellants. However, they knew that because they did not engage in political speech themselves, but rather leased billboard space to others who might engage in such speech, for them to credibly argue the political speech issue before the Court would be difficult. Accordingly, Metromedia's attorneys, including former Bush Administration Solicitor General Theodore Olson,[71] enlisted the aid of the American Civil Liberties Union (ACLU), a celebrated First Amendment advocate, to file an amicus curiae brief arguing the political speech aspects of the case (Ennis 1984: 607). In addition to the ACLU's amicus brief, four others were filed in support of Metromedia, representing a diverse spectrum of groups including the conservative Pacific Legal Foundation (PLF) and the American Newspaper Publishers Association (ANPA). Five amicus briefs were filed in opposition to Metromedia's position, representing amici with equal, if not more substantial, clout as the ACLU, including President Carter's Solicitor General, the states of Hawaii, Maine, and Vermont, and the National Institute of Municipal Law Officers (NIMLO), an organization composed of local law officials representing more than 1,500 municipalities throughout the United States.

Each of these amici supplied the Court with unique insights into the potential legal and policy ramifications stemming from the decision. While the liberal ACLU focused on the First Amendment issue as it involved the suppression of political speech, the conservative PLF centered its arguments on the commercial law consequences that might result from upholding the San Diego law, going so far as to claim that the law violated the Fifth Amendment's prohibition against the deprivation of property without due process of law. The ANPA took a broader stance than the ACLU, arguing that the First Amendment is absolute, thus barring any governmental interference with the dissemination of information. The two remaining amicus briefs in support of Metromedia were filed by the Outdoor Advertising Association of America (OAAA), a trade association of the outdoor advertising industry, and by Robert and

---

70 See, e.g., *Central Hudson Gas and Electric v. Public Service Commission* (1980) and *Virginia Pharmacy Board v. Virginia Citizens Consumer Council* (1976), noting that, while purely commercial speech enjoys First Amendment protection, it does not enjoy such protection on an equal footing with noncommercial speech.

71 Olson served as Solicitor General from June of 2001 to July of 2004.

Barbara Pope, proprietors of a small, family-owned outdoor advertising business in San Diego. While the Pope brief highlighted the detrimental effects upholding the San Diego law would have on small business owners like themselves, thus putting a human face on the regulation, the OAAA presented the Court with statistical evidence involving the repercussions of upholding the ordinance for the industry at large, including a historical discussion of the billboard industry in America. Clearly, each amicus offered the Court novel information that might not otherwise be available to the justices.

Supporting the San Diego ordinance, the Carter Administration's Solicitor General, Wade McCree, argued that the ban was a perfectly acceptable exercise of the city's police powers and highlighted for the Court the potential problems that might arise for the federal Highway Beautification Act of 1965, should the Court determine that the San Diego regulation was invalid. The states of Hawaii, Maine, and Vermont, which joined a single amicus brief, noted to the Court that should it opt to invalidate the San Diego ordinance, such a decision would also judicially invalidate the statewide ban on commercial advertising in Maine and render similar bans in Hawaii and Vermont unenforceable. Amici City and County of San Francisco submitted a brief to the Court arguing that the proper standard for considering the ban was not the rigorous strict scrutiny standard, but instead a more relaxed rational basis test.[72] Further, San Francisco contended that the case was not really about the First Amendment, but instead involved a zoning regulation with only an incidental relation to freedom of speech, plainly framing the case differently than appellant amici ACLU and ANPA. In the amicus brief filed by seven California cities, evidence was presented suggesting that commercial advertising would continue in the city even with the ordinance in place, albeit on a much smaller scale, thus offering the Court a potential means to sidestep the First Amendment issue. In NIMLO's amicus brief, it was argued that the proper Court decision was to decline to accept the appellant's view and declare that billboards are a distinct and valuable medium for expression, thus requiring stringent First Amendment

---

72 Strict scrutiny is the most rigid level of scrutiny used by the Court to evaluate alleged violations of First Amendment law in cases involving issues of freedom of speech and expression. To survive this level of scrutiny, it must be shown that a law is narrowly tailored to serve a compelling government interest. Conversely, the rational basis test evaluates a law to determine only if it is reasonably related to a legitimate government interest; if such a finding is made, then the law is not in violation of the First Amendment.

protection, but instead defer to the desires of democratically elected city councils who have determined that such bans are beneficial to their constituents. Though the San Diego amici offered very different arguments than the amici supporting Metromedia, they, nonetheless, offered the Court distinctive insights into the legal and policy ramifications stemming from the outcome of the case.

The Supreme Court announced its decision on July 2, 1981. Unable to reach a majority, a plurality of the Court determined that although the City of San Diego had a legitimate reason for enacting the ban, the ordinance violated the First Amendment because it restricted both commercial and noncommercial speech, with the latter enjoying a greater degree of protection.[73] Writing for the plurality, Justice White explained that because the ban allowed for the advertising of goods and services sold onsite, it favored commercial speech at the expense of noncommercial speech, such as speech involving political and social activism, which is traditionally accorded a greater degree of First Amendment protection.[74] As such, White's opinion relied heavily on the arguments provided by appellant amici, most notably the ACLU.

In his concurring opinion, Justice Brennan, joined by Justice Blackmun, expressed the view that the San Diego ordinance violated the First Amendment because it amounted to a total prohibition of outdoor advertising in the city.[75] In so doing, Brennan incorporated the arguments of the ACLU, OAAA, and the other appellant amici by accepting the position that billboards are a valuable medium of expression warranting stringent First Amendment protection.[76] In addition, Brennan rejected the argument of the seven California cities—that outdoor advertising would continue in the city, even with the ban in place[77]—as well as that of

---

73 While the Court was only able to reach a plurality as to its rationale, a 6–3 majority of the justices agreed that the ban was invalid under the First Amendment. Because the Court was unable to form a majority opinion coalition, the case was decided by a judgment of the Court, compromising its authority as legal precedent since "Only the decision is authoritative, not necessarily the reasoning whereby the Court reached its conclusion" (Segal, Spaeth, and Benesh 2005: 335).

74 453 U.S. 490, at 513 (1981).

75 453 U.S. 490, at 522 (1981). The primary distinction between Brennan's concurrence and White's plurality opinion is that Brennan believed that the case involved the question of whether municipalities could totally ban outdoor advertising, while the plurality did not focus on that specific issue.

76 453 U.S. 490, at 523 (1981).

77 453 U.S. 490, at 525 (1981).

the Solicitor General, who argued that striking down the ban would render the federal Highway Beautification Act unenforceable.[78]

In addition to Brennan's concurring opinion, three justices wrote dissenting opinions in the case. Justice Stevens argued that the total prohibition of billboards in the city, with the exception of those billboards advertising goods and services sold onsite, was a constitutionally permissible use of the city's police powers.[79] In this dissent, Stevens rejected the ANPA's stance that the First Amendment is absolute, at the same time endorsing the view of NIMLO that the proper role of the Court in adjudicating disputes such as this is to defer to the desires of democratically elected city councils who believe that such bans are advantageous for improving the appearance of the city.[80] Justice Burger dissented on the grounds that the plurality's decision was an unwise use of judicial power because it trampled on subject matter traditionally reserved to local authority—protecting the safety of motorists and enhancing the environment of an urban area.[81] As with Stevens' dissent, Burger's opinion reflected arguments presented by NIMLO, the Solicitor General, and the city and state amici. Finally, Justice Rehnquist also dissented, arguing, in a very brief opinion,[82] that the plurality erred in its ruling since aesthetic justification alone is sufficient to justify a total ban on billboards.[83] As with Stevens and Burger, Rehnquist also relied heavily on the arguments of the appellee amici in concluding that "little can be gained in the area of constitutional law, and much lost in the process of democratic decision making, by allowing individual judges in city after city to second-guess such legislative or administrative determinations."[84]

Metromedia v. San Diego provides important insights into Supreme Court decision making for a number of reasons. First, it highlights the fact that the Court adjudicates disputes that have far-reaching implications for public policy. In this sense, it is clear that the Court's jurisprudence is not simply about the parties to litigation. Instead, the Court's decisions involve a wide range of societal interests, including cities, states, the federal government, small business owners, and civil rights and liberties organizations.

---

78 453 U.S. 490, at 534 (1981).
79 453 U.S. 490, at 541 (1981).
80 453 U.S. 490, at 552 (1981).
81 453 U.S. 490, at 556 (1981).
82 Rehnquist's dissent is only 385 words long.
83 453 U.S. 490, at 570 (1981).
84 453 U.S. 490, at 570 (1981).

Second, it provides an unambiguous example of how arguments supplied by the amici bring to light the broader legal and political ramifications of a decision, in the process presenting the justices with numerous alternative and reframed arguments that might not otherwise be available to them. Finally, and perhaps most important, the above analysis of *Metromedia* reveals the need for systematic analysis to determine whether amicus briefs influence the decision making of the justices. Though all of the justices' opinions reflect arguments presented by the amici, to determine whether these amicus briefs influenced the justices' decision making or whether the arguments in the briefs were simply used as *ex post* justifications for decisions made on the basis of other influences is virtually impossible (Segal and Spaeth 2002). As such, it is impractical to use a case study to determine whether the Court's liberal plurality was influenced by the Metromedia amici or whether they reached their decision on the basis of their own pro-free speech values. Likewise, we cannot determine whether the conservative dissenters were influenced by the San Diego amici or simply reached a conclusion they were predisposed to believe. To be sure, even after comparing the Court's opinion with the briefs filed by the parties and the amici, only the justices know for sure "whether and to what extent a decision rests upon what was said by an amicus" (Stern, Gressman, Shapiro, and Geller 2002: 664; see also Imre 2001). Accordingly, systematic and controlled analysis is required to rigorously evaluate the influence of amicus curiae briefs on the Supreme Court.

I. Chapter Overview

Arguably, the central controversy surrounding Supreme Court decision making involves the extent to which judicial behavior is influenced by legal as opposed to ideological factors (e.g., Baum 1997; Frank 1930; Holmes 1897; Mendelson 1963). On the one hand, advocates of the attitudinal model argue that the justices are almost entirely motivated by their policy preferences and therefore the language of the law serves as little more than *post hoc* justification for attitudinally driven decision making (e.g., Segal and Spaeth 1993, 2002). On the other hand, proponents of the legal model assert that while attitudes may influence judicial choice, legal factors also play a significant role in shaping Supreme Court decision making (e.g., Dworkin 1978; Epstein and Kobylka 1992; Gillman 2001; Richards and Kritzer 2002). In part, this debate is fueled by the adversarial nature of the American legal system in which compelling argumentation is presented to jurists on both sides of a case (Kagan 1991, 2002). Because this institutional structure requires the litigants and amici to act as their own advocates, adversarialism enables the justices to process information in a biased manner, reaching decisions not on the legal merits of a case but instead in accord with what they are predisposed to believe (e.g., Baum 1997: 64–65; Segal and Spaeth 2002: 433; Wrightsman 2006: 119–120). Despite the fact that Supreme Court justices are often assumed to engage in this type of cognitive response to persuasion, few have explicitly subjected this motivated reasoning hypothesis to empirical scrutiny (but see Braman 2006; Braman and Nelson 2007). The purpose of this chapter is to offer insight into this question by examining whether the justices' responses to amicus curiae briefs are most consistent with attitudinal (i.e., motivated reasoning) or legal accounts of judicial decision making.

Ascertaining the influence of amicus curiae briefs provides a particularly auspicious opportunity for detecting whether the justices' responses to persuasion attempts are most consistent with the attitudinal or the legal model. First, although there is substantial evidence that the justices read and make use of amicus briefs in their opinions (e.g., Breyer 1998; Douglas 1962; O'Connor 1996; see also Kearney and Merrill 2000; Lynch 2004; Samuels 2004), scholars have yet to develop rigorous theories to explain the influence of amicus briefs consistent with these extant models of judicial choice. I redress this deficiency by developing, and subjecting to empirical scrutiny, two theories for the influence of amicus briefs: one consistent with the attitudinal model and one consistent with the legal model. Importantly, the empirical predictions derived from these theories are competing. Therefore, this analysis is not subject to the condemnation that systematic support for one model also provides support for another (Segal and Spaeth 1996: 974).[85] Second, the strategy employed here is particularly useful for examining whether the justices engage in motivated reasoning because it closely mimics an experimental design in that instruments of persuasion (amicus briefs) are presented to subjects (justices), offering leverage over how subjects with different policy preferences respond to identical information (e.g., Braman and

---

85 In this sense, the hypotheses developed here do not involve behaviorally equivalent predictions which occur when two or more theoretically divergent hypotheses nonetheless predict identical outcomes.

Nelson 2007). Third, because amicus briefs are adversarial in nature (e.g., Krislov 1963), they can be readily coded on the identical liberal and conservative dimension as the justices' votes in a case. In addition, analyzing justices' responses to amicus briefs contributes to both the interest group and judicial decision making literatures more broadly as a significant debate exists as to whether these briefs structure the choices justices make.

This chapter proceeds as follows. I begin with a discussion of the legal model, followed by an exposition of the attitudinal model. Next, I integrate amicus curiae briefs into each of these models by explaining how amicus briefs are expected to influence the individual justices' decision making consistent with these two divergent approaches to judicial choice. I then present the research design and methodology used in this chapter, followed by the empirical results. I close with a brief discussion of the major findings and their implications for understanding judicial decision making.

II. Models of Judicial Decision Making

A. The Legal Model

According to the legal model of judicial decision making, judges base their decisions on neutral principles internal to the law (consistent with their legal training), leaving personal preferences aside (Cross 1997; Dworkin 1978). Three of the central tenets of this view are the plain meaning of words approach,[86] framers' or legislators' intent,[87] and precedent[88] (Cross 1997: 262; Segal and Spaeth 2002: 48). Though scholars generally focus only on these three aspects of the legal model, a fourth exists, which I refer to as *legal persuasion*. This facet of the legal model encompasses each of the previous versions discussed and is very intuitive.[89] As decision makers, unaffected by their personal policy preferences,

---

86 Justices utilizing plain meaning are said to base their decisions on the plain meaning of the relevant language of the constitutional provision(s), legislative statute(s), or judicial rule(s) at issue.

87 This view of judicial decision making asserts that the justices construe statutes and provisions of the Constitution according to the preferences of those who authored and supported them.

88 Precedent is the tenet that justices adhere to what has previously been decided.

89 The legal persuasion model proposed is said to encompass each of the previous versions discussed in that the other tenets of the legal model (plain meaning, framers'

the justices seek to resolve cases before them correctly, in light of their legal training, and as defined by the complex norms of the legal profession. These complex norms include the notion of judges as neutral decision makers who strive to make accurate legal decisions, as well as the expected influences of plain meaning, legislative and framers' intent, and *stare decisis*. Further, these norms include a consideration of the societal consequences stemming from the adoption of different legal rules or perspectives (Kearney and Merrill 2000: 778).

To reach what they believe to be the correct decision, the justices must explore alternative legal perspectives relating to how cases should be resolved. The justices are expected to be receptive to information that offers alternative interpretations of precedents or statutes, likely societal consequences regarding the application of particular rules or tests, as well as any other information relevant to the case at hand. Central to this view is the idea that all of this information can be persuasive. In other words, for the justices to reach a decision they believe to be correct, they must be persuaded as to which outcome is the correct one (e.g., Spriggs and Wahlbeck 1997: 368). When the justices are supplied with a myriad of options regarding the interpretation of these legal principles, it is expected that the justices will be better equipped to reach what they believe to be the legally correct decision. Relating this to the central component of American jurisprudence, the adversarial system, it follows that the justices should act favorably toward the position most persuasively argued.

To be clear, the legal persuasion model differs from strict interpretations of the other tenets of the legal model in that it does not assume that the justices engage in mechanical jurisprudence. That is, it rejects the perspective that the justices can robotically apply precedent and other legal rules to any given case to reach an objectively correct decision. In fact, the legal persuasion model does not assert that there are truly objectively correct legal answers. Instead, it proposes that some answers are more correct than others, although it cannot definitively tell us what those answers are. Rather, its explanatory capability rests on the idea that some arguments are more persuasive than others and that the justices will make good faith efforts to discover which answers are most accurate. Thus, it does not require judges to follow Justice Robert's mechanical perspective, articulated in *U.S. v. Butler* (1936), that states "the judicial branch of the

---

intent, and precedent) can be thought of as falling under the more general rubric of legal persuasion when they are advanced by the parties and amici.

government has only one duty; to lay the article of the Constitution which is invoked beside the statute which is challenged and to decide whether the latter squares with the former" (297 U.S. 6, at 62). Instead, it posits that while not having the same authoritative force as plain meaning, precedent, and framers' intent, persuasion is important because it asks judges—consistent with their legal training and as unbiased decision makers—to endorse the position that is best supported by the tools of doctrinal analysis that make up the traditional legal model.

While legal persuasion has not yet found a prominent place along-side the dominant tenets of the legal model, I join a wide array of scholars who discuss persuasion as an aspect of the legal model. Indeed, law professors have discussed legal persuasion in connection to the legal model for almost a century. For example, Powell's (1917) analysis of minimum-wage legislation notes that though the law is indeterminate on this issue, judicial decision making in this area is best explained through a careful analysis of which position is able to marshal the language of the law to make the strongest argument.[90] Dworkin (1978, 1985, 1991) like-wise acknowledges the role of persuasion in the formulation of his "right answers" thesis by noting that it means little more than the idea that it is possible for one side to present the better argument (1991: 365).[91] More recently, a number of legal scholars have addressed persuasion as an aspect of the legal model. In his analysis of constitutional argument, Bobbitt (1991) argues that legal argumentation and persuasion should *not* be viewed as little more than instrumental devices that judges can apply to further ideological ends. Instead, "the modalities of constitu-tional argument are the ways in which law statements in constitutional matters are assessed" (1991: 22). Similarly, Kearney and Merrill (2000: 777) point out:

> The fact that the cases reaching the Supreme Court are those that produce disagreement among lawyers does not mean that the law is irrelevant to the resolution of those disputes. The lawyers appearing before the Court debate these issues in terms of legal

90 Interestingly, Powell quickly became disillusioned with this view, later positing that the Court's minimum-wage decision making was predominately driven by the justices' personal views (Powell 1924).

91 It should be noted, of course, that Dworkin then infers that, if a neutral decision maker can conclude that one side has a better argument than the other, this leads to a rejection of the idea of uncertainty in the law, resulting in objectively correct legal answers (at least on a case-by-case basis).

doctrine, and they frequently reach a consensus about which outcomes are most appropriate.

Tamanaha (2006) echoes this sentiment in his discussion of judges as neutral decision makers who rely on reasoned deliberation to reach their decisions. According to Tamanaha (2006: 242), "legal rules allow for more than one legally plausible outcome, though usually one outcome can be ranked as more legally compelling or defensible than the others."

It is important to note that the concept of legal persuasion as a part of the legal model is not unique to law professors. Indeed, a number of political scientists, associated with a range of approaches to the study of judicial decision making, view persuasion through the lens of the legal model. For example, Songer and Haire (1992: 968) incorporate a discussion of persuasion into their conception of the legal model, noting that "judges' decisions will depend in part on which issues and arguments are offered by the litigants and the quality and persuasiveness of those arguments." In a related analysis, Traut and Emmert (1998) analyze persuasion through a legal perspective, concluding that argumentation can act as a constraint on the ability of judges to pursue their policy preferences. Howard and Segal (2002) note that under the legal model, Supreme Court justices actively seek to endorse the most correct answer before them. The justices determine which of the multitude of possible answers is most correct by examining the persuasion presented through legal briefs. In a similar vein, Epstein and Kobylka (1992: 310) conclude their analysis of legal change by noting that interest groups, by using legal persuasion to pursue their policy preferences, influence the justices' decision making in a manner consistent with legalist conceptions of judges as reasoned and deliberative legal thinkers. Gillman (2001), who incorporates legal persuasion into his conception of the legalist judge, presents a lucid overview of a "postpositivist" legal model that is consistent with the legal persuasion model advanced here.[92] Under this conception

---

92 Postpositivist approaches assert that legal influences play an important role in judicial decision making in that judges utilize their *subjective* interpretations of the law to render their decisions (e.g., Burton 1992). Conversely, positivist approaches hold that the law is capable of providing *objectively* correct answers. As such, positivists argue that judges endeavor to limit any subjective influences on their decision making, instead following value free considerations, such as framers' intent or the meaning of words (e.g., Davis 1989; Sebok 1998).

a legal state of mind does not necessarily mean obedience to conspicuous rules; instead, it means a sense of obligation to make the best decision possible in light of one's general training and sense of professional obligation. On this view, decisions are considered legally motivated if they represent a judge's sincere belief that their decision represents their best understanding of what the law requires. (2001: 486)

This last variant of the legal model of judicial decision making, legal persuasion, offers leverage over judicial choice that many of the others do not. First, it is relatively intuitive: the justices should be influenced by persuasive argumentation. As such, this version of the legal model is based on the expectation that the justices will find some arguments more persuasive than others and make good faith efforts to endorse those positions, regardless of whether the outcomes are at odds with their ideological preferences (e.g., Epstein and Kobylka 1992: 310; Lindquist and Klein 2006). Second, and related, it offers an a *priori* hypothesis that is both falsifiable and easily testable using a variety of measures at different stages of Supreme Court review. For example, this model is applicable at the certiorari stage (e.g., petitioners who are most persuasive as to why the Court should take their case should be granted certiorari more often as compared with those who are less persuasive), the briefing stage (e.g., litigants who are more persuasive than their opponents should prevail more often), as well as the oral argument stage (e.g., attorneys whose oral arguments are more persuasive should win more often). As such, this view offers an empirically falsifiable and testable account of judicial decision making applicable to numerous fields of inquiry. This rather intuitive theory of legal persuasion serves as the foundation of the legal explanation for the influence of amicus briefs that follows.

B. The Attitudinal Model

Although there are divergent explanations as to exactly what constitutes the legal model of judicial decision making, it clearly does *not* view judicial decisions as politically motivated (Cross 1997: 263). And, although the legal model of judicial decision making dominated early perspectives of judicial choice, it was taken to task as early as the late nineteenth century by the legal realists (e.g., Frank 1930; Holmes 1897; Llewellyn 1931; Pound 1908). In stark contrast to formulistic views of the law, the legal realists recognized that judicial opinions that contain references to concepts such as precedent and plain meaning might be little more than *post hoc* rationalizations for decisions, not the causes of them. Instead, the legal realists called for the scientific study of law and judicial decision making to uncover the "true" determinants of judicial choice. Given that both political scientists and legal scholars openly welcomed this call to arms, it should be of no surprise that "realism is generally regarded today as the most significant development in American legal theory in the years between the two world wars" (Rumble 1968: 3).

The behavioral revolution of the late 1940s initiated the scientific study of judicial decision making for political scientists. In his pioneering work on the Roosevelt Court, Pritchett (1948) was among the first to recognize the role of ideology in judicial decision making. Though he failed to provide evidence as to exactly how the justices made their decisions, Pritchett acknowledged that they are motivated by their own preferences. Similarly, Murphy (1964: 4) viewed the justices as policy oriented, willing to take advantage of their power to further their own particular policy aims. Building from these notions that ideological factors are central to judicial decision making in the Court, Schubert (1965, 1974) provided the first "detailed attitudinal model of Supreme Court decision making" (Segal and Spaeth 1993: 67), which was later expanded on by Rohde and Spaeth (1976). This latter view of justices argues that

> the primary goals of Supreme Court justices in the decision-making process are *policy goals*. Each member of the Court has preferences concerning the policy questions faced by the Court, and when the justices make decisions they want the outcomes to approximate as nearly as possible those policy preferences. (Rohde and Spaeth 1976: 72)

Following these earlier studies, Segal and Spaeth (1993, 2002) provide the most compelling account of the attitudinal model as it applies to the Supreme Court. These authors argue, "Members of the Supreme Court further their policy goals because they lack electoral or political account-ability, ambition for higher office, and comprise a court of last resort that controls its own jurisdiction" (1993: 69). All these factors combine to promote the personal policy making capacities of Supreme Court justices. Indeed, through these works, Segal and Spaeth provide sound theory and compelling evidence that "the Supreme Court decides disputes in light of the facts of the case vis-à-vis the ideological attitudes and values of the justices. Simply put, Rehnquist [voted] the way he [did] because he [was] extremely conservative; Marshall voted the way he did because he [was] extremely liberal" (1993: 65). By the 1990s, scholars recognized the attitudinal model as the predominant view of judicial decision making on the Supreme Court (Segal, Epstein, Cameron, and Spaeth 1995: 812) and this view stands essentially unchallenged as the "best representation of voting on the merits in the nation's highest court" (Hall and Brace 1996: 238; but see Epstein and Knight 1998).[93] This perspective on judicial choice will serve as the foundation for the proposed attitudinal explanation for the influence of amicus briefs.

C. The Legal and Attitudinal Models: A Shared Characteristic

While legal and attitudinal explanations of judicial decision making differ dramatically, they, nonetheless, share a similar implicit characteristic. Specifically, both theories view the justices as policy generalists. From the legal perspective, this suggests that the justices must seek out information that enables them to reach what they believe to be the correct legal decision. From the attitudinal perspective, this suggests that the justices must seek out information that enables them to maximize their policy preferences. It is well established that no matter how sophisticated the justices on the Court may be, they operate in an environment of incomplete information (Epstein and Knight 1998; Maltzman, Spriggs, and Wahlbeck 2000; Murphy 1964). Because the Supreme Court's docket covers a multitude of legal and social policy issues, the justices are necessarily limited in their ability to become policy specialists. This has resulted in a Court composed primarily of policy generalists. Though some justices may be considered experts in particular areas of policy and law, the complexity and diversity of the Court's workload limits the ability of the justices to become specialists in all areas of law and social policy

---

93 It is important to note that the attitudinal model's "undisputed" nature applies to voting only and not to the Court's policy outputs contained in its opinions. In other words, the attitudinal model's substantial ability to predict the liberal or conservative nature of the justices' votes is generally accepted, although the model's ability to predict the content of the legal policies endorsed by the justices as enunciated in their opinions is debatable (e.g., Spriggs 2003).

(Breyer 1998). Justice O'Connor makes this reality evidently clear in noting that

> the breadth of cases now heard by judges in the United States has reminded us that humility is a virtue still worth pursuing. Faced with a staggering variety and complexity of problems, the Justices of the Supreme Court have in recent years learned—some would say relearned—that there are limits on our judicial authority, expertise, and ability to resolve social issues couched in terms of individual rights. By and large, we are not trained economists, educators, social workers, or criminologists. (2003: 247)

As O'Connor observes, the justices are not omniscient decision makers. As a result, to reach decisions that maximize their policy preferences and/or create what they believe to be efficacious law, the justices often must seek out information to realize these sometimes divergent goals. Below, I propose a theoretical framework fitting amicus participation into this view of justices as policy generalists from both the legal and attitudinal perspectives.

III. Amici Curiae and Judicial Decision Making: Two Approaches

In this section, I detail two approaches potentially useful for explaining what affect, if any, amicus briefs have on judicial decision making. I begin with an explanation derived from the legal persuasion framework highlighted above, and move onto a discussion based on the attitudinal framework. The theories that follow offer falsifiable, and mutually exclusive, hypotheses for the possible influence of amicus briefs on the decision making of members of the Supreme Court.

A. Legal Persuasion and Amici Curiae

To recall, the legal model of judicial decision making asserts that justices, uninfluenced by their ideological predispositions, seek to arrive at a correct legal decision, as defined by the complex norms of the legal profession. To reach what they believe to be the correct decision, the justices often must explore alternative legal perspectives relating to how cases should be resolved. While the briefs of the parties, along with the lower court record, certainly provide such information, these sources are generally limited in scope, focusing only on the outcome of the case at hand and not the broader legal implications of a decision (Birkby and Murphy 1964). Contrary to this, amicus briefs often inform the justices of the wide-ranging implications that may result from a particular decision (Collins 2004a; Epstein and Knight 1998). "Frequently, this additional information presents the dispute from another legal perspective, discusses policy consequences, or comments on the norms governing the interpretation of precedents or statutes" (Spriggs and Wahlbeck 1997: 372). In addition, amicus briefs also present the justices with statistical information regarding the likely societal impact of a decision in the form of Brandeis briefs. As Rustad and Koenig (1993: 94) note, "The most common method of introducing social science evidence to the Court is through 'non-record evidence' in amicus curiae briefs."

The legal model posits that all of this information might serve to persuade the justices to reach what they believe to be the correct legal decision. For example, Collins (2004a) notes that justices who are not particularly pleased by the arguments presented by the litigants might seek out information in amicus briefs supporting that litigant's preferred disposition. In other words, because amicus briefs present the justices with numerous alternative or reframed legal arguments, this information might serve to persuade the justices that the amici's preferred disposition is the decision most consistent with their legal training (i.e., the correct one). Further, even if the justices are predisposed toward an argument presented by a party to litigation (e.g., they believe it to be the correct legal decision), amicus briefs can serve to strengthen these beliefs, further persuading the justices that their initial thinking was correct. Such is the case because amicus briefs allow for the expansion of legal argumentation that the parties were only able to make in abbreviated form due to page constraints (Sungaila 1999: 190).

Legal scholars have accumulated little systematic knowledge as to how legal persuasion relates to Supreme Court decision making. A review of that small extant literature is, however, useful. Building on Galanter's (1974) notion that superior litigation experience breeds success, McGuire's (1995, 1998) studies suggest that experienced attorneys are more persuasive than their inexperienced counterparts, resulting in an increased likelihood of litigation success for the party supported by the more experienced litigator (see also Johnson, Wahlbeck, and Spriggs 2006; Kearney and Merrill 2000). Collins (2004a) finds that a litigant with amicus briefs supporting its position has an increased probability of victory. Likewise, Johnson and Roberts (2003) find that the justices are more likely to vote in favor of a litigant supported by amici appearing at oral arguments. Collins argues that this is the case because a large number of amicus briefs supporting a particular litigant allows for the introduction of numerous alternative and reframed legal arguments supporting that litigant's position. In a similar vein, Vigilante, Hettinger, and Zorn (2001) find that in a legal-experimental context, undergraduate students who receive only one-sided information (e.g., only a petitioner's brief) are more likely to vote in favor of the position supported by the information they receive. Using similar methodology, several studies in social psychology reveal that the number of arguments presented to a subject influences that subject's decision making (Chaiken 1980), particularly in regard to jury trials (e.g., Calder, Insko, and Yandell 1974; Insko, Lind, and LaTour 1976). In other words, subjects who receive 10 arguments supporting a particular outcome are more likely to support that outcome relative to subjects who receive only one argument supporting the same outcome.[94] As a whole, these studies reveal that even after controlling for other factors such as ideology and institutional factors, the arguments made by litigants and amici can have a genuine impact on judicial choice.

Above, I have depicted the justices as neutral decision makers, uninfluenced by their ideological predispositions, who seek to arrive at the correct legal decision, as defined by the complex norms of the legal profession. Central to this view is the notion that the justices often must explore alternative legal perspectives relating to how cases should be resolved. As is argued above, amicus briefs provide this information to the justices. Further, unlike the lower court record and the briefs of the parties, amicus briefs generally focus on the broader consequences of a decision. This fits squarely with Forston's (1975: 283) advice to appellate practitioners: "To be effective in persuading [the court], the advocate should deemphasize his own case and emphasize instead the merits of adopting his position for the benefit of the citizens who may in the future be in the same situation as his client." Indeed, this is exactly what amicus

---

94 The idea that the number of arguments presented to the justices can have a genuine impact on their decision making is familiar to both Supreme Court practitioners and the justices. In fact, in an effort to prevent the parties to litigation from filing two briefs—one as a litigant and one as an amicus—the Court adopted Rule 37.6 requiring amici to report whether a party to litigation or its counsel contributed to an amicus brief (e.g., Mauro 2007).

briefs do—offer the justices alternative and reframed legal arguments aimed at illuminating the broader ramifications of the case. Accordingly:

legal model

> Legal Persuasion Hypothesis: As the number of liberal (conservative) amicus curiae briefs increases, so too will the likelihood of observing a liberal (conservative) vote.

B. The Attitudinal Model and Amici Curiae

The legal persuasion hypothesis posited above treats the justices uniformly in that attitudes are *not* expected to mediate the influence of amicus briefs. Rather, this hypothesis simply holds that the justices are neutral decision makers who seek to render decisions that are consistent with the complex norms of the legal profession. To do this, the justices need to be persuaded as to which decision is most consistent with these norms. By supplying the justices with a diverse array of information regarding the interpretation of precedent, framers' intent, plain meaning, and the likely societal repercussions stemming from a decision, amicus briefs are said to influence the justices' decision making. However, this theory ignores decades of research regarding the role of ideology in judicial decision making. Below, I offer an alternative account of amicus briefs consistent with the attitudinal model.

To recall, the attitudinal model of judicial decision making holds that the justices' decision making is driven by their policy preferences (Segal and Spaeth 1993, 2002). Although the justices take their ideological preferences to the bench with them, they, nonetheless, operate in an information-poor environment. As policy generalists, the justices may seek out information available in amicus briefs to assist them in realizing the application of their preferences. Amicus briefs enable the justices to make very precise calculations regarding the potential impact of a decision, for both the law and for public policy, because the briefs are aimed at the issues surrounding any given case (Epstein and Knight 1998: 221–222).

Unlike the legal persuasion hypothesis offered above, which treats the justices uniformly, the attitudinal model does not. Rather, the attitudinal theory of the influence of amicus briefs, based largely on the cognitive response model developed in social psychology (e.g., Greenwald 1968; Petty, Ostrom, and Brock 1981), considers the possibility that ideology might play a mediating role with regard to how the justices respond to amicus briefs. "The cognitive response model views receivers as active participants in persuasion, producing cognitions (thoughts) in response to a stimulus (the persuasive communication)" (Benoit 1987: 182–183). The basic logic behind the cognitive response model is that the degree to which persuasive argumentation influences the decision making of receivers depends predominately upon whether the persuasive communication supports or refutes the receiver's predetermined attitudes. "To the extent that a communication elicits predominantly favorable thoughts, persuasion is enhanced. To the extent that the message evokes predominantly unfavorable thoughts, persuasion is inhibited" (Eagly and Chaiken 1984: 282). As it relates to the Supreme Court and the attitudinal model, the cognitive response model treats ideology as a mediating variable that conditions how the justices respond to amicus briefs. Below, I explore how the justices are expected to react to amicus briefs when the arguments presented in the briefs support or contradict the justices' ideological predispositions.

When an increasing number of amicus briefs are present in a case that support a justice's ideology, it is expected that this will increase the likelihood of observing that justice cast a vote congruent with her ideology. This expectation is based on three reasons. First, because an ideologically motivated justice might lack information that informs her of how her ideological preferences dictate voting in a particular case, amicus briefs can provide this information. For example, when several amicus briefs are filed in a case that are congruent with her ideological preferences, the justice is better equipped to realize the application of her policy preference in this particular issue and apply it accordingly. That is, the presence of amicus briefs in a case that are ideologically congruent with the justice's beliefs guides the justice toward locating, and voting in favor of, her optimal policy preference as it relates to the case at hand.

Second, past research in social psychology reveals that when confronted with ideologically congruent information, receivers are less motivated to develop counterarguments or ignore this information and instead use this information to develop thoughts favorable to their ideological predispositions (Benoit 1989; Petty, Ostrom, and Brock 1981: 13). Related to the above discussion, this might "push" a justice toward more confidently invoking her policy preferences in the case, thus increasing the likelihood of observing an ideologically congruent vote. Further, a justice might use this congruent information as a means to further reinforce an ideologically driven vote, as well as to justify that vote in conference and during the give-and-take that occurs in the opinion writing process.

Finally, the notion that ideologically congruent information increases the likelihood of observing a justice cast an ideologically congruent vote follows from Segal and Spaeth's (2002: 433) argument that the justices engage in motivated reasoning (e.g., Kunda 1990). In this sense, justices are said to make unconscious decisions to accept arguments consistent with their preferences as valid, while viewing arguments inconsistent with their preferences as weak or inapplicable (see also Lord, Ross, and Lepper 1979). This argument, though clearly attitudinal in nature, suggests that the justices may act as if they *believe* the law matters, in that their decisions to accept only ideologically congruent information as valid occur on an unconscious level. As Braman and Nelson (2007) note, this helps explain jurists' affirmations that their decisions are predominantly driven by law rather than personal preferences. If the justices engage in motivated reasoning, this further reinforces the notion that the justices will be influenced only by ideologically congruent information because that is the only information they view as legitimate. Simply put, when the justices are faced with an increasing number of amicus briefs congruent with their ideological preferences, this enables the justices to maximize the application of their policy preferences in a given case. Accordingly:

> *Attitudinal Congruence Hypothesis: As the number of liberal (conservative) amicus curiae briefs increases, so too will the likelihood of observing a liberal (conservative) justice cast a liberal (conservative) vote.*

When increasing numbers of amicus briefs that refute a justice's ideology are present in a case, the expectation is that there will be no effect on the likelihood of observing that justice cast an ideologically congruent vote. In fact, under the attitudinal model, incongruent information should have no influence whatsoever on the justices' voting behavior for two reasons. First, if the justices consciously seek out information that will aid them in employing their policy preferences in a given case, they should make effective use of their time by almost wholly ignoring information that is inconsistent with their preferences. Instead, the justices should seek out congruent information that will allow them to maximize their policy preferences. Such information can likely be found in congruent amicus briefs, a litigant brief, the lower court record(s), or during oral argument (although the latter three means of gathering information focus primarily on the outcome of the case at hand and not the

engage in motivated reasoning.

Posner

Confirmation Bias

broader policy ramifications of the decision). Even in the rare instances in which this information cannot be obtained from one of these sources, the justices are free to use their law clerks to uncover such information or perform the research themselves. In so doing, policy driven justices are able to maximize the application of their policy preferences in the case— at the same time minimizing their likelihood of deciding in error (i.e., inconsistent with their preferences)—while still assembling the legal authorities that might be necessary to justify their votes in conference and during the inter-chambers bargaining that occurs while opinions are crafted (e.g., Maltzman, Spriggs, and Wahlbeck 2000).

Second, following from the notion that the justices partake in motivated reasoning, they should dismiss or discount information that contradicts their established policy preferences. This notion of biased information assimilation can be traced back almost four centuries to Francis Bacon's intuitions on human behavior:

> The human understanding, once it has adopted opinions, either because they were already accepted and believed, or because it likes them, draws everything else to support and agree with them. And though it may meet a greater number and weight of contrary instances, it will, with great and harmful prejudice, ignore or condemn or exclude them by introducing some distinction, in order that the authority of those earlier assumptions may remain intact and unharmed. (Bacon [1620] 1994: 57)

As Bacon makes clear, humans do not process information impartially but rather filter their impressions as to the validity and reliability of persuasive communications through their attitudes and values. Indeed, a multitude of research in social psychology provides a compelling basis for this view of the human condition (e.g., Benoit 1989; Kahneman, Slovic, and Tversky 1982; Lord, Lepper, and Preston 1984), particularly with regard to those who hold strong opinions on complex social issues (Lord, Ross, and Lepper 1979). To be sure, the justices are among those who hold such strong opinions in that they constantly deal with multi-faceted legal and policy issues while maintaining a relatively enduring and well-established set of preferences (e.g., Baum 1988; Schubert 1974; Segal and Spaeth 1993; but see Epstein, Hoekstra, Segal, and Spaeth 1998). Given this, under the attitudinal perspective of judicial decision making, there is little reason to believe that the justices will view incongruent amicus briefs as valid information sources.

This view of how the justices process incongruent information clearly suggests that such information will likely never undermine their pre-existing beliefs (while the legal explanation for amicus briefs posits that this is likely to occur). In this sense, the expectation is that the justices are driven by attitudinal consistency. This perspective of the justices has prima facie support in the existing literature. For instance, Spaeth and Segal (1999) find that the justices stick to their publicly announced positions in precedent-setting cases when the opportunity to overrule such precedents arises, almost 90% of the time, and that this finding holds over their tenure on the Court (i.e., is not subject to change over time). This provides evidence that the justices, having developed their policy preferences prior to their ascension to the high Court, are expected to maintain a psychological commitment to these attitudes.[95] In this sense, the justices exhibit what Lewin (1951) calls a "freezing effect"—they are committed to their policy preferences and highly resistant to pressures for change. Given this, from the attitudinal perspective, it can be said that the justices' policy preferences are foundational beliefs and, therefore, should not be subject to great change when faced with contradictory information in amicus briefs. As such, the justices, like other political actors (e.g., Jervis 1968), are expected to fit incongruent persuasion into their existing attitudinal cognitions and discount such information. Therefore, the expectation is that the mere availability of contradictory evidence will not be sufficient to cause the justices to abandon their well-established attitudes and values (Lord, Ross, and Lepper 1979: 2108).

The above attitudinal hypothesis applies only to those justices who have relatively extreme policy preferences and, thus, excludes the moderate justices on the Court. The expected influence of amicus briefs on moderate justices under an attitudinal perspective matches that of the legal persuasion hypothesis developed above. This is the case because there is no expectation that moderate justices' preferences are extreme enough to mediate the influence of amicus briefs. Rather, moderate

---

95 Epstein, Martin, Quinn, and Segal (2007) offer an alternative perspective on this issue, providing fairly substantial evidence that preference change occurs over time on the Court. However, because they base their conclusions on the actual votes justices cast, it is unclear whether their results are entirely a function of preference change or are indicative of the influence of other factors, such as acclimation effects (e.g., Brenner 1983), alterations to the Court's docket (e.g., Baum 1988), the constraint of precedent (e.g., Richards and Kritzer 2002), oral arguments (e.g., Johnson, Wahlbeck, and Spriggs 2006), the Solicitor General (e.g., Segal 1988), and amicus curiae briefs.

justices are expected to respond to the presence of amicus briefs by voting consistent with the positions advocated in the briefs.

C. Overview and Clarification

The two theories regarding the relationship between amicus curiae participation and judicial decision making discussed above offer testable and divergent hypotheses as to how we might expect the justices to respond to amicus briefs. While both of these theories treat the information contained in amicus briefs uniformly, they do not treat the justices' responses homogeneously. The legal persuasion theory views the justices as neutral decision makers seeking to make a correct legal decision. Amicus briefs serve to educate the justices as to which choice meets these expectations. As such, the legal persuasion theory views the justices as uniform receivers of information. Conversely, the attitudinal theory presented above takes into account the possibility that attitudes serve to mediate how the justices respond to information contained in amicus briefs. In other words, while the message remains the same, the receivers' responses vary. For example, liberal justices are expected to react to liberal briefs by locating and employing their attitudinal preferences more frequently. Liberal justices are expected to respond to conservative briefs by ignoring information that differs from their cognitive beliefs (e.g., attitudes).

Table 4.1 summarizes the hypotheses relating to the influence of amicus briefs on judicial decision making. The purpose here is to highlight where the legal and attitudinal explanations diverge. However, first note that both the legal and attitudinal hypotheses suggest that as the number of liberal (conservative) amicus briefs filed increases, so too will the likelihood of observing a liberal (conservative) justice cast a liberal (conservative) vote. Thus, the predictions are identical, although the theoretical reasons for them are not. The legal persuasion model, in effect, "black boxes" ideology in that it is inconsequential for the model. The fact that a justice is liberal or conservative is of no import to the legal model. Rather, the model's predictions stem from the expectation that as the number of amicus filed supporting a particular outcome increases, so too will the likelihood of observing a justice vote in favor of that outcome. Accordingly, the key test for which theory best explains the justices' behavior comes from an examination of how a liberal (conservative)

attitudinal model,
Justice disregards non partisan (their)
signals

Table 4.1. Explanations for the Influence of Amicus Curiae Briefs on Judicial Decision Making

Justice's Ideology	Direction of Amicus Briefs	Direction of Relationship	Hypothesis Supported
Conservative	Conservative	−	Attitudinal
Liberal	Liberal	+	Congruence/ Legal Persuasion
Conservative	Liberal	+	Legal Persuasion
Liberal	Conservative	−	
Conservative	Liberal	n.s.	Attitudinal
Liberal	Conservative	n.s.	
Moderate	Conservative	−	Legal Persuasion
Moderate	Liberal	+	

Note: n.s. = not significant. Dependent variable is coded such that 1 = liberal vote; 0 = conservative vote.

justice responds to an increasing number of conservative (liberal) amicus briefs. The attitudinal model suggests no meaningful relationship should exist because the briefs are ignored or viewed as invalid. The legal model suggests that this should increase the likelihood of observing a conservative (liberal) vote because this is additional argumentation supporting the conservative (liberal) position.[96]

IV. Modeling the Influence of Amici Curiae

To test whether the influence of amicus curiae briefs is most consistent with an attitudinal or legal explanation, I estimate a statistical model that

other popular model

---

96 In this sense, the hypotheses tested here are analogous to Brenner and Spaeth's (1995) test for the influence of precedent on the justices' voting behavior. Briefly, the authors note that both attitudinal and precedential accounts of the justices' voting behavior often yield the same predictions. For example, the attitudinal model holds that the justices reveal a preference for the rule of law announced by the Court in a precedent-setting case and should subsequently vote to uphold this precedent if it is challenged. The legal model asserts that the justices should uphold the precedent, regardless of their prior vote, because this is a norm of judicial decision making. Thus, in these examples, the divergent models' predictions are identical, although the theoretical explanations differ. In order to uncover which explanation is more empirically valid, Brenner and Spaeth look to instances in which the justices voted *against* the establishment of a precedent and subsequently voted *in favor* of upholding the precedent. The authors argue that only under this condition, in which the justices revealed a preference against the rule of law established in the precedent but subsequently voted to uphold it, can precedent be said to constrain the justices' decision making.

A ⟶ dependent

calculates the influence of liberal and conservative amicus briefs on the likelihood of observing a justice cast a liberal vote.[97] The dependent variable captures the ideological direction of the individual justices' voting behavior. This is scored 1 for a liberal vote and 0 for a conservative vote. Spaeth (2002, 2003) codes this variable according to contemporary definitions of liberalism and conservatism. In criminal cases, liberal votes support the rights of the criminally accused, while conservative votes favor the government. In civil liberties cases, liberal votes support the litigant claiming a violation of its freedoms, such as free expression, freedom of religion, and the right to privacy, while conservative votes are the opposite. The liberal position in a civil rights case is pro-civil rights claimant, while the conservative position is, for example, supportive of the curtailment of the rights in question. The liberal position in cases involving labor unions takes the pro-union position (except in cases involving union antitrust), while the conservative position is pro-business/employer. The liberal position in economic activity cases takes, for example, a pro-liability position, while the conservative position supports limiting liability claims against a business or government. The liberal position in a federalism case takes a pro-federal government power position, while a conservative position takes a pro-state power position. In cases involving federal taxation, a liberal vote supports the government at the expense of the taxpayer or, alternatively, the federal government at the expense of a state government. Recall that Chapter 3 provided a more detailed treatment of the distinction between liberal and conservative positions with regard to amicus briefs. Because the amicus briefs are coded on the exact same dimension as the justices' votes, I forgo a more detailed discussion here.[98]

---

97 Following standard practice (e.g., Segal, Epstein, Cameron, and Spaeth 1995), I identified relevant cases using the case citation plus split vote (meaning that each case is counted once, with the exception of a small number of split vote cases, comprising less than 1% of the data, in which one or more of the justices joined the majority on one aspect of a case, but dissented on another aspect of the case). The unit of analysis is the justice-vote. The data contain information on the justices' voting behavior in all orally argued cases decided during the 1946–2001 terms. The data, including the independent variables, were primarily obtained through the Spaeth (2002, 2003) databases, with exceptions discussed below.

98 As noted in Chapter 3, the small number of cases dealing with interstate relations are not coded as taking conservative or liberal positions because these cases generally involve boundary disputes between states, which do not lend themselves to such ideological classifications.

Because the dependent variable is dichotomous, probit is used (e.g., Aldrich and Nelson 1984; Pampel 2000).[99] Note that understanding the technicalities of the probit model is not necessary to obtain an intuitive comprehension of what the model tells us with respect to the influence of amicus briefs. This is the case because, in addition to reporting the variables' parameter estimates and standard errors, I use the results of the statistical model to graphically plot the influence of the amicus variables on the likelihood of observing a liberal vote across varying judicial ideologies. Further, I calculate substantively interesting changes in the predicted probability that a justice will cast a liberal vote for the other independent variables in the model.[100]

The primary variables of interest in the model represent each justice's ideology and the number of liberal and conservative amicus briefs filed in each case. *Ideology* is measured by employing the Martin and Quinn (2002) ideology scores, which have substantial face validity. For example, Martin and Quinn classify Rehnquist, Scalia, and Thomas as the most conservative justices on the Court from 1946 to 2001, while Brennan, Douglas, and Marshall constitute the most liberal justices during this time frame. These scores are based on the actual votes cast by justices for each term served on the Court. The justices are scaled using a dynamic item response model with Bayesian inference and thus the ideal point estimates vary over time. To facilitate interpretation, I have rescaled these scores by adding 6.331 to each ideal point; accordingly this variable ranges from 0 to 10.641. Higher scores on this variable reflect more conservative ideologies.[101] The expected sign of this variable is negative,

---

99 To control for the nonindependence of observations, the model is estimated using robust standard errors, clustered on case citation (Giles and Zorn 2000).

100 The marginal effects for the noninteractive variables reported throughout this book were calculated altering the variables of interest from 0 to 1 for dichotomous variables and from the mean to one standard deviation above the mean for continuous variables, holding all other variables constant at their mean or modal values. The marginal effects for the interactive variables, and their constituent terms, were calculated using the method described in Brambor, Clark, and Golder (2006).

101 Note that I have performed alternative analyses using the Segal and Cover (1989) scores, which are based on editorial commentary involving the justices' perceived ideologies made between their nomination and Senate confirmation, in place of the Martin and Quinn (2002) scores. None of the results decidedly altered. I have opted to report results that use the Martin and Quinn scores because their endogenous nature makes the test of the legal persuasion hypothesis conservative from a social scientific standpoint. This is the case because the Martin and Quinn scores, as a function of being based on the justices' actual voting behavior, potentially capture the influence of non-ideological factors, including amicus curiae briefs. As such, any

indicating that conservative justices are more likely to cast conservative votes than liberal justices.

Conservative Amicus and *Liberal Amicus* capture the number of amicus briefs filed in support of the conservative and liberal positions, respectively. A full discussion of the data collection and coding of these variables appears in the Appendix. In order to examine whether ideology mediates the influence of amicus curiae briefs, I include two interaction terms in the model: *Ideology × Conservative Amicus* and *Ideology × Liberal Amicus*.[102] Because I cannot infer from the magnitude and significance of the interaction terms whether ideology mediates the influence of amicus briefs (Ai and Norton 2003), it is necessary to calculate the marginal effects and confidence intervals for these interaction terms, holding all other variables at their mean or modal values. To do this, I use the technique developed by Brambor, Clark, and Golder (2006).

To illustrate the expected predictions for each model of the influence of amicus briefs, consider Figure 4.1, which plots the hypothetical marginal effects for a one standard deviation change in the number of liberal amicus briefs (from one to three) against ideology with the dependent variable representing the ideological direction of the justices' votes. The figure on the top illustrates support for the attitudinal explanation of the influence of amicus briefs. Looking first at the slope (the dash-dot line), the results indicate that compared with a case in which a single liberal amicus brief is filed, when three liberal briefs are filed a justice is 3% more likely to cast a liberal vote. However, this result only holds for justices whose ideologies are at or below 6.0. For justices whose ideologies fall above 6.0 (i.e., moderate to strongly conservative ideologues), there is no statistically significant effect of liberal amicus briefs as evidenced by the fact that the confidence intervals straddle zero (Brambor, Clark, and Golder 2006). Thus, in interpreting these interaction terms, one must pay close attention to not only the slope of the effect but also the confidence

---

results supporting the legal persuasion hypothesis should be viewed as particularly robust.

102 The purpose of using interaction terms is to capture the conditional relationship between two or more variables (e.g., Brambor, Clark, and Golder 2006). In this analysis, the use of interaction terms allows for the examination of whether, for example, all justices respond to the persuasion attempts forwarded in conservative amicus briefs or if only conservative justices are receptive to conservative briefs.

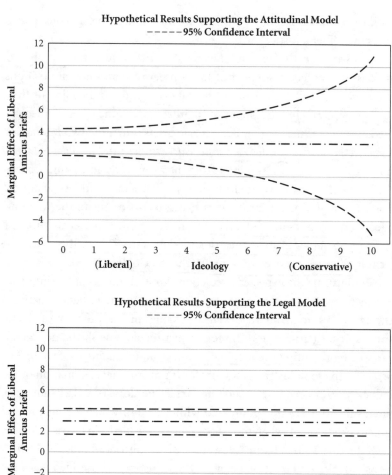

Figure 4.1. An Illustration of Hypothesized Results for Each Model

intervals surrounding that slope, which indicate significance levels. The marginal effects are significant whenever the upper and lower bounds of the confidence intervals are *both* above (or below) the zero line. The graph on the bottom of Figure 4.1 indicates hypothetical support for the legal model. In that figure, the marginal effect of liberal amicus briefs is both uniform in its impact and statistically significant regardless of a justice's ideology.

Controls

A. Other Influences on the Ideological Direction of the Vote

To capture the effects of other influences on judicial choice, several control variables are included in the model. First, I account for the resource status of the parties to the case. Judicial scholars have long noted that the status of litigants plays a role in the choices judges make (e.g., Collins 2004a; Galanter 1974; Wheeler, Cartwright, Kagan, and Friedman 1987). This line of research began with Galanter's (1974) famed speculation that the judiciary favors the "haves" over the "have-nots." The advantage that high-resource litigants enjoy stems from their ability to hire better lawyers on appeal and their selectivity regarding which cases to appeal or defend when the lower court loser appeals (Wheeler, Cartwright, Kagan, and Friedman 1987: 441). Their resources (i.e., wealth) allow them to hire the best team of lawyers available, retain the best expert witnesses, and take on additional expenses that might increase their litigation success, such as dedicating a great deal of time to legal research (Songer, Kuersten, and Kaheny 2000: 540). Accordingly, the expectation is that as the resource status of a liberal (conservative) litigant increases, so too will the likelihood of observing a justice cast a liberal (conservative) vote. To control for litigant resources, I use the status continuum of litigants adopted generally from Sheehan, Mishler, and Songer (1992; see also Collins 2004a; McGuire 1995, 1998; Wheeler, Cartwright, Kagan, and Friedman 1987). That is, I ranked litigants, according to increasing resources, as follows: poor individuals = 1, minorities = 2, individuals = 3, unions/interest groups = 4, small businesses = 5, businesses = 6, corporations = 7, local governments = 8, state governments = 9, and the federal government = 10.[103] From this resource continuum, I then calculated two variables, *Liberal Resources* and *Conservative Resources*, depending on whether the litigants were advocating the liberal or conservative position, respectively. While this scoring may be suboptimal because it relies on the use of such broad categories, it nonetheless serves as a parsimonious means of accounting for the influence of resources in Supreme Court litigation and has been used successfully in earlier studies (e.g., Collins 2004a; McGuire 1995, 1998; Sheehan, Mishler, and Songer 1992).

---

103 See Sheehan, Mishler, and Songer (1992) for the inclusion of litigants in these categories. In addition, I have coded litigants as fitting into an interest group category. This includes all litigants identified in the Spaeth (2002, 2003) databases as the American Medical Association, political action committees, unions, union members, and environmental organizations. Litigants that did not fit into any of the categories discussed above were assigned the mean resource score for all litigants.

To control for the justices' well-known practice of accepting cases on appeal that they seek to reverse (Caldeira and Wright 1988; Perry 1991; Schubert 1959; Segal and Spaeth 1993), I include a variable called *Lower Court Direction*. This variable is coded 1 if the decision that the Supreme Court is reviewing was liberal and 0 if it was conservative. The expected sign of this variable is negative, indicating that a justice is more likely to vote conservatively given that the lower court handed down a liberal decision.

The final control variables in the model account for the Office of Solicitor General's participation as amicus curiae. Created by the Judiciary Act of 1870, the Office of Solicitor General (SG) consists of the principal attorneys for the executive branch in the Supreme Court, headed by the SG, who is the only federal government official required to be "learned in the law" (Waxman 1998). The SG is generally selected by the Attorney General, nominated by the president, and confirmed by the Senate (Salokar 1992: 3). As such, the SG is very much a part of the Justice Department, reporting either to the president or the attorney general. However, he also maintains an office in the Supreme Court. This makes the SG one of only two federal officials (the other being the vice president who has an office in the Capitol building) who keep formal offices in two branches of government.

While the SG is theoretically ideologically neutral before the Court— being an agent of the Court (e.g., Caplan 1987)—in fact the Office is very political in nature. This is perhaps most evident in the SG's selection process. "The selection process is designed to ensure that the solicitor general will share the basic political values of the administration. 'The Candidate for the Office must be in basic accord with the philosophical tenets of the President and Attorney General'" (Salokar 1992: 3). While the SG enjoys some independence from the administration in terms of his day-to-day decision making, the selection process ensures that the SG will not stray too far from the ideological bent of the president and attorney general.[104] Should this occur, there are well documented accounts

---

104 The justices appear to be cognizant of the fact that, because the SG serves at the pleasure of his appointing president, he acts as an advocate for the president's interests in the Court. For example, Justice Sutherland noted in *Humphrey's Executor v. United States* (1935) that "it is quite evident that one who holds his office only during the pleasure of another, cannot be depended upon to maintain an attitude of independence against the latter's will" (295 U.S. 602, at 629).

of the president and/or attorney general reining in the SG (e.g., Caplan 1987; Days 2001; Salokar 1992).

Since 1872, the executive branch's litigation efforts in the Supreme Court have been handled solely by the SG, although during the late nineteenth century this was occasionally in conjunction with the attorney general (Waxman 1998). In his capacity as the executive branch's representative before the Court, the SG performs three primary functions. First, the SG reviews potential appeals to the Court. In this role, the SG acts as a gatekeeper for the Court, either directly appealing or endorsing, via an amicus brief in support of review, only the worthiest of cases (e.g., Perry 1991). This gatekeeping role is not lost on the justices. Caldeira and Wright (1988, 1998) report that an appeal brought by the SG constitutes one of the three most influential variables with regard to the justices' certiorari decisions.

Second, the SG argues all cases in which the federal government is a litigant. This is the most visible function of the SG before the Court. During the 1946–2001 terms, the SG represented the federal government as a petitioner or respondent in more than 41% of all cases argued before the Court. In this role, the SG is extremely successful. During this time frame the SG prevailed in over 65% of cases in which he participated. Though there are divergent explanations for the SG's success in the Court, such as institutional deference (e.g., Yates 2002) and strategic litigation decisions (e.g., Zorn 2002), recent research suggests that the quality of the SG's legal argumentation might be the best explanation for his success (e.g., Lindquist and Klein 2003; McGuire 1998; Merrill 2003).

Finally, and central to this analysis, is the SG's role as amicus curiae. During the 1946–2001 terms, the SG filed more than 1,000 amicus briefs, making amicus participation in decisions on the merits the SG's second most visible litigation strategy in the Court. Past studies reveal that the SG is even more successful as an amicus than as a litigant. For example, Deen, Ignagni, and Meernick (2003; see also Segal 1988) report that the SG prevailed as an amicus at a high of 85% during the Warren Court and a low of 73.1% during the Rehnquist Court (overall success rate = 75%). To account for the well-documented success of the Office of Solicitor General as amicus curiae, two variables are included. *SG Liberal* is scored 1 if the Office of Solicitor General filed an amicus brief advocating the liberal position and 0 otherwise. *SG Conservative* is scored 1 if the SG filed an amicus brief arguing for the conservative position and 0 otherwise. A liberal amicus brief filed by the Solicitor General is expected to increase the likelihood of observing a liberal vote, while a conservative amicus brief by the Solicitor General is expected to decrease the likelihood of observing a liberal vote.

V. Empirical Results

Table 4.2 reports the results of the probit model. The model correctly predicts 66% of votes, for a percent reduction in error of 28%. The parameter estimates for the *Conservative Amicus* and *Liberal Amicus* variables indicate the influence of amicus briefs when both interaction terms are at zero. The marginal effects of these variables reveal that a justice whose ideology is at 0 (i.e., the most liberal justice in the data) is approximately 2% more likely to cast a conservative vote as the number of conservative briefs increases from one to three and 3% more likely to cast a liberal vote as the number of liberal amicus briefs increases from one to three. Though this table is useful, the information it provides is very

Table 4.2. Probit Model of the Influence of Amici Curiae in the U.S. Supreme Court, 1946–2001 Terms

Predictor	Coefficient	Marginal Effect
Liberal Amicus	.094 (.017)***	+3.1%
Conservative Amicus	−.034 (.017)*	−2.2%
SG Liberal	.349 (.048)***	+13.3%
SG Conservative	−.335 (.046)***	−13.1%
Liberal Resources	.024 (.005)***	+2.6%
Conservative Resources	−.039 (.006)***	−3.6%
Lower Court Direction	−.419 (.024)***	−16.5%
Ideology	−.190 (.004)***	−16.1%
Ideology × Liberal Amicus	−.008 (.002)**	see figure 4.2
Ideology × Conservative Amicus	−.0005 (.002)	see figure 4.2
Constant	1.62 (.069)***	
N	57,327	
Wald χ^2	3,250.9***	
Percent Correctly Predicted	66.5	
Percent Reduction in Error	28.0	

Dependent variable indicates the ideological direction of the individual justices' vote (1 = liberal, 0 = conservative). Numbers in parentheses indicate robust standard errors, clustered on case citation. * p <.05; ** p <.01; *** p <.001 (one-tailed).

limited because it does not offer leverage over the influence of amicus briefs when a justice's ideology is above zero. These nonzero observations constitute 99.8% of all data points and include all justice-observations except Douglas in the 1974 term. Accordingly, I graphically illustrate the marginal effect of amicus briefs on the ideological direction of the vote across the observed range of ideology in Figure 4.2.

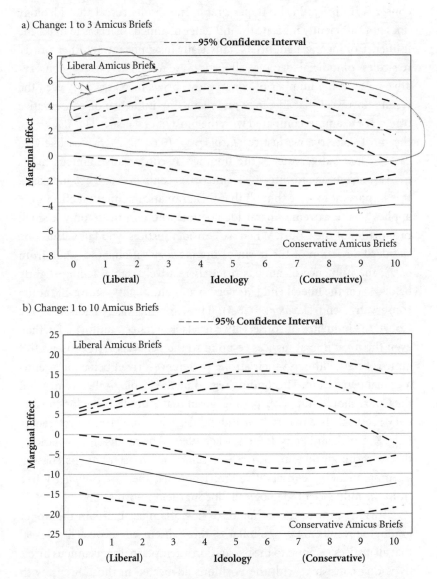

Figure 4.2. The Marginal Effect of Amicus Curiae Briefs on Supreme Court Decision Making

The solid line in each figure indicates how the marginal effects of conservative amicus briefs change as a justice becomes more conservative, while the dash-dot line reports the same information with respect to liberal amicus briefs. Significance levels are denoted by the 95% confidence intervals drawn around these lines. The effect of amicus briefs is significant whenever the upper and lower bounds of these confidence intervals are both above (or below) the zero line. Beginning with conservative briefs in the upper graph, the results reveal that ideology does not sufficiently mediate the influence of amicus briefs as to make the influence of incongruent briefs statistically insignificant. In other words, regardless of judicial ideology, all justices are more likely to cast conservative votes as the number of conservative briefs increases. However, the results do reveal that ideology attenuates the influence of conservative briefs. For example, compared with the most liberal justice (*Ideology* = 0), the most conservative justice (*Ideology* = 10.641) is twice as likely to cast a conservative vote as the number of conservative amicus briefs increases from one to three (a 2% increase, compared to a 4% increase). It is important to note though that this dramatic attenuation effect only applies to the extreme liberal ideologues, who constitute only a small proportion of the Court. When we consider justices who fall within one standard deviation of the mean of the *Ideology* variable (+/− 2.06 from 6.27), the influence of amicus briefs is relatively stable, falling slightly below 4% at the liberal end (*Ideology* = 4.2) and slightly above 4% at the conservative end (*Ideology* = 8.3). Thus, for the vast majority of the Court, the influence of conservative briefs is, in effect, uniform. Further, even the most liberal justices respond to the persuasion in conservative amicus briefs, although their strong preference-driven behavior attenuates that persuasion. This finding regarding the ideological extremists on the Court should not be surprising, given that attitude-behavior consistency is especially enhanced for individuals who hold strong preferences (e.g., Krosnick and Petty 1995; Wicker 1969). The results simply indicate that exceedingly liberal justices are *somewhat* resistant to persuasion attempts made by conservative amici not that they are *completely* free from the influence of ideologically incongruent information.

Turning now to the influence of liberal amicus briefs in the upper graph, the results are very similar to those discussed above. They reveal that all justices respond to the persuasion attempts in liberal amicus briefs by voting consistent with the positions advocated in those briefs, with one caveat. That is, liberal amicus briefs do not appear to influence the decision making of extremely conservative justices whose ideologies are above 9.5 as evidenced by the fact that the lower bound of the 95% confidence interval crosses zero. This is an interesting result, particularly as it is the only finding that supports the attitudinal explanation for the influence of amicus briefs. The identity of these justices is also intriguing, though hardly surprising. The justice-observations that do not respond to liberal briefs are Justice Scalia during the 1999–2000 terms, Justice Thomas during the 1994–2001 terms, and Associate Justice Rehnquist from 1971 to 1985. Cumulatively these observations make up only 5% of the data points in the analysis and do not span the entire career of any of these three. Given his staunch conservatism and resistance to liberal argumentation, it should not be shocking that Rehnquist is referred to as the "poster child" for the attitudinal model (Spaeth 2005), while the other two will likely receive similar accolades following their departures from the bench. Setting these justices aside, for those justices who fall within one standard deviation of the mean of the *Ideology* variable, the influence of amicus briefs is again relatively stable, at 5% for liberal justices (*Ideology* = 4.2) and 4% for conservative justices (*Ideology* = 8.3). Thus, as with conservative briefs, for the vast majority of the Court, the influence of liberal briefs is essentially uniform.

Though there is clearly a statistically significant influence of amicus briefs for virtually all of the justices, the substantive effect of only a few briefs is somewhat marginal. However, when the justices are faced with asymmetric amicus participation—in the sense that a large number of briefs are filed supporting a particular ideological position—the influence of the briefs is rather dramatic. Consider, for example, the lower graph in Figure 4.2, which plots the marginal effects of a 10-brief increase against judicial attitudes on the ideological direction of the justices' votes. With regard to conservative briefs, the results indicate that compared with a case in which a single conservative brief is filed (and a single liberal brief), when 10 conservative briefs are filed (and one liberal brief), the most liberal justice in the data (*Ideology* = 0) is 6% more likely to vote conservatively. This increases to about 14% for the vast majority of the Court (*Ideology* >4.2 and <8.3) and is slightly attenuated for the most conservative justices in the sample (*Ideology* >10), who are 12% more likely to vote conservatively in this situation. The results are virtually identical for liberal amicus briefs: the most liberal justice in the data is 6% more likely to cast a liberal vote as the number of liberal briefs moves from 1 to 10, while the majority of the Court is about 14% more likely cast a liberal vote. As discussed above, once a justice's ideology moves past 9.5, the effect of liberal amicus briefs is insignificant. These are particularly noteworthy findings, given that disparities between amicus briefs advocating for different outcomes have increased quite dramatically over time. For example, during the Vinson Court, the average disparity between liberal and conservative briefs was only 0.37 briefs compared with 1.72 briefs in the Rehnquist Court era. The substantively significant influence of a large number of amicus briefs urging a particular disposition likely offers partial leverage over decisions such as the affirmative action case of *Grutter v. Bollinger* (2003), in which the conservative Rehnquist Court handed down a liberal decision on a significant issue of public policy; in *Grutter*, 83 amicus briefs were filed supporting the liberal position, compared with only 19 for the conservative side of the debate (Devins 2003; Gray and LeBlanc 2003).[105]

Taken as a whole, the results are striking: 100% of justices positively respond to the persuasion attempts in conservative briefs, while the vast majority of the justices positively respond to the persuasion attempts in liberal briefs. Only three extremely conservative justices, constituting only 5% of the 56-year sample, fail to conform to the expectations of the legal model, and none do so over their entire tenure on the Court. Even though ideology slightly attenuates the influence of amicus briefs, it only does so at the far ends of the spectrum, as evidenced by the bell-shaped curves corresponding to liberal briefs and the inverse bell curves corresponding to conservative briefs in Figure 4.2. Thus, the evidence is overwhelmingly supportive of the legal persuasion model as it applies to the influence of organized interests in the Court.

The results indicating that ideology slightly attenuates the influence of incongruent amicus briefs deserves some attention as it provides evidence that justices who sit at or near the center of the Court are especially susceptible to the powers of legal persuasion. This is an especially significant finding in light of the fact that the Supreme Court operates

---

105 For reasons that are not entirely apparent, determining the number of amicus briefs filed in *Grutter* has proved rather elusive: reports range from 93 amicus briefs (e.g., Evans, McIntosh, Lin, and Cates 2007) to 107 amicus briefs (e.g., Coyle 2008). As Devins (2003) presents an authoritative and detailed overview of the amicus filings in *Grutter*, for the purposes of the examples used throughout this book, I accept his count. Of course, it is important to note that, regardless of the total number of amicus briefs filed in the case, the significant point is that liberal amicus briefs outnumbered conservative amicus briefs by a wide margin, a fact on which scholars agree.

under the principle of majority rule for its decisions on the merits. Because of this rule, cases are often determined by the votes of the median or swing justice, whose vote is crucial for obtaining a favorable outcome (e.g., Baker 1996; Blasecki 1990; Edelman and Chen 1996, 2001; Martin, Quinn, and Epstein 2005; Schmidt and Yalof 2004). The fact that justices who occupy positions at or near the center of the Court are particularly receptive to legal persuasion corroborates the utility of targeting the median or swing vote through amicus briefs (Ennis 1984; Kolbert 1989). Through these advocacy efforts, groups can potentially capture the decisive vote of the median justice while persuading more ideologically extreme justices to cast votes in their favor.

The figures discussed above allowed me to evaluate the validity of the attitudinal and legal persuasion hypotheses by plotting the influence of an increasing number of liberal or conservative amicus briefs across judicial ideology. Though central to this analysis, those figures are somewhat limited in that they do not provide information as to how the justices respond to amicus briefs under conditions in which the number of amicus briefs advocating the liberal and conservative positions deviate in other meaningful ways. Table 4.3 supplies this information by reporting the predicted probability of observing a liberal vote across a range of scenarios, holding all other variables at their mean or modal values. For the purposes of this table, conservative justices are classified as having an ideal point score one standard deviation below the mean, while liberal justices are categorized as having an ideology score one standard deviation above the mean. Moderate justices' scores are at the mean. To foster comparison, the first example summarizes the probability of observing a liberal vote for conservative, moderate, and liberal justices in a case with no amicus briefs. In such a dispute, a conservative justice's probability of casting a liberal vote is 45%. For moderate justices, this increases to 61%, and liberal justices have a 75% chance of casting a liberal vote.[106]

---

106 The astute reader will notice that these predictions are skewed in the liberal direction. This is the case because the modal category of the *Lower Court Direction* variable is conservative. As Table 4.2 reveals, a justice is 17% more likely to vote liberally when the lower court rendered a conservative decision. Because lower court decisions are discrete choices (i.e., they are either liberal or conservative), in order to calculate predicted probabilities, it is necessary to hold such a dichotomous variable at one value or the other. Following standard practice, this variable is held at its modal category, thus explaining why the predicted probabilities in Table 4.3 lean toward a liberal vote. Note that the results do not substantively change when the *Lower Court Direction* variable is held at its nonmodal value.

Table 4.3. Predicted Probabilities of Amicus Curiae Influence on the U.S. Supreme Court, 1946–2001 Terms

Liberal Briefs	Conservative Briefs	Probability of Liberal Vote		
Ideology		_Conservative_	_Moderate_	_Liberal_
0	0	45.3	60.5	74.5
3	3	44.2	61.4	76.8
6	3	47.6	66.4	82.0
9	3	51.1	70.1	86.4
12	3	54.5	75.5	90.0
15	3	57.9	79.5	92.9
3	6	39.7	57.0	73.4
3	9	35.2	52.5	69.6
3	12	31.0	48.1	65.7
3	15	27.1	43.6	61.6
20	5	60.5	83.4	95.5
25	10	58.6	84.2	96.5
30	15	56.8	85.1	97.4
5	20	22.9	39.7	59.2
10	25	21.4	41.1	64.0
15	30	20.0	42.4	68.5

In this table, the conservative justice's ideology score is one standard deviation above the mean (8.3), the moderate justice's ideology score is at the mean (6.3), and the liberal justice's ideology score is one standard deviation below the mean (4.2). All predictions are significant at $p < .05$.

Table 4.3 conveys two important pieces of information. First, it corroborates research that indicates a relative advantage of amicus briefs influences judicial choice (e.g., Collins 2004a; McGuire 1990, 1995). For example, compared with a case in which three amicus briefs are filed supporting the liberal and conservative positions, in a case in which 15 liberal briefs are filed and three conservative briefs are present, a conservative justice is 14% more likely to vote liberally, a moderate justice is 18% more likely to vote liberally, and a liberal justice is 16% more likely to cast a liberal vote. Second, this table reveals that the influence of amicus briefs is not linear.[107] In this sense, there are diminishing returns once a

---

107 As a methodological point, note that the probit model, as with maximum likelihood models in general, does not assume or preclude the possibility of a linear influence of amicus briefs (e.g., Greene 2000: 812–827).

relatively large number of briefs are filed. In other words, the model captures the fact that the substantive change from three to six briefs is different than the change from nine to twelve briefs. For example, compared with a case with three amicus briefs filed for each ideological outcome, in a case with six liberal briefs and three conservative briefs, the probability of observing a liberal justice cast a liberal vote increases by 5.2%. With the addition of three more liberal briefs (nine liberal briefs total), this increases by 3.6%. For a case with 12 liberal briefs the probability of observing a liberal justice cast a liberal vote increases by only 2.9%. Thus, it appears that once a case has been thoroughly briefed by the amici, the influence of concomitant amicus briefs is somewhat attenuated.

Finally, all of the control variables are signed in the correct direction and achieve conventional statistical significance. First, note the important role that amicus briefs filed by Solicitors General play in the Court. When the SG argues a liberal position, a justice is 13% more likely to cast a liberal vote; conversely, when the SG advocates for the conservative position, the likelihood of observing a justice cast a conservative vote increases by 13%. This provides strong support for the Solicitor General's influence in the Court. The results also indicate that as a litigant moves up the resource continuum reported above, the justices are increasingly likely to support that litigant's position. For example, compared to an individual litigant, when a corporation argues the conservative position, this results in a 4% increase in the likelihood of observing a justice cast a conservative vote. Third, the results show that when the Supreme Court is reviewing a liberal decision, the justices are 17% more likely to vote conservatively than when the Court is reviewing a conservative decision. Finally, note the strong role of ideology in the justices' decision making. For example, compared with an extremely conservative justice (with a Martin and Quinn score of 10.0, as in Associate Justice Rehnquist), an extremely liberal justice (with a Martin and Quinn score of 0, as in Douglas in 1974) is more than 60% more likely to cast a liberal vote (in cases without amicus participation). Thus, although ideology generally fails as an explanation for the influence of amici in the Court, it, nonetheless, ranks among the most important influences on the justices' decision making overall.

VI. Summary and Conclusions

The purpose of this chapter was to determine whether the law structures judicial choice by analyzing justices' responses to amicus curiae briefs.

The results indicate that ideology does not act as a mediating variable in the justices' processing of information contained in amicus filings, with the exception of three extremely conservative justices for short periods of their careers. Rather, these results indicate that the legal persuasion model best explains the influence of amicus briefs in the Court. In this sense, the justices do not use information contained in congruent amicus briefs to better realize the application of their policy preferences in a given case, nor do they engage in motivated reasoning with respect to the briefs. Instead, amicus briefs are processed as persuasive communication in its simplest form. Specifically, amicus briefs serve to persuade the justices to endorse the conclusions advocated in the briefs. Because this implies that the briefs are able to persuade even ideologically driven justices to support the positions advanced in the briefs, these results can be interpreted to imply that the law matters to the justices. Clearly, the justices' attitudes play a role in their decision making. But, by providing the justices with persuasive communication regarding how the *law* should be applied in any given case, amicus briefs illustrate that judicial decision making on the Court is more than a function of the justices' ideological preferences. Of course, this is not to say that amicus briefs lead the justices inexorably to an outcome supported by the briefs. Rather, the important point is that by persuading the justices to adopt positions consistent with the *legal argumentation* in the briefs, amicus briefs provide us with an insight into one way in which the law matters to Supreme Court decision making.

These results also speak to the assumption that the justices engage in motivated reasoning and provide particularly compelling evidence that they do not do so, at least with regard to amicus briefs. Interestingly, if the justices engaged in this type of cognitive response to persuasion, we might expect those responses to manifest themselves strongly in reaction to amicus briefs because no legal norms compel the justices to use amicus briefs in their decision-making processes. Thus, unlike precedent, in which a norm violation occurs if it is disregarded, the justices are free to ignore amicus briefs. But, the justices do not do so. As such, although the justices may engage in motivated reasoning in other aspects of their decision making, amicus briefs appear to constrain the justices' ability to do so as they limit the capacity of the justices to construct judgments supporting their preferences in the face of contrary information (e.g., Kunda 1990).

CHAPTER 5

Amici Curiae and the Consistency of Judicial Decision Making

American jurisprudence is based on the adversarial system. Under this arrangement, parties to litigation marshal facts and present evidence to promote the validity of their claims: they seek to be as persuasive as possible. Adversarialism operates under the assumption that when parties act as their own advocates, the truth—or some version of the truth—is best discovered by a theoretically neutral decision maker. One characteristic of the adversarial system is the substantial amount of uncertainty as to how decisions are rendered. As Kagan (1991: 374) argues, the adversarial system leads to reduced consistency in the application of the law, resulting in law being treated as malleable, used as a means to achieve a party's ends (Tamanaha 2006). This uncertainty becomes exacerbated at the appellate stages. For example, Supreme Court justices are charged with adjudicating disputes that typically involve divergent applications of the law from two or more lower courts (e.g., Caldeira and Wright 1988). Indeed, Supreme Court Rule 10 identifies these cases as particularly appropriate for review. In cases in which several lower courts disagree with the application of the law, the potential for certainty is diminished. Moreover, once the Supreme Court agrees to review a case, uncertainty is further enhanced when organized interests use the case as a means to promote their own policy interests, presenting the justices with a host of alternative perspectives as to the correct application of the law that are frequently not addressed by the parties to litigation. Inasmuch as certainty can only be achieved when options are eliminated (Casagrande 1999: 7), the introduction of novel argumentation in the form of amicus briefs has the potential to increase inconsistency at the Court.

I. The Importance of Understanding Variability in Decision Making

Consistency plays a central role in decision making for both the citizenry and political elites (e.g., Abelson, Aronson, McGuire, Newcomb, Rosenberg, and Tannenbaum 1968; Festinger 1957; Heider 1946; Kirkpatrick, Davis, and Robertson 1976). Individuals regularly evaluate politicians based on an expectation of consistency in their behavior. This was perhaps no more evident than in the presidential election of 2004. John Kerry, the Democratic candidate, was viewed as a "flip-flopper" by the American public for his seemingly inconsistent views on a host of policies, most notably his initial support for the Iraq War in 2002 and his opposition to funding the war effort only a year later (Harris 2004). Because the public evaluates politicians with an expectation of consistency, this creates a strong incentive for political actors to behave, at least publicly, in a consistent fashion. While consistency plays a key role in the elected branches of government, influencing the citizenry's perceptions of elected officials and thus their subsequent behavior, the expectation of consistency is arguably strongest in the judicial arena.

This is the case because, within the legal realm, expectations of consistency drive both normative and empirical perspectives of judicial decision making. From a normative standpoint, consistency is essential to insure the smooth operation of the judiciary because it permits individuals to plan their activities under a shared expectation of how their actions will be viewed by others, including the government. When individuals can anticipate judicial decisions with a high degree of certainty, a legitimizing effect occurs as faith in the judiciary is enhanced. Conversely, when judicial decisions appear inconsistent, the citizenry may view the outcome of judicial decisions as "a crapshoot," causing decreased confidence in the legal system (Tamanaha 2006: 129, 233, 236). Because Supreme Court justices must rely on the goodwill of the citizenry to follow their decisions, this creates a strong incentive on the part of the justices to behave in a consistent manner, thereby enhancing public confidence in the Court. Moreover, lower court judges benefit from consistent decision making by the Supreme Court because it augments their ability to avoid making costly and reversible errors (Shavell 1995). In this respect, because Supreme Court decisions act as precedent for the entire American legal system, when the justices render decisions in a consistent fashion, this makes it easier for lower court judges to follow vertical precedent by rendering decisions consistent with those set by the nation's highest court.

Empirically, the hunt for consistency in decision making is at the core of scientific investigation. The search for predictability leads researchers toward the formulation of theories and hypotheses that later allow for generalization (Severin and Tankard 1997: 159). In judicial politics, the expectation of consistency drives both attitudinal and legal theories of Supreme Court decision making. From the attitudinal standpoint, preferences are assumed to be foundational beliefs that are stable over time and resistant to great change. For example, consistent with standard psychological definitions (e.g., Cacioppo, Harkins, and Petty 1981: 31–32; Miller and Colman 1981: 105), political scientists in the attitudinal tradition recognize attitudes as a relatively *enduring* set of interrelated beliefs regarding at least one object and the situation in which it is encountered (Rohde and Spaeth 1976: 72; Segal and Spaeth 1993: 69). From a legal standpoint, consistency also plays a key role. For example, precedent dictates that similar cases must receive like treatment.

Despite the normative and empirical importance of consistency, few analyses explicitly address variability in judicial decision making. Those that do focus primarily on consistency as it relates to voting in precedent-setting cases and cases that challenge those precedents (e.g., Brenner and Spaeth 1995; Collins 2004b; Spaeth and Segal 1999) or fluidity involving alterations from the initial conference vote to the final vote on the merits (e.g., Brenner 1980; Brenner, Hagle, and Spaeth, 1989; Hagle and Spaeth, 1991; Howard, 1968). The purpose of this chapter is to contribute to this small, but significant, line of inquiry by investigating the causes of consistent and inconsistent voting in the Supreme Court, focusing on how organized interests reduce the certainty in the justices' decision-making process, leading to more variable voting behavior.

This analysis differs from previous efforts to address the consistency of judicial choice in that I do not compare a justice's previous votes (either in conference or in a precedent-setting case) with his or her consequent voting behavior. Instead, I focus on consistency as it relates to an individual justices' vote in a given case. To do this, I employ a heteroskedastic probit model. While I address this estimation technique in more detail later in the chapter, a few brief words are appropriate here to avoid the potential for unnecessary confusion. Scholars who use statistical inference to examine the voting behavior of judicial decision makers almost exclusively focus on variables that influence the mean of the distribution of a dependent variable (e.g., the causes of liberal or conservative voting). When using dichotomous dependent variables, researchers typically employ a logit or probit model, which assumes that the error variance around the justices' choices is constant. Unlike these models, the heteroskedastic probit model relaxes the assumption of uniformity in the error term and instead allows the error term to alter with respect to predictor variables. Thus, it allows for the estimation of factors that are hypothesized to influence the change in the variance of the distribution of the dependent variable. In simpler terms, it offers a researcher the opportunity to examine the causes of consistent or inconsistent voting. As such, the hypotheses advanced below should not be confused with more traditional expectations that posit some influence on the mean of the distribution of the dependent variable. Instead, they should be understood in terms of how the variables of interest effect the variance surrounding the justices' choices; that is, the causes of consistency in judicial choice.

II. Amici Curiae and the Consistency of Judicial Choice

Life is filled with uncertainty. Every day, individuals are charged with making decisions that involve choosing between two or more alternatives. To make these decisions, we are forced to weigh a number of factors, even for the most mundane of choices. Consider, for example, Festinger's (1957: 45) illustration of the decision to attend a dinner party or go to a concert. In making this rather routine choice, an individual contemplates a number of factors, including whether the host of the dinner party will be offended if he or she declines, the likelihood of deriving pleasure from social interaction with the other attendees of the dinner party, as well as an assessment of the expected level of enjoyment from attending the concert (Simon, Snow, and Read 2004). One could add to this a number of other considerations, such as the amount of travel time required to attend the party vis-à-vis the concert. As this narrative makes clear, incertitude is a hallmark of individual choice.

Life on the Supreme Court is similar in this regard. In adjudicating cases, the justices are regularly faced with choosing between two or more alternatives. But, unlike the decision to attend a dinner party or go to a concert, the justices' choices have far more significant consequences. In their role as policymakers, the choices justices make have profound implications for society at large. In recent terms, the justices have adjudicated whether public displays of the Ten Commandments violate the First Amendment's Establishment Clause (*McCreary County v. ACLU* 2005), whether the execution of mentally retarded individuals constitutes cruel and unusual punishment (*Atkins v. Virginia* 2002), in addition to determining whether Congress can prohibit the medical use of marijuana, despite state laws to the contrary (*Gonzales v. Raich* 2005). Moreover, in their capacity as legal actors, the justices are expected to be attentive to norms that have the potential to constrain their behavior. This is perhaps no more evident than society's expectation that judging be accomplished in an objective and neutral manner. With this in mind, the justices must address a number of important questions before casting their votes. For example, which is the most legally compelling resolution to the dispute? Which side marshaled the most persuasive evidence? Is this decision in line with my previous votes in similar cases and those of the previous Courts? Which position allows me to best pursue my policy goals? How will society react to this decision? How will other actors in government react to this decision? Will lower court judges follow the decision in good faith?

Considerations like these are present in every case the Court accepts for review. As such, the justices are continually confronted with uncertainty. However, it is important to note that some cases are more uncertain than others. Consider, first, a Supreme Court case without amicus participation. In such a case, the justices consider two fundamental perspectives: those of the petitioner and respondent. While both of these litigants will attempt to present the justices with as much persuasive evidence as possible to make their claims, page limitations restrict the number of arguments that the parties can advance.[108] Because of this, the parties to litigation must estimate which arguments will be most persuasive and center their briefs (and oral arguments) on those positions. Because the parties are primarily concerned with their direct interest in the case, and not the broader social consequences of the decision, the parties generally

---

108 Under Supreme Court Rule 33, parties' briefs are limited to 50 pages, while their reply briefs are capped at 20 pages.

focus their arguments on presenting evidence that corresponds to their central goal: to win. Thus, in cases without amicus participation, both the overall amount of information and the type of information available to the justices are somewhat limited as the dispute is framed in a manner that focuses on the direct outcome of the case for the parties to litigation, not as it affects society at large (Birkby and Murphy 1964).

Now consider a case with amicus participation. In such a case, the justices are the recipients of a wide array of information as the amici expand the scope of the conflict (e.g., Schattschneider 1960). In addition to receiving the somewhat narrow argumentation presented by the parties, the justices also receive an extensive assortment of information presented by the amici. This information is focused, not on the outcome of the case as it relates to the parties to litigation, but instead on the broader legal and policy aspects of the decision. Since amici raise new issues in the Court—focusing on the legal, policy, and separation of powers issues implicated in the case—the amici further confound the justices' already uncertain decision making. By bringing new issues to the justices' attention, the amici make it difficult for the justices to determine what the correct application of the law is in any given case. Therefore, I argue that the justices' voting behavior will be more variable in cases attracting a relatively large number of amicus briefs.

The notion that increased information can lead to uncertainty for decision makers is well documented in a variety of literatures, ranging from consumer research (e.g., Malhotra 1984), to management studies (e.g., Iselin 1993), to social psychology (e.g., Simon 1979), to political science (e.g., Robertson 1980), to law (e.g., Grether, Schwartz, and Wilde 1986). Known as information overload, this is the concept that when decision makers receive a great deal of information, they have difficulty processing this information. As a result of the arduous nature of this type of information processing, decisional uncertainty is increased. One consequence of this uncertainty is increased variability; that is, a reduction of consistency. From the standpoint of information overload, the primary focus involves how the performance of a decision maker is affected by the amount of information that decision maker receives. When a decision maker is the recipient of a great deal of information relating to a decision, it creates a burden that can lead to confusion, resulting in increased uncertainty as to the utility of each choice (Eppler and Mengis 2004: 326). For the justices, a great deal of information can reduce their ability to effectively evaluate the consequences of the choices they face, thus resulting in increased ambiguity as to the correct application of the law. Because certainty can only be accomplished when options are eliminated or narrowed, by expanding the scope of the conflict, amicus briefs can contribute to the uncertainty in the justices' decision making, leading to more variable voting behavior. In this way, the justices' decisional processes have the potential to become unstable as the overall volume of information increases (e.g., Millburn and Billings 1976).

The results presented in the previous chapter, indicating that the justices respond to persuasion attempts in amicus briefs essentially regardless of whether they are predisposed to agree with the argumentation in the briefs, lends preliminary support for the overload hypothesis. In that analysis, I found that, while ideology plays a major role in explaining judicial choice, amicus briefs are capable of persuading the justices to vote against their ideological preferences. Incorporating this finding into my expectations regarding the variance in the justices' decision making, this suggests that a liberal justice, when confronted with several amicus briefs supporting the conservative position, may be persuaded to support the conservative position, thus violating expectations of the attitudinal model. Clearly, this would result in an increase in the variability of this justice's behavior.[109]

Of course, it is important to note that the presence of information that is incongruent with an individual's prior beliefs is not a necessary condition for overload to occur. Rather, information overload has the potential to transpire whenever information increases uncertainty. In other words, overload can manifest itself whenever a decision maker becomes saturated with a great deal of information. By raising issues not addressed by the litigants, amici can expand the scope of the conflict, even when amicus briefs are filed on only one side of the case. For example, in *El Al Israel Airlines v. Tseng* (1999), a case involving whether an airline passenger's allegations that an international airline's preboarding security search caused her to suffer personal injuries is ripe for state court review, three amicus briefs were filed for the petitioner and none were

---

109 This view of variance in judicial decision making is analogous to the information persuasion model posited by Alvarez and Brehm (2002: 32–33). These authors argue that, when an individual encounters new information that suggests a deviation from his or her predispositions, this new information might alter that person's underlying belief, leading to an increase in the observed variance in that individual's belief system. In other words, as informational uncertainty increases, the consistency of observed behavior should decrease.

filed on behalf of the respondent. In its amicus brief, the U.S. Solicitor General argued that the respondent's personal injury claim cannot be brought in state court because this is prohibited by the Warsaw Convention, an international treaty that established uniform regulations for international air travel. The International Air Transport Association, an organization of 256 air carriers, addressed the industrywide implications of allowing passengers to bring liability claims in state courts as they relate to the ability of airlines to modernize the Warsaw Convention's limitations on liability claims. The Air Transport Association of America, an association of 28 foreign and domestic airlines, devoted substantial attention to a treatment of its belief that by allowing passengers to bring liability claims in state courts, the security of airlines and airline passengers is threatened since the decision to do so would compromise the complex web of international agreements that govern liability claims made by injured passengers. As this case makes clear, even amici supporting only one litigant have the potential to influence the justices' decision making by raising new issues and reframing arguments already presented by the parties. Following from this, I expect that as the number of amicus briefs filed in a case increases, these briefs present the justices with new information that increases the amount of uncertainty regarding the correct application of the law in that case. Accordingly, I hypothesize:

> *Variance Hypothesis: As the number of amicus curiae briefs increases, so too will the variance in a justice's voting behavior.*

III. Modeling the Influence of Amici Curiae

To test this hypothesis, I utilize the same data used in Chapter 4. As before, the dependent variable captures the ideological direction of the individual justice's vote, scored 1 for a liberal vote and 0 for a conservative vote.[110] While my interest in this chapter is to evaluate whether amicus curiae briefs increase the variability in the justices' decision making, it is also necessary to account for factors that influence the justices' choices. As such, I include the same variables reported in the previous chapter in the choice portion of the model.

---

110 Following the previous chapter, I control for the nonindependence of observations by estimating the model using robust standard errors, clustered on case citation.

I employ a heteroskedastic probit model to estimate the variability in the justices' choices. This model simultaneously estimates the effect of explanatory variables on both the mean and variance of a dichotomous dependent variable. It does so by relaxing the assumption that the variance is equal to one (as in a homoskedastic probit model). Instead, it allows the variance to alter with respect to predictor variables, such as the number of amicus briefs filed in a case. As with the standard probit model used in Chapter 4, it is not necessary to understand the technicalities of the heteroskedastic probit model to gain an intuitive understanding of its results. This is the case because, in addition to reporting the model's coefficients and standard errors, I use the model's estimates to graphically plot the variance in the justices' decision making. It should be noted, however, that, unlike the previous chapter, in which I presented marginal effects—changes in the predicted probability of observing a liberal vote given a shift in the value of an independent variable—the variance portion of the heteroskedastic probit model cannot be interpreted in this way. Nonetheless, the results can easily be understood by plotting the predicted changes in the error variance for a range of substantively interesting situations. This allows me to elucidate the relative magnitude of the variables that contribute to the error variance in the justices' decision making.[111]

---

111 To more clearly differentiate between the two models, consider the log likelihood function of the standard, homoskedastic probit model (Equation 1) as compared with the log likelihood function of the heteroskedastic probit model (Equation 2):

(1) $$\log L = \sum_{i=1}^{n} yi \ \log(\Phi(Xi\beta)) + (1 - yi)\log(1 - \Phi(Xi\beta))$$

(2) $$\log L = \sum_{i=1}^{n} \left(yi \ \log\Phi\left(\frac{Xi\beta}{\exp(Zi\gamma)}\right) + (1 - yi)\log\left[1 - \Phi\left(\frac{Xi\beta}{\exp(Zi\gamma)}\right)\right] \right)$$

In these equations, β represents the parameter estimates for the independent variables (X) in the choice model, γ is the parameter estimates for the independent variables in the variance model (Z), and Φ represents the standard normal (probit) distribution. As these equations make clear, the primary difference between the likelihood functions of the two models is the inclusion of the variance model ($\exp(Zi\gamma)$) in the denominator of the unrestricted heteroskedastic probit model (Alvarez and Brehm 1995: 1062). Accordingly, the heteroskedastic model provides two types of estimates: those related to the mean of the distribution of the dependent variable (i.e., the causes of liberal or conservative voting) and those related to the variance of the distribution of the dependent variable (i.e., the causes of consistent or inconsistent voting). If the effects of the variables expected to influence the variance of the distribution of the dependent variable are constant, I cannot reject the null hypothesis of homoskedasticity

To determine whether the justices' decision making is more variant in cases attracting a relatively large number of amicus briefs, I include a variable labeled *Total Amicus Briefs*. This is simply the sum of the *Liberal Amicus* and *Conservative Amicus* variables reported in the previous chapter (which are included in the choice model). I expect that this variable will be positively signed, indicating that a justice's decision making is more variable in cases in which interest groups expand the scope of the conflict through amicus participation.[112]

A. Other Influences on the Consistency of Judicial Decision Making

To capture the effects of other influences on the consistency of the justices' decision making, I include several control variables in the variance portion of the model. Unless otherwise noted, all of these variables were derived from the Spaeth (2002, 2003) databases. First, I account for a case's salience to capture the possibility that the justices rely even more on their attitudes in important cases than in relatively trivial disputes (e.g., Segal 1986: 939; Spaeth and Segal 1999: 309–311; Unah and Hancock 2006). Past research indicates that in such cases, the justices ask more questions during oral arguments in an attempt to clarify issues in order to maximize the application of their policy preferences (Schubert, Peterson, Schubert, and Wasby 1992) and that chief justices self-assign salient cases to maximize control over the ideological content of the opinions (e.g., Brenner and Arrington 2002; Epstein and Segal 2000; Segal and Spaeth 1993; 2002). Accordingly, in landmark cases, I expect the justices will become more cognitively engaged (than in relatively routine cases), leading to more stable voting behavior. Following this, I expect that the justices' voting behavior will be more consistent in politically salient cases.

---

and the model reduces to the standard probit model. If, as expected, the results of the variables predicted to influence the consistency of the justices' decision making are nonconstant, I can reject the null hypothesis of homoskedasticity and conclude that the model is systematically heteroskedastic.

112 I ran an alternative specification of the model including the *Liberal Amicus* and *Conservative Amicus* variables in place of the *Total Amicus Briefs* variable in the variance vector, as well as a model that included a variable indicating that amicus briefs were filed on only side of the case. The results of the former specification (breaking up the *Total Amicus Briefs* variable by the ideological direction of the briefs) corroborate the results reported here, while the variable indicating amicus briefs were filed on only one side of the case failed to achieve statistical significance.

As a proxy for *Political Salience*, I employ a variable scored 1 if the case appeared on the front page of the *New York Times* following the decision and 0 if it did not.[113] I expect this variable will be negatively signed, indicating that a justice's voting behavior is more stable in salient cases.

Supreme Court Rule 10 provides the only official instructions regarding what factors the justices consider when evaluating petitions for writs of certiorari, although the Court recognizes that the rule is "neither controlling nor fully measuring the Court's discretion." Parts (a) and (b) of Rule 10 state that the Court is particularly interested in accepting cases for review that involve conflicting decisions from two or more lower courts.[114] As such, this rule codifies the Court's perspective that one of its main purposes is to resolve uncertainty among lower courts. While scholars have evaluated whether the Court follows this rule in a host of studies relating to certiorari decisions (e.g., Caldeira and Wright 1988; Perry 1991; Ulmer 1984), researchers have yet to investigate whether the presence of lower court conflict influences the variability in the justices' decision making on the merits. Accordingly, I do so here. I hypothesize that the justices' decision making will be more variable in cases in which the reason for granting certiorari was due to the presence of lower court conflict. In such cases, there are two or more divergent applications of the law from lower federal or state courts, indicating that each "litigant" has successful persuaded at least one lower court to endorse its position on the merits, suggesting that both perspectives carry legal validity. This means that for the justices, there are two binding (in the lower courts' jurisdictions), and presumably sound, decisions from lower courts. This suggests that there is a substantial amount of uncertainty with regard to the correct application of the law in the case, which may contribute to variability in the justices' decision making. To determine whether this hypothesis comports with reality, I include a *Lower Court Conflict* variable in the model, scored 1 if the reason for granting certiorari is lower court conflict and 0 otherwise. I expect this variable will be positively signed, indicating that the justices' decision making is less consistent in cases where lower courts diverged in their application of the law.

---

113 The data that compose this variable were collected by Epstein and Segal (2000) for the 1946–1995 terms and collected by the author for the remaining terms, using the coding rules established by Epstein and Segal.

114 Part (c) of Rule 10 states that the Court is interested in cases involving important questions of federal law that have not been decided by the Court, as well as those cases in which a lower court decision conflicts with a Supreme Court precedent.

Scholars of the Supreme Court are increasingly attentive to the fact that the Court does not operate in isolation from the other branches of government (e.g., Epstein and Knight 1998; Eskridge 1991; Murphy 1964; Segal 1997). Rather, it has been suggested that the justices are constrained in their decision making in statutory cases by the fact that their decisions might be overridden by Congress or indifferently enforced by the executive branch.[115] Insofar as Congress or the president might reverse these decisions, this creates a strong incentive for the justices to consider these actors' preferences when rendering their decisions to ensure the institutional legitimacy of the Court. As such, I hypothesize that the justices' decision making will be more variable in cases involving statutory interpretation, as opposed to constitutional cases, because the justices may be more willing to defer to the desires of the elected branches of government and vote in a manner that is inconsistent with their sincere policy preferences in these cases (e.g., Bartels 2005). To test this theory, I include a *Statutory Interpretation* variable in the model, scored 1 if the case at issue involves statutory interpretation and 0 if it involves constitutional interpretation. I anticipate that this variable will be positively signed, indicating that the justices' decision making is more variable in statutory interpretation cases.

In addition to these case specific factors, a particular attribute of the justices is expected to influence the variability in their decision making. That is, I expect that as a justice's length of service on the Court increases, the variability in his or her decision making will decrease. Known as an acclimation effect, this is the idea that a justice goes through a period of initial disorientation on the Court, which weakens over time as his or her policy preferences become more firmly developed (e.g., Brenner 1983; Hagle 1993; Pacelle and Pauly 1996; Snyder 1958). Thus, the acclimation hypothesis predicts that the justice's decision making patterns will stabilize over time (Howard 1968: 45). To determine whether the variability in a justice's decision making decreases over time, I include a *Tenure* variable that is a count of each justice's length of service on the Court. I expect this variable will be negatively signed, indicating that the variability in a justice's decision making decreases over time.

---

115 Statutory interpretation differs from constitutional interpretation in that federal statutory cases involve the adjudication of, e.g., an act of Congress, while constitutional cases involve the interpretation of some aspect of the constitution.

IV. Empirical Results

Table 5.1 reports the heteroskedastic probit model that predicts the influences of the included variables on both the mean and the variance of the justices' decision making. The model correctly predicts 66.6% of cases, for a percent reduction in error of 28.2%. The heteroskedasticity test is particularly important because it reveals that I can reject the null hypothesis of homoskedasticity, indicating that the heteroskedastic probit model provides a better fit than the homoskedastic model that assumes the variance is constant.[116] Though my primary purpose in this chapter is to investigate the influence of amicus curiae briefs as the briefs relate to the variance surrounding the justices' choices, it is useful to begin by addressing the choice portion of the model.

As the choice component of the model indicates, the results of the variables that influence the liberal or conservative nature of the justices' decision making remain consistent with those reported in the previous chapter, although the marginal effects do exhibit minor fluctuations. This reveals that the homoskedastic model (Table 4.2), by failing to account for heteroskedasticity in the data, provided slightly biased parameter estimates. For example, the homoskedastic model indicated that when the Solicitor General files a liberal amicus brief, the likelihood of observing a justice cast a liberal vote increases by 13.3%, while the heteroskedastic model reports this influence slightly lower, at 11.9%. Likewise, the heteroskedastic model indicates that the influence of the ideological direction of the lower court's decision is slightly smaller than in the homoskedastic model: 14% (heteroskedastic) compared to 16.5% (homoskedastic). As for the other control variables in the choice portion of the model, they confirm the results of the homoskedastic model, falling within approximately one percentage point of the homoskedastic model's results in terms of their marginal effects.

---

116 This heteroskedasticity test compares the heteroskedastic model with the homoskedastic model using the likelihood ratio test where L_0 is the log likelihood for the homoskedastic probit model, L_H is the log likelihood for the heteroskedastic probit model, and k is the number of estimated parameters in the variance portion of the model. The likelihood ratio is $2 \times (L_H - L_0)$, which is distributed by χ^2 with k degrees of freedom (e.g., Alvarez and Brehm 1995). The results of this test are confirmed through the use of the asymptotically equivalent Wald test statistic (Wald χ^2, $\sigma^2 = 185.6$, significant at $< .001$).

Table 5.1. Heteroskedastic Probit Model of the Influence of Amici Curiae in the U.S. Supreme Court, 1946–2001 Terms

Predictor	Coefficient	Marginal Effect
CHOICE MODEL		
Liberal Amicus	.236 (.052)***	see figure 5.1
Conservative Amicus	.009 (.036)	see figure 5.1
SG Liberal	.519 (.074)***	+11.9%
SG Conservative	−.507 (.073)***	−12.5%
Liberal Resources	.034 (.007)***	+2.3%
Conservative Resources	−.052 (.007)***	−3.2%
Lower Court Direction	−.569 (.036)***	−14.0%
Ideology	−.270 (.010)***	−15.5%
Ideology × Liberal Amicus	−.034 (.007)***	see figure 5.1
Ideology × Conservative Amicus	−.011 (.006)*	see figure 5.1
Constant	2.28 (.112)***	
VARIANCE MODEL		
Total Amicus Briefs	.042 (.012)***	
Political Salience	−.313 (.0 49)***	
Statutory Interpretation	.183 (.042)***	
Lower Court Conflict	.166 (.057)**	
Tenure	.018 (. 002)***	
N	57,327	
Wald χ^2	833.4***	
Heteroskedasticity Test $\left(\chi^2_{df=5}\right)$	453.9***	
Percent Correctly Predicted	66.6	
Percent Reduction in Error	28.2	

Dependent variable indicates the ideological direction of the individual justices' vote (1 = liberal, 0 = conservative). Numbers in parentheses indicate robust standard errors, clustered on case citation. * $p < .05$; ** $p < .01$; *** $p < .001$ (one-tailed).

Figure 5.1 reports the marginal effects of the amicus variables in the choice model across the range of ideology.[117] The top graph indicates the marginal effects of amicus briefs as they increase from one to three, while the bottom graph reports the predicted change in observing a liberal vote as the number of amicus briefs increases from one to ten. The upper portion of each graph, containing the dash-dot line, indicates the marginal effects of liberal amicus briefs as a justice becomes more conservative. The lower portion of each graph, containing the solid line, designates the influence of conservative amicus briefs across the same ideological spectrum. The confidence intervals are indicated by the dotted lines. The marginal effects are significant whenever the upper and lower bounds of the confidence intervals are both above (or below) the zero line.

These graphs corroborate the results reported in the previous chapter. Beginning with conservative briefs, the results illustrate that an increasing number of conservative amicus briefs decreases the likelihood of observing a liberal vote, regardless of judicial ideology. For example, the most liberal justice in the data (*Ideology* = 0) is 2% more likely to cast a conservative vote as the number of conservative amicus briefs increases from one to three. For the most conservative justice (*Ideology* = 10.6), this increase is more pronounced, at 5%. For the bulk of the Court, those justices whose ideologies fall within one standard deviation of the mean, the influence of conservative amicus briefs is more-or-less uniform, at 5% on the liberal end (*Ideology* = 4.2) and 6% at the conservative end

---

117 In the previous chapter, I was able to directly interpret the marginal effects of the *Conservative Amicus* and *Liberal Amicus* variables, which indicated the influence of amicus briefs when both of the interaction terms were held at zero. In other words, those constitutive variables provided information as to the marginal effects of amicus briefs for a justice whose ideology is at 0 (i.e., the most liberal justice in the data—Justice Douglas during the 1974 term). Unlike the homoskedastic model, I cannot directly interpret the influence of amicus briefs by examining the constituent variables in the heteroskedastic model. This is the case because the parameter estimates for the *Conservative* and *Liberal Amicus* variables do not consider the value of the *Total Amicus Briefs* variable in the variance vector, which is essential because that variable is made up of the two directional amicus variables. In other words, in order to uncover the marginal effects, it is required that I fit the model's predictions given the fact that the *Total Amicus Briefs* variable is composed of the *Conservative* and *Liberal Amicus* variables. Thus, nothing should be made as to the impact of these constituent terms. Instead, in order to establish whether the influence of amicus curiae briefs changes depending on whether I use a homoskedastic or heteroskedastic model, it is necessary to calculate the marginal effect and confidence intervals for these variables across the range of the *Ideology* variable, holding all other variables at their mean or modal values. To do this, I adapt the method developed by Brambor, Clark, and Golder (2006) for use with the heteroskedastic probit model.

a) Change: 1 to 3 Amicus Briefs

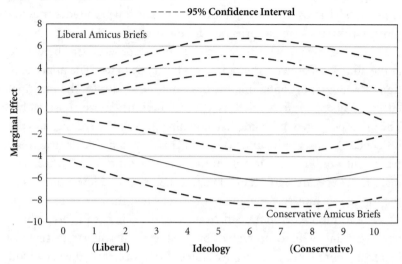

b) Change: 1 to 10 Amicus Briefs

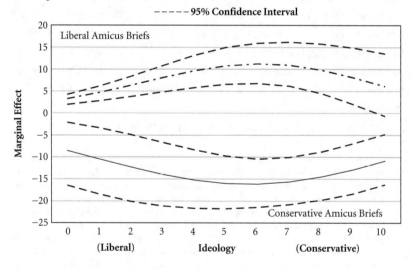

Figure 5.1. The Marginal Effect of Amicus Curiae Briefs on Supreme Court Decision Making

(*Ideology* = 8.3) of the spectrum. The bottom graph indicates that the marginal effects of conservative amicus briefs are more pronounced as their number increases. For example, the most liberal justice in the data is almost 10% more likely to cast a conservative vote in a case where 10 briefs are filed for the conservative position, compared with a case with a single conservative brief. For the most conservative justice in the data, this figure increases to about 12%. For those justices whose ideologies fall within one standard deviation of the mean, this influence increases to 15% on average.

The upper portion of each graph illustrates the marginal effect of liberal amicus briefs on the justices' decision making. Again, these results corroborate the findings of the homoskedastic model, although the marginal effects are slightly smaller in the heteroskedastic model. This graph indicates that liberal amicus briefs influence the decision making of all justices, with the exception of those justices whose ideologies are above 9.5. For those extremely conservative justices, liberal briefs do not wield an influence. As before, it is important to note that those observations correspond to only a few justices for only a portion of their tenures on the Court.[118] Turning to a substantive interpretation of these findings, the results in the top graph indicate that the most liberal justice in the data is 2% more likely to cast a liberal vote as the number of liberal amicus briefs increases from one to three. For the bulk of the Court—those justices whose ideologies fall within one standard deviation of the mean—this influence increases twofold. Examining the bottom graph, the results illustrate that the most liberal justice is about 4% more likely to cast a liberal vote as the number of liberal briefs increases from one to ten. For the more moderate justices, this effect is enhanced, at about 7% for moderate liberals, 12% for moderates, and 9% for moderate conservatives. Taken as a whole, these results again confirm the expectations of the legal persuasion model: 100% of justices are influenced by conservative amicus briefs, while liberal amicus briefs shape the decision-making proclivities of all justices except for three extreme conservatives constituting less than 5% of the observations in the data.

Turning now to the central purpose of this chapter, the variance portion of the model reports influences on the consistency or inconsistency in the justices' voting behavior. The primary variable of interest, *Total Amicus Briefs*, is signed in the expected direction and achieves statistical significance. Thus, as the number of amicus briefs filed in a case increases, so too does the variability in the justices' decision making. This indicates that by presenting information that might not otherwise be available to

---

118 Recall these data points involve Justice Scalia during the 1999–2000 terms, Justice Thomas during the 1994–2001 terms, and Associate Justice Rehnquist during the 1971–1985 terms, cumulatively constituting less than 5% of the observations under analysis.

the justices, organized interests expand the scope of the conflict causing the justices' choices to become more variant than in cases with no (or less) amicus participation. As such, these results suggest that theories of information overload developed in a multitude of disciplines are applicable to Supreme Court justices: as the information available to the justices increases, it becomes more difficult for the justices to determine the correct application of the law, thus increasing the uncertainty and variability in their decision making.

Three justices—liberal, conservative, and moderate—illustrate this finding nicely. On the liberal end, Earl Warren voted liberally in 74% of cases with no amicus briefs. In cases with four or more amicus briefs, Warren voted liberally in only 62% of cases. On the conservative end, William Rehnquist voted liberally in 27% of cases with no amicus briefs. For cases with four or more amicus briefs, this increased to 31%. Sandra Day O'Connor, a moderate conservative, voted liberally in 37% of cases in which no amicus briefs were filed. In cases with four or more briefs, O'Connor voted liberally 41% of the time. When considered in tandem with the results of the choice model, this reveals that amicus briefs are capable of persuading the justices to vote in accordance with the positions they espouse, effectively regardless of whether the justices are predisposed to support the positions advocated by the amici, and this persuasion increases the variability in the justices' voting behavior. A clear implication of this is that the predictive power of the attitudinal model is attenuated in cases with amicus participation.

The *Political Salience* variable indicates that, as expected, the variance in the justices' decision making is decreased in salient cases, as compared to relatively routine disputes. This reveals that a justice's ideology plays a more prominent role in salient cases, reducing the probability of observing nonattitudinal behavior. As such, this finding corroborates research in social psychology that indicates that attitude-behavior consistency is enhanced when an individual views the issues implicated in the decisional process as important (e.g., Posavac, Sanbonmatsu, and Fazio 1997). Consider, for example, two justices at the polar ends of the ideological spectrum. In nonsalient cases, conservative Clarence Thomas cast liberal votes in 32% of cases. For salient cases this decreased to 27%. William Douglas, a liberal, cast liberal votes in 76% of nonsalient cases. In salient cases, Douglas voted liberally 90% of the time.

This finding has an important implication in light of the results of the amicus variable in the variance vector. That is, the results illustrate that researchers should be particularly attentive as to the appropriateness of using amicus briefs as a proxy for a case's import (e.g., Hettinger, Lindquist, and Martinek 2004; Maltzman, Spriggs, and Wahlbeck 2000; Wahlbeck, Spriggs, and Maltzman 1999). More specifically, if amicus briefs serve as a surrogate for a case's importance, then the expected sign of the *Total Amicus Briefs* variable would be negative in direction, indicating less error variance in cases attracting a relatively large number of amicus briefs. However, this expectation does not comport with reality. Instead, it illustrates that the relationship between amicus briefs and error variance is most consistent with theories of information overload and not theories of cognitive consistency.[119] As such, this implies that it is inappropriate to use amicus briefs as a proxy for case salience for the Court's decisions on the merits.[120]

Table 5.1 also provides support for the role that lower court conflict plays in shaping the variability in judicial choice. In cases in which the justices granted certiorari to resolve conflict between two or more lower courts, the consistency in the justices' decision making is decreased. This suggests that when two or more lower courts diverge as to the correct application of the law, this increases the uncertainty in the justices' decision making. For example, conservative Antonin Scalia cast liberal votes in only 31% of cases in which lower court conflict was not identified

---

119 Further corroborating this point is the fact that the *Total Amicus Briefs* variable and the *Political Salience* variable are only correlated at 0.24.

120 However, it is important to note that using amicus briefs as a measure of salience at the Court's agenda setting stage might still prove appropriate. At that stage, the Court mulls over some 8,000 appeals, choosing to hear less than 100 cases in recent terms. Seeking to limit the amount of time allocated to this process, the justices and their clerks inevitably look for readily identifiable cues or signals to separate the wheat from the chaff (e.g., Tanenhaus, Schick, Muraskin, and Rosen 1963). One obvious signal is organizational amicus curiae participation, which highlights the potentially broad social consequences of a decision (Caldeira and Wright 1988). In this sense, the justices need not even read the briefs; they must only be aware of their presence. However, at the merits stage, a different picture emerges. Here the briefs do not merely signal the salience of a case, but instead act as adversarial weapons, advocating for a particular disposition of the case (Krislov 1963). At this stage, it is well established that the briefs are not only read, but have the potential to influence either the result of a case or the reasoning announced in the Court's opinions, a point the justices themselves corroborate (Breyer 1998; Douglas 1962; O'Connor 1996). As such, it is extremely important that we are attentive to the underlying information that a variable transmits and how this information might differ across different levels of decision making (e.g., Sartori 1970). What might tap into salience at one stage, might measure something entirely different at a different stage. Put succinctly, while it is ultimately desirable to develop indicators that are applicable to multiple stages of Supreme Court decision making, we cannot substitute a variable's validity for the sake of parsimony.

as the reason for granting certiorari. In cases with lower court conflict, this increased to 41%, illustrating how Scalia's reliance on his attitudes decreased when lower courts disagreed in their interpretations of the law.

The results of the heteroskedastic probit model also indicate that the justices' decision making is more variable in statutory interpretation cases, as compared to cases that implicate constitutional issues. This suggests that the justices are attentive to the fact that in statutory cases, Congress and the president might overrule or indifferently enforce their decisions, providing support for separation of powers perspectives on the Court (e.g., Epstein and Knight 1998; Eskridge 1991; Murphy 1964; Segal 1997). For example, Thurgood Marshall voted liberally in 76% of cases that did not involve statutory interpretation. In statutory interpretation cases, he cast liberal votes only 67% of the time, an 9 point decrease.

Contrary to my expectation, it does not appear that a justice's decision making becomes more stable as his or her tenure on the Court increases. In fact, this variable indicates that as a justice's length of service on the Court increases, so too does the variability in his or her decision making. While inconsistent with my theoretical expectations, a plausible explanation for this finding is that justices who are new to the bench may bring with them extreme policy preferences as a function of the contentious nature of the appointment process (e.g., Epstein and Segal 2005), along with a lack of understanding for Court rules and norms (Kaheny, Haire, and Benesh n.d.). Over time, justices gradually submit to Court norms, downplaying their reliance on their attitudes, resulting in less consistent voting behavior later in their careers (Kaheny, Haire, and Benesh n.d.). This alternative theoretical perspective suggests that we should observe more consistent voting behavior for justices new to the bench, and that variability should increase over time.[121] While this finding is consistent with this account, it should be noted that, as explained below, I am hesitant to make much of this finding since the substantive effect of the *Tenure* variable is relatively weak.

Thus far, I have only been able to interpret the variables that make up the variance portion of the model in terms of their direction and statistical significance. Though informative, the above discussion is unable to

---

121 Alternatively, it is possible that the justices improve on their strategic calculations as their tenure on the Court increases and are, hence, more likely to vote contrary to their attitudes later in their careers for strategic gains, depending on the context of any given case and the policy preferences of the President and Congress (e.g., Epstein, Knight, and Martin 2001).

provide information as to the relative magnitude of the variables' effects. To provide this information, Figure 5.2 plots the predicted error variance that corresponds to various substantively interesting scenarios. The solid lines indicate the predicted error variance, while the dotted lines report 95% confidence intervals. Figures A, B, and C plot the error variance as the number of amicus briefs increases, while Figure D plots the predicted error variance as a justice's tenure on the Court increases. The scenarios depicted in the figures are indicated in the upper left hand corner of each table. For example, Figure A plots predicted error variance as the number of amicus briefs increases for a justice who is serving in his or her eleventh term on the Court in a nonsalient case that does not involve statutory interpretation or lower court conflict. Figure A indicates that compared with a case in which only two amicus briefs are filed, in a case in which 10 amicus briefs are filed, the error variance increases by 46%. For a case

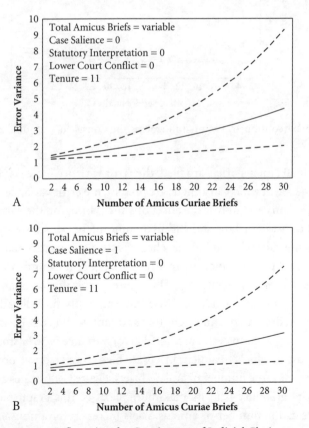

Figure 5.2. Factors Influencing the Consistency of Judicial Choice

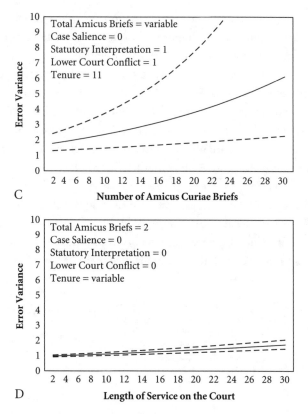

Figure 5.2. (continued) Factors Influencing the Consistency of Judicial Choice

in which 20 amicus briefs are filed, the error variance increases by 123% and, in a case in which 30 amicus are present, the error variance increases by 236%. Thus, not only is the effect of amicus briefs on the variability in judicial decision making statistically significant, but its substantive influence on the variability in judicial choice is strong in relative magnitude.

Figure B plots the increase in error variance as the number of amicus briefs increases in a salient case. This figure reveals that compared with a nonsalient case, in a landmark case, the variability in judicial decision making is decreased, although the substantive impact is somewhat marginal. For example, the predicted error variance is 36% smaller in a salient case in which 10 amicus briefs are filed compared to a non-salient case with the same number of amicus briefs. Figure C illustrates a scenario in which variability is at its maximum. That is, this graph plots error variance as the number of amicus briefs increases for a nonsalient case involving statutory interpretation and lower court conflict. This table reveals that, for example, compared with a case involving a constitutional provision with no lower court conflict and 10 amicus briefs, the variability in a justice's decision making increases by 42% for a case involving both lower court conflict and statutory interpretation. Finally, Figure D reports predicted error variance as a justice's length of service on the Court increases. As this figure makes clear, while the *Tenure* variable is statistically significant, its substantive influence is quite marginal, suggesting that the justices' decision making patterns are relatively stable over the course of their careers.

V. Summary and Conclusions

The purpose of this chapter was to analyze the influence of amicus briefs as they relate to the variability in the justices' decision making (i.e., the error variance associated with the justices' choices). Expanding on the previous chapter's findings that amicus briefs serve to attenuate the justices' reliance on their attitudes, I found evidence for my hypothesis that amicus briefs increase the ambiguity in the justices' already uncertain decision making, leading to more variable behavior. That is, by raising new issues in the Court, and persuading the justices to adopt positions that are attitudinally incongruent, amicus briefs confound the certainty surrounding the justices' perspectives as to the correct application of the law in a case. A novel perspective to understanding the influence of legal considerations, my approach sheds light on how legal influences—by undermining the justices' policy preferences and creating incertitude with respect to the correct application of the law—are capable of reducing consistency in judicial decision making. This indicates that while stability is generally viewed as normatively desirable in judicial decision making, not all legal explanations for judicial decision making provide for stability in the law.

CHAPTER 6

Amici Curiae and Dissensus on the Supreme Court

On May 23, 1957, police officers arrived at the home of Dollree Mapp in response to a tip that an alleged bomber was hiding in her residence. When the law enforcement officials demanded entrance to search Mapp's home, she immediately contacted her attorney, who advised her to refuse to admit the police without a search warrant. Acting on the advice of her counsel, she denied the officers access to her home. Three hours later, the police again sought to enter Mapp's residence. When Mapp did not respond to the officers' commands for admittance, the police forcibly entered her home. At this point, she demanded to view the warrant and the police handed her a piece of paper they claimed was a warrant, which she stuffed into her blouse. After a brief scuffle, the police recovered the "warrant," took her into custody, and searched her home. While the police found no evidence that Mapp was harboring the alleged bomber, they did find some pornographic pictures, a pencil drawing, and a few erotic comic books focused on the sexual adventures of Popeye the Sailor, referred to in the popular parlance as "Tijuana bibles" (Dickson 2001: 485). Viewing the materials as lewd and lascivious, the police arrested Mapp for violating an Ohio statute that prohibited the possession of obscene materials. Somewhat mysteriously, at her trial, neither the police nor the prosecution produced the warrant. Nonetheless, Mapp was found guilty of violating the obscenity statute.

On October 24, 1960, the Supreme Court noted probable jurisdiction in *Mapp v. Ohio* (1961). The attorneys for both the petitioner and respondent argued the case on First Amendment grounds. Thus, through the eyes of the litigants, *Mapp* centered primarily on the constitutionality of the Ohio obscenity statute in light of freedom of speech concerns. However, in an amicus curiae brief filed by the ACLU and the Ohio Civil Liberties Union, a second issue was raised on which the case would ultimately rest. That is, these amici addressed the possibility of extending the exclusionary rule—the dictate that illegally obtained evidence cannot be admitted at trial—to state prosecutions:

> This case presents the issue of whether evidence obtained in an illegal search and seizure can constitutionally be used in a State criminal proceeding. We are aware of the view that this Court has taken on this issue in *Wolf v. Colorado*. It is our purpose by this paragraph to respectfully request that this Court re-examine this issue and conclude that the ordered liberty concept guaranteed to persons by the due process clause of the Fourteenth Amendment necessarily requires that evidence illegally obtained in violation thereof, not be admissible in state criminal proceedings (citations omitted).[122]

The exclusionary rule was created by the Supreme Court in *Weeks v. United States* (1914). However, it was only made applicable to the actions of federal law enforcement officials in federal criminal trials. Thus, illegally obtained evidence could still be admitted against criminal defendants in state courts, where the majority of criminal trials take place. In *Wolf v. Colorado* (1949), the Supreme Court had the opportunity to extend the exclusionary rule to state prosecutions but opted not to do so, noting that the exclusionary rule was but one of many methods of enforcing the Fourth Amendment's protection from illegal searches and seizures. Appropriating the arguments advanced by the ACLU, *Mapp* overruled *Wolf*, making the exclusionary rule applicable to both state and federal criminal trials.[123]

---

122 See amicus curiae brief of the ACLU and Ohio Civil Liberties Union, *Mapp v. Ohio* (1961).

123 While both of the litigants' attorneys addressed the Fourth Amendment aspects of the case as a secondary issue, they did not focus on the exclusionary rule's applicability to

Mapp is often celebrated as one of the most important Supreme Court decisions of the twentieth century (e.g., Katz 2001: 475; Long 2006; Stewart 1983: 1368). Moreover, the importance of the ACLU's amicus brief in *Mapp* is widely touted as evidence of the significance of amicus briefs in influencing the justices' decision making (e.g., Day 2001; Epstein and Walker 2004: 544; Spriggs and Wahlbeck 1997). While I agree with both of these assessments, my purpose in addressing *Mapp* is to highlight how amicus briefs can contribute to dissensus on the Supreme Court. To illuminate this point, consider the events that transpired during the conference at which the justices decided *Mapp*.[124]

When the justices met to adjudicate *Mapp*, their discussion began with a treatment of the case as a relatively routine obscenity dispute, a somewhat common occurrence on the Warren Court (Woodward and Armstrong 1979: 192–204). Indeed, five justices voted to reverse Mapp's conviction on First Amendment grounds, noting that the Ohio statute was unconstitutional. Justice Douglas, however, viewed the case as implicating the exclusionary rule, indicating that he would reverse Mapp's conviction on both First Amendment and Fourth Amendment grounds. Douglas, in seeking to overrule *Wolf*, was joined by three other justices: Brennan, Warren, and Clark. Thus, while all of the justices voted to reverse Mapp's conviction, five based their decision to do so on obscenity grounds, while four sought to do so by extending the exclusionary rule to state prosecutions. Ultimately, Justice Black switched his position and voted to overturn *Wolf* on both Fourth and Fifth Amendment grounds. So, what began as a 9-0 vote to reverse the lower court ended up as a 5-4 decision to overturn Mapp's conviction and apply the exclusionary rule to state prosecutions.

Mapp provides useful insight on the role of amicus briefs in contributing to a justice's decision to write a separate opinion, highlighting how the ACLU's amicus brief contributed to two types of uncertainty with regard to the correct application of the law for the justices. The first issue

---

state prosecutions. Rather, they concerned themselves with whether the police officers' behavior violated the "shock the conscious standard" articulated in *Rochin v. California* (1952). This rule holds that, if the police behavior in question would shock the conscious of a reasonable person, that behavior violates the Due Process Clause of the Fourteenth Amendment. In fact, during oral arguments, Ohio's attorney general was questioned about the applicability of *Wolf v. Colorado* and responded that he was not familiar with the case (Stewart 1983: 1367).

124 The discussion that follows is based on the conference notes of Justices Brennan and Douglas, as reported in Dickson (2001: 485–487).

related to this involves the appropriateness of using *Mapp* as a vehicle for extending the exclusionary rule to state prosecutions. This point was raised in the dissenting opinion of Justice Harlan, which was joined by Justices Frankfurter and Whittaker. Harlan indicated his belief that the Court's majority violated its long-standing tradition of refusing to consider issues *sua sponte*; that is, without having been presented by the parties to litigation. While Harlan acknowledged that the exclusionary rule issue was advanced in the ACLU's amicus brief, citing its argument in its entirety (367 U.S. 643, at 675), he nonetheless contended that *Mapp* was a bad vehicle for applying the rule to state court proceedings. Instead, he proposed that the Court should either schedule the case for rehearing, directing the litigants to focus on the constitutionality of *Wolf*, or wait until a more appropriate case arrived to determine the applicability of the exclusionary rule to the states. In light of this, the ACLU's amicus brief contributed to the dissenting justices' decision to address whether *Mapp* was an appropriate opportunity to overrule *Wolf*. In so doing, the dissenters made clear their uncertainty as to whether the case was suitable for extending the exclusionary rule to state criminal trials.

Second, the case illustrates the justices' uncertainty as to the legal basis for the exclusionary rule. In its amicus brief, the ACLU suggested that the Court make the exclusionary rule applicable to state criminal proceedings but did not address the legal foundation for the exclusionary rule with regard to the Fourth and Fifth Amendments. In *Mapp's* majority, four justices viewed the exclusionary rule as grounded in the Fourth Amendment. However, Justice Black, the crucial fifth vote in the case, wrote in a concurring opinion that the exclusionary rule was not grounded solely in the Fourth Amendment but instead found its footing in both the Fourth and Fifth Amendments (367 U.S. 643, at 662).[125] As such, there was substantial uncertainty with regard to the correct application of the law in the case as evidenced by the fact that even the justices in the majority were not of like mind as to the legal basis for the exclusionary rule. Taken as a whole, *Mapp* illustrates that amicus briefs can play a transformative role by lobbying the justices to consider the legal and policy issues implicated in the Court's jurisprudence through different perspectives than

---

125 This fact was addressed in Justice Harlan's dissenting opinion, in which he opined that the majority's decision was limited to the judgment to overrule *Wolf* since only four justices viewed the Fourth Amendment as the basis for the exclusionary rule (367 U. S. 643, at 685).

those of the parties to litigation. In so doing, amicus briefs can create ambiguity for the justices, at the same time providing the justices with legal argumentation that can be used as the basis for a separate opinion. The purpose of this chapter is to investigate the role of amicus curiae briefs in contributing to a justice's decision to author or join a separate opinion.

I. The Importance of Understanding Separate Opinions

For the first three decades of its existence, the Supreme Court disposed of cases in one of two primary manners. First, the majority of cases were decided in a *per curiam* fashion, with opinions being announced "by the Court." These *per curiam* decisions were not attributed to a single justice, but rather to the Court as a whole. Second, a large number of cases were decided through a seriatim opinion process, in which all of the justices wrote separate opinions. In 1801, this changed when John Marshall became Chief Justice and moved to initiate norms of unanimity (Kelsh 1999). Marshall was quite successful in this effort and put an end to the practice of releasing opinions seriatim. In its place, opinions were announced by a single justice who spoke for the Court, only rarely accompanied by separate opinions (Kelsh 1999).

The days of the Marshall Court are a far cry from today's standards. That is, separate opinion writing is now a custom on the Supreme Court (e.g., Caldeira and Zorn 1998; Halpern and Vines 1977; Smyth and Narayan 2006; Walker, Epstein, and Dixon 1988). To provide some perspective, during the Marshall Court era (1801–1835), dissenting opinions appeared in an average of 6% of cases, while concurring opinions were written in only 2% of cases. In the Rehnquist Court era (1986–2004), dissents were filed in more than 60% of cases, while concurring opinions were published in more than 40% of cases (Epstein, Segal, Spaeth, and Walker 1994; Spaeth 2007). In the contemporary Supreme Court, decisions are commonly accompanied by four types of opinions. First, the controlling rule of law in the case is announced by a majority opinion that indicates the disposition of the case (e.g., affirm or reverse), as well as the reasoning behind that outcome.[126] Second, a justice can file a regular

---

126 If there is no majority, the Court publishes a plurality opinion that expresses the views of a plurality of the Court's members. While a plurality opinion is a decision of the Court, it lacks the binding precedential authority of a majority opinion.

concurring opinion. In this capacity, the justice agrees with the majority's disposition of the case but expounds on the majority's logic behind that opinion. Third, a justice in the majority can file a special concurring opinion. In this mode, a justice is in concord with the majority's disposition of the case but writes separately to express disharmony with the majority's explanation for its reasoning. Finally, a justice in the minority can file a dissenting opinion, signaling his or her disagreement with both the majority's disposition of the case and the majority's reason for reaching that result.

Justices who opt to write or join separate opinions frequently speak to a number of benefits they perceive from writing separately. For example, the justices have indicated that they derive personal satisfaction in writing separately because they are generally free to do so without having to engage in bargaining with other justices over the content of their opinions (Hettinger, Lindquist, and Martinek 2006: 18; Kelsh 1999: 172). Justice Scalia expresses this point in discussing separate opinion writing:

> To be able to write an opinion solely for oneself, without the need to accommodate, to any degree whatever, the more-or-less-differing views of one's colleagues; to address precisely the points of law that one considers important and *no others*; to express precisely the degree of quibble, or foreboding, or disbelief, or indignation that one believes the majority's disposition should engender – that is indeed an unparalleled pleasure. (1994: 42)

In addition to deriving personal satisfaction from writing separately, in partaking of this type of behavior justices actively engage in a form of institutional disobedience by protesting perceived errors in the majority opinion. As Campbell (1983: 306) notes, this serves the democratic end of reinforcing the principle of self-choice, which is a fundamental tenet of free government. In other words, through separate opinion writing, the justices are enabled to point out flaws in the majority opinion, while presenting their own interpretation of the correct application of the law in a case. In so doing, justices can separate themselves from bearing responsibility for the majority's decision (Kelsh 1999: 159). For example, in *Fontain v. Ravenel* (1854), a case involving the execution of a will, Justice Daniel wrote:

> In expressing my dissent, I shall not follow the protracted argument throughout its entire length; my purpose is, chiefly, to free

myself on any future occasion from the trammels of an assent, either expressed or implied, to what are deemed by me the untenable, and, in this case, the irrelevant positions, which that argument propounds. (58 U.S. 369, at 396)

The decision to write separately can also foreshadow doctrinal development in the Court (Hettinger, Lindquist, and Martinek 2006: 19). In this sense, today's dissent (or concurrence) can become tomorrow's majority opinion. Indeed, Justice Cardozo was especially vocal about this benefit of separate opinions in arguing that:

The voice of the majority may be that of force triumphant, content with the plaudits of the hour, and recking little of the morrow. The dissenter speaks to the future, and his voice is pitched to a key that will carry through the years. Read some of the great dissents ... and feel after the cooling time of the better part of a century, the glow and fire of a faith that was content to bide its hour. The prophet and martyr do not see the hooting throng. Their eyes are fixed on the eternities. (1939: 505)

Cardozo's view on the utility of separate opinions in their capacity as a stimulus for future doctrinal change has come to fruition in a number of cases (e.g., Campbell 1983; Kelsh 1999). For example, in *Betts v. Brady* (1942), the Court's majority refused to provide the right to counsel to indigent defendants who were not charged with rape or murder. In dissent, Justice Black, joined by Justices Douglas and Murphy, protested, arguing that due process of law requires an attorney be made available to indigent defendants. Two decades later, Black's dissent became the law of the land in the landmark decision of *Gideon v. Wainwright* (1963).[127]

Finally, and perhaps most important for the present analysis, is the notion that through separate opinions, the Court is able to partially overcome its so-called countermajoritarian difficulty. While more traditional conceptions of this conundrum focus on the Court's isolation from the public and its secretive nature (e.g., Bickel 1962), Bennett (2001) presents an alternative perspective, highlighting the ability of the Court to engage

---

127 Similarly, Justice Harlan's dissent in *Plessy v. Ferguson* (1896), in which the Court's majority declared that separate facilities for the races are constitutionally permissible so long as they are equal, was etched into law some 60 years later in *Brown v. Board of Education* (1954). In *Brown*, the Court overruled *Plessy* on the grounds that separate facilities are inherently unequal in the context of public education.

in a colloquy with the public. According to this view, greater utility is derived from considering how the Court engages in democratic conversation, rather than focusing solely on its countermajoritarian institutional features. Bennett argues that the two primary means available to the Court to partake of this type of constitutional dialogue are its receptivity to amicus participation and the presentations the justices make to the public through their opinions. Amicus briefs, it is argued, provide a medium for the justices to interact with nonparties to a case, while judicial opinions permit the justices to expound on the reasons for their decisions. Consequently, both foster democratic involvement in the legal system. Indeed, this might be particularly true for separate opinions, which can soften disappointment with the Court's majority opinion by demonstrating to members of the thwarted public that their position is supported by at least a minority of the Court. Thus, much can be gained by exploring the interplay between these two methods for redeeming the nondemocratic nature of the Court, particularly with regard to how the primary mechanism for democratic input into the judiciary (amicus briefs) might be related to the Court's primary instruments for democratic output (opinions).

Of course, it is important to note that not all subscribe to a sanguine view of separate opinions. For example, it is commonly noted that the presence of dissenting and concurring opinions weakens the Court's prestige since nonunanimous opinions indicate to the public that the Court is unable to speak in a unified voice (e.g., Hettinger, Lindquist, and Martinek 2006: 19; Kelsh 1999: 144). Indeed, this perspective was forwarded by Justice White in *Pollack v. Farmers' Loan and Trust* (1895) when he explained that "The only purpose which an elaborate dissent can accomplish, if any, is to weaken the effect of the opinion of the majority, and thus engender want of confidence in the conclusions of courts of last resort" (157 U.S. 429, at 608). Since nonunanimous decisions indicate the existence of strife on the bench, this can lead the Court's audiences to view it not as a deliberative and unbiased legal body but instead as an institution composed of political actors seeking to etch their personal policy preferences into law.

In addition, nonunanimous decisions can disrupt the consistency of federal law, because they are more likely to be overruled (Spriggs and Hansford 2001). This is the case because separate opinions point out flaws in the logic of the majority opinion and signal ideological cleavages on the Court, leading to "uncertainty and instability in the law"

(Ray 1990: 811). Moreover, when a case is accompanied by separate opinions, litigants have a reduced ability to make efficient decisions about pursuing litigation because it compromises their facility to predict the outcome of potential disputes (Hettinger, Lindquist, and Martinek 2006: 20). Finally, separate opinions can cause confusion for lower courts since they inhibit the ability of lower courts to correctly interpret the rule of law announced in a Supreme Court precedent (Corley 2005). This is particularly significant since lower courts are charged with complying with the Court's decisions and handle the vast majority of litigation in the United States. If lower courts have difficulty interpreting the rule of law inherent in the Supreme Court's precedent, this damages the capacity of the Court to perform its institutional role as the final authority on federal law.

Regardless of one's position as to the utility of separate opinions, it is clear that they can have potentially profound implications for the administration of justice. Whether serving to reduce the legitimacy of the Court or as a means to promote democratic dialogue with the public, understanding the occurrence of separate opinions is unmistakably a topic worthy of investigation. The remainder of this chapter is dedicated to analyzing how amicus briefs can contribute to a justices' decision to write or join a separate opinion. I begin with a discussion of extant studies that have considered the influence of amicus briefs on dissensus, concluding that those previous studies have mistakenly viewed amicus briefs solely as a proxy for a case's salience. Instead of viewing amicus briefs as signaling the importance of the case, I build on the previous chapter and argue that by providing the justices with a host of information regarding how cases should be resolved, organized interests create ambiguity in the justices' already uncertain decision making. At the same time, amicus briefs supply the justices with a substantial foundation for a concurring or dissenting opinion, which reduces the resource-costs of engaging in this type of nonconsensual behavior.

II. Amicus Curiae Briefs: A Misapplied Surrogate for Salience

Although scholars have not provided a persuasive theoretical explanation for including amicus curiae participation in models of judicial dissensus, several studies have, nonetheless, used the number of amicus briefs filed in a case—or some derivation thereof—as a proxy for a case's political salience, finding that separate opinion writing is more likely in cases that attract a large number of amicus briefs (e.g., Hettinger, Lindquist, and Martinek 2004; Maltzman, Spriggs, and Wahlbeck 2000; Wahlbeck, Spriggs, and Maltzman 1999). Using this measure as a surrogate for salience is, however, problematic. Consider, for example, Epstein and Segal's (2000) discussion of the drawbacks associated with assorted proxies for case salience. First, these authors argue that various measures of salience suffer from content bias, in that salience is weighted toward particular types of issues. Using the number of amicus briefs filed in a case suffers from this concern as amicus briefs are most often filed in civil rights and liberties cases. For example, during the 1946–2001 Supreme Court terms, civil rights and liberties issues accounted for 53% of cases with amicus briefs, followed by cases involving economics and unions (26%), judicial power (11%), federalism (6%), and federal taxation (3%). Second, Epstein and Segal posit that measures of salience suffer from recency biases, in that the proxies overcount contemporaneous cases to the detriment of older cases. Again, an amicus-based measure of salience is afflicted by this criticism. For example, amicus briefs were present in less than 30% of cases during the 1946–1955 terms, compared with more than 90% since the 1990s. Third, Epstein and Segal note that many measures of salience suffer from time dependency, overcounting cases from particular eras of the Court. As a result of the increase in amicus participation over time, this criticism is also applicable to using amicus briefs as a surrogate for salience.[128] Fourth, the authors contend that many measures of salience are not transportable to other institutions. Though one might use interest group testimony at legislative hearings as a proxy for amicus participation in the Court to bridge these institutions, there is substantial evidence of an elite bias in the legislature (e.g., Salisbury 1984) that does not comport with the wide array of interest groups participating in the Supreme Court (e.g., Caldeira and Wright 1990; Collins and Solowiej 2007). In other words, because one of the primary reasons groups turn to the judicial arena is due to a lack of access to more traditional venues of influence, such as the legislative and executive branches (e.g., Cortner 1968; Vose 1959), that these seemingly-related concepts are actually tapping into the same underlying dimension is unlikely.

---

128 While recency bias and time dependency are related in the above example, these two criticisms of salience measures are not always concomitant. For example, a hypothetical salience measure that overcounts cases decided by the Burger Court (1969–1985) would suffer from time dependency but not recency bias.

Fifth, Epstein and Segal argue that a contemporaneous measure of salience is more useful than a retrospective measure. Of the five condemnations levied by these authors, this is the only criticism that is not applicable to amicus briefs.

In addition to the concerns addressed by Epstein and Segal (2000), it is appropriate to reiterate the results of the previous chapter in light of previous studies' use of amicus briefs as a proxy for a case's political salience. In Chapter 5, I examined the influence of amicus briefs on the consistency of judicial choice, finding that a justices' voting behavior is *more* variable in cases attracting a large number of amicus briefs. Conversely, I demonstrated that a justice's voting behavior is *less* variable in salient cases. Because the empirical result associated with the influence of amicus briefs was divergent from that of case salience, this indicates that the justices' responses to amicus briefs do not mimic that of case salience. Instead, amicus briefs confound the correct application of the law for the justices, increasing the ambiguity in their already uncertain decision making. Therefore, the results of this empirical test corroborate the fact that amicus briefs are an unsuitable measure of a case's broad significance. Moreover, by viewing briefs as a proxy for a case's broad import, scholars have ignored the informational value of the briefs, which Chapter 4 illustrated was an important factor in predicting the ideological direction of the justices' voting behavior. All of this suggests the need for a rigorous theory to explain why amicus briefs increase the likelihood that a justice will author or join a separate opinion, as demonstrated by past research.

III. The Influence of Amicus Briefs on Concurrences and Dissents

I propose that amicus curiae briefs will contribute to a justice's decision to write or join a separate opinion for two reasons, both based on the informational content of the briefs. The first reason is derived from the theoretical argument developed in the previous chapter. This account proposes that by providing the justices with novel argumentation regarding the correct application of the law in a case, amicus briefs create ambiguity for the justices. That is, as compared with cases with no amicus briefs, in cases with amicus briefs, the justices are the recipients of information that expands the scope of the conflict (e.g., Schattschneider 1960).

By raising such issues in the Court, amicus briefs confound the justices' already uncertain decision making. This uncertainty is argued to contribute to a justice's decision to write or join a separate opinion (e.g., Snyder 1959; Wrightsman 2006: 100). In cases without amicus participation, the scope of the conflict is narrow and the justices generally only consider issues raised by the litigants (e.g., Epstein, Segal, and Johnson 1996). In cases with amicus participation, the scope of the conflict is broad because the amici bring new issues to the justices' attention. By introducing or expanding on issues that the direct litigants were only able to raise in abbreviated form, amici obfuscate the justices' ability to discover the correct application of the law.

In this sense, because amicus briefs contribute to the justices' interpretations of the intricacy of a case, it is expected that the justices will become increasingly attentive to the case's multifaceted nature and, recognizing its ambiguity, will seek to shape the direction of the policy pronounced in the case (e.g., Snyder 1959). Because only a single justice can author the majority opinion, save for the extremely rare joint opinion (e.g., *Planned Parenthood v. Casey* 1992), if a justice desires to shape the content of the Court's policy, while avoiding bargaining with the majority opinion author, he or she is relegated to authoring a separate opinion (e.g., Scalia 1994). As Justice Ginsburg (1990: 148) notes, "Hard cases do not inevitably make bad law, but too often they produce multiple opinions." Insofar as the reduction of uncertainty in decision making is only accomplished when options are narrowed (Casagrande 1999: 7), amicus briefs, by presenting the justices with information that might be otherwise unavailable, act to overload the justices' cognitive processes (e.g., Robertson 1980). With regard to concurring opinions, the legal ambiguity that exists in cases with amicus participation can contribute to the decision to author such opinions since the majority opinion author might be unwilling to address all of the issues implicated in the case. As such, a justice who is interested in fleshing out an argument raised by an amicus can do so in a concurring opinion, while still illustrating his or her support for the majority's disposition of the case. As it relates to dissenting opinions, the legal uncertainty evinced in cases with amicus briefs can contribute to the decision to author a dissent since the majority often approaches the legal doctrine in the case from a different standpoint than that of the dissenters (e.g., Kelsh 1999; Scalia 1994). Because cases with amicus briefs typically involve a multitude of legal provisions (Hansford 2004a), a justice who desires to focus on how the majority erred in its interpretation of the rule of law implicated by the case can express this sentiment by authoring or joining a dissenting opinion.

In addition to bringing issues to the justices' attention that have the potential to light the fires of dissensus, amicus briefs also provide a substantial basis from which a justice can cultivate a separate opinion (e.g., Parker 1999). In so doing, amicus briefs marginalize the resource-costs of engaging in nonconsensual behavior as the justices are able to draw the justifications for this behavior from the arguments of the organized interests. Because partaking in nonconsensual behavior requires that the justices expend resources that might be spent otherwise—for example, dealing with certiorari petitions and authoring assigned opinions—choosing to dissent or concur is costly. By presenting the justices with a foundation for a separate opinion, amicus briefs can reduce the costs of writing separately. To illustrate this point, consider the separate opinions in the following two cases.

Gilmer v. Interstate/Johnson Lane Corporation (1991) began when Robert Gilmer, the manager of a financial services company, registered as a securities representative with a number of stock exchanges. By registering, Gilmer consented to arbitrate any future controversies that might arise between himself and his employer, Interstate/Johnson Lane. The company fired Gilmer at the age of 62, and he brought suit claiming that his termination was related to his age, in violation of the Age Discrimination in Employment Act of 1967 (ADEA). When his former employer moved to initiate arbitration, a district court judge denied this motion on the grounds that Congress intended to protect individuals bringing age discrimination suits from waiving their right to trial. The United States Court of Appeals for the Fourth Circuit reversed this decision. When the case reached the Supreme Court, seven amicus briefs were filed in the case. On the conservative side of the debate, advocating for the affirmation of the lower court decision, amicus briefs were filed by the Center for Public Resources, the U.S. Chamber of Commerce, the Equal Employment Advisory Council (EEAC), joined by the Professional Employment Research Council, and the Securities Industry Association (SIA). The three briefs supporting the liberal position were filed by the American Association of Retired Persons (AARP), the American Federation of Labor and Congress of Industrial Organizations (AFL-CIO), and the Lawyers' Committee for Civil Rights Under Law (Lawyers' Committee). The Supreme Court's majority upheld the circuit court decision, finding that age discrimination claims can be subjected to mandatory arbitration since the ADEA does not prohibit arbitration.

In dissent, Justice Stevens, joined by Justice Marshall, argued that the majority erred in its ruling because the Federal Arbitration Act explicitly exempts employees who are engaged in interstate commerce, such as financial securities managers, from being forced to engage in binding arbitration. Importantly, Stevens acknowledges that Gilmer did not raise this issue, either in the lower courts or in the Supreme Court. Rather, the issue was initially introduced by all three of the petitioner amici and subsequently briefed in opposition by two respondent amici, the SIA and EEAC. In his dissent, Stevens cited 27 authorities (e.g., cases, statutes, and other forms of doctrinal analysis) to buttress his position. Attesting to the reality that Stevens relied heavily on the arguments advanced by the amici as a basis for his dissenting opinion is the fact that these authorities were introduced to the Court primarily through amicus briefs. For example, Stevens referenced eight authorities presented by the petitioner, comprising 30% of all authorities, and cited 10 authorities addressed by the respondent (37%). The authorities cited by Stevens stemming from amicus briefs ranged from a low of 26% (Chamber of Commerce; SIA) to highs of 44% (AFL-CIO) and 56% (AARP). Moreover, 30% of the authorities that Stevens relied on were presented solely by the amici (40% were cited by both the parties and amici). Further telling is the fact that eight of these authorities (the remaining 30%), which were not presented by either the amici or parties, were used by Stevens to illustrate the Court's established practice of relying on arguments introduced in amicus briefs as a basis for past precedents "because the issues were so integral to the decision of the case" (500 U.S. 20, at 37).[129] In supporting this point, Stevens highlighted the central role that amicus briefs played in *Teague v. Lane* (1989) and *Mapp v. Ohio* (1961). As this discussion makes clear, the amicus briefs provided Stevens a well researched basis on which to base the central theme of his dissent.

Lilly v. Virginia (1999) provides an illuminating example of a justice's reliance on amicus briefs as the basis for separate opinion with regard to concurrences. This case began when the petitioner, Benjamin Lilly, along with his brother, Mark Lilly, and Gary Barker, was arrested by police following a two-day felony extravaganza during which the outfit allegedly

---

129 Thus, if the eight authorities not addressed by the parties or amici are excluded from consideration, the extent to which Stevens relied on authorities presented in amicus briefs is even more pronounced, ranging from a low of 37% (Chamber of Commerce; SIA) to a high of 79% (AARP).

stole liquor and guns and kidnapped and killed Alex DeFilippis. During police questioning, Mark admitted to stealing the liquor but claimed that the other two individuals pilfered the guns and that his brother Benjamin shot DeFilippis. At Benjamin's trial, Mark was called as a witness but refused to testify citing his Fifth Amendment privilege against self-incrimination. Although he was not compelled to testify, the trial court judge admitted Mark's custodial confession pursuant to a declaration of an unavailable witness against penal interest. This exception to the hearsay rule authorizes the admittance of statements that incriminate both the declarant and the defendant. Benjamin argued that the inculpatory statements should not be admitted because they shifted the responsibility for the murder from Mark to Benjamin and would thus violate the Sixth Amendment's Confrontation Clause. The trial court judge rejected these arguments and Benjamin was found guilty, a decision that was upheld by the Virginia Supreme Court.

When the case reached the U.S. Supreme Court, four amicus briefs were filed. The ACLU and the National Association of Criminal Defense Lawyers advocated the liberal position, arguing that the Court should reverse the lower court decision. On the conservative side, the Criminal Justice Legal Foundation and 17 U.S. states and territories filed briefs. In a plurality decision, with a 9-0 vote to reverse, the Court's plurality overturned the lower court, holding that admitting the confession violated the petitioner's Sixth Amendment right "to be confronted with the witnesses against him."

In his concurring opinion, Justice Breyer argued that the Court's plurality gave insufficient attention to the manner in which the hearsay rule is connected to the Confrontation Clause. Relying explicitly on arguments presented by the amici, Breyer opined that the Court's current hearsay-based Confrontation Clause test is both too narrow and too broad. With regard to its narrowness, Breyer argued that the Court's plurality viewed the hearsay exception as only appropriate when the statements fall within established out-of-court statements, such as those declarations occurring during police questioning, but might not cover statements made during a videotaped confession or deposition. As to the rule's generality, Breyer argued that the rule is too broad because it might cover statements that are only tangentially related to the facts of the case or those declarations made long before a crime was committed without being related to the potential for a future criminal act. Significantly, Breyer's concurrence draws heavily on amicus briefs. For example, Breyer used 17 authorities as the basis for his concurrence. Of these, 35% were drawn from the petitioner's brief, while 29% were appropriated from the respondent's brief. Citations to authorities in amicus briefs were much more prevalent, particularly with regard to the ACLU's amicus brief, which made up 76% of the authorities in his opinion. Moreover, 41% of the authorities cited in Breyer's concurrence were introduced by the amici, not the parties.[130] Further, Breyer's reliance on the ACLU's amicus brief was so heavy that he even cited the same edition of Hale's ([1660–1676] 1971) *History of the Common Law of England* that appeared in the ACLU's brief. Thus, again it is clear that the justices use amicus briefs as the foundation of separate opinions.[131]

By increasing the already ambiguous nature of the Court's information environment and by providing the justices with a well-researched basis for a separate opinion, I argue that amicus curiae briefs will influence a justice's decision to engage in this type of dissensus. Accordingly, I hypothesize:

> *Dissensus Hypothesis: As the number of amicus curiae briefs increases, so too will the likelihood that a justice will write or join a separate opinion.*

IV. Modeling the Influence of Amici Curiae

To test this hypothesis, I use the same data relied upon for analysis in the previous two chapters but exclude majority opinion authors from consideration. Majority opinion authors are eliminated from the model since they do not have the option to write a separate opinion. As such, their inclusion in the statistical analysis would introduce bias into the model. The dependent variable indicates whether a justice joined the majority, authored or joined a regular concurring opinion, authored or joined a special concurring opinion, or authored or joined a dissenting opinion.[132] Since the dependent variable is nominal, I use a multinomial

---

130 Signaling his literary tastes, two of the three authorities cited in Breyer's opinion that were not presented by either the amici or the parties involved citations to the works of William Shakespeare (Henry VIII and Richard II).

131 For another example of this phenomenon, see *Estes v. Texas* (1965), in which Justice Harlan filed a five-page appendix to his concurring opinion drawn directly from the amicus brief of the American Bar Association (381 U.S. 532, at 596–601).

132 To control for the nonindependence of observations, I utilize robust standard errors, clustered on case citation.

probit model, which estimates a single decision among two or more unordered alternatives (e.g., Greene 2000: 871).[133] And because the multinomial probit model estimates the likelihood that a justice will make a particular decision (dissent, regularly concur, or specially concur), relative to a base decision (join the majority), the model produces three estimates. That is, the model indicates the effects of the independent variables on the probability change from: (1) joining the majority to authoring or joining a dissenting opinion, (2) joining the majority to authoring or joining a regular concurring opinion, and (3) joining the majority to authoring or joining a special concurring opinion. As in the previous chapters, it is unnecessary to understand the technicalities of this model to comprehend its results because I interpret the effects of the independent variables on the decision to write or join a separate opinion through the use of predicted probabilities.

To determine whether a justice is more likely to author or join a separate opinion in cases attracting a relatively large number of amicus briefs, I include a *Total Amicus Briefs* variable representing the number of amicus briefs filed in the case. I expect that this variable will be positively signed, indicating that a justice is more likely to write or join a separate opinion in cases accompanied by a relatively large number of amicus filings.

A. Other Influences on Dissensus

To account for other influences on the decision to write or join a separate opinion, I include a number of control variables in the model. Unless otherwise noted, all of these variables were derived from the Spaeth (2002, 2003) databases. First, I expect that a justices' ideological proximity to the majority opinion author will influence the decision to write or join a separate opinion. As previously discussed, a long line of research on Supreme Court decision making reveals the importance of attitudes in shaping the choices justices make (e.g., Pritchett 1948; Shubert 1965; Segal and Spaeth 1993, 2002). Because the author of the majority opinion wields substantial control over the content of that opinion (e.g., Maltzman,

---

133 The multinomial probit model is preferable to the multinomial logit model because it relaxes the assumption of the independence of irrelevant alternatives (e.g., that the likelihood of authoring or joining a special concurring opinion is independent of authoring or joining a regular concurring opinion). Note that I obtain substantively identical results when the multinomial logit model is employed.

Spriggs, and Wahlbeck 2000: 35; Rohde and Spaeth 1976: 172), the extent to which a justice views the majority opinion as an appropriate representation of his or her preferences will depend substantially on the ideological proximity between the majority opinion author and that justice. If the justice is ideologically close to the majority opinion author, I expect the justice will be less likely to write or join a separate opinion because the majority opinion is likely to reflect that justice's policy preferences. If, however, a justice is ideologically distant from the majority opinion author, I propose that the justice will be more likely to write or join a separate opinion since the majority opinion is likely to be in discord with the justice's policy preferences. To capture this possibility, I use a measure based on the Martin and Quinn (2002) ideology scores. This variable, labeled *Ideological Distance*, is the absolute difference between each justice's ideology score and that of the majority opinion author.[134] Because higher values on this variable reflect increased ideological distance between a justice and the majority opinion author, I expect this variable will be positive in direction.

I also expect that a case's legal complexity will influence the decision to write or join a separate opinion. In legally complex cases, it is difficult for the majority opinion author to adequately address the multiple concerns of each individual justice, thus making separate opinions more likely because numerous opportunities exist to depart from the majority opinion author as to the correct application of the law (e.g., Hettinger, Lindquist, and Martinek 2006; Wahlbeck, Spriggs, and Maltzman 1999). To control for this possibility, I derive a measure of *Legal Complexity* based on the number of legal provisions relevant to the case and the number of issues raised in the case (Wahlbeck, Spriggs, and Maltzman 1999).[135] A factor analysis of these two variables produced a single factor with an eigenvalue greater than one.[136] I expect that this variable will be positively signed, indicating that a justice is more likely to write or join a separate opinion in a legally complex case.

---

134 For cases decided per curiam, the ideology score of the median justice in the majority is used as a surrogate for the majority opinion author's score.

135 Legal provisions involve the provision(s) of the constitution, statutes, and case law that the justices considered in the dispute. The number of issues raised in a case refers to the general issues involved in the case, such as school desegregation, residency requirements, and/or the rights of Native Americans (Spaeth 2007).

136 Factor analysis is a statistical technique that is used to condense the information contained in two or more interrelated variables into a smaller constructs (factors) without losing information from the original variables (e.g., Gorsuch 1983).

In addition to these factors, I hypothesize that a justice will be more likely to write or join a separate opinion in a case in which the majority overrules a precedent or declares a law unconstitutional. Because deference to precedent is a norm on the Court (e.g., Spriggs and Hansford 2001), when the majority chooses to overrule a previous decision, this provides an incentive for a justice to author or join a separate opinion to signal his or her displeasure with this norm violation. Correspondingly, because the Court rarely declares local, state, or federal laws unconstitutional (e.g., Keck 2004; Keith 2007), when the majority violates the Court's traditional support for the elected branches of government, this might entice a justice to write or join a separate opinion in order to signal his or her unhappiness with the majority's decision to declare a law unconstitutional. To evaluate this possibility, I include a measure of *Legal Salience* that is scored 1 if the majority formally altered precedent or declared a local, state, or federal unconstitutional and 0 otherwise. I expect that this variable will be positively signed, indicating that a justice is more likely to author or join a separate opinion in a legally salient case.

A number of studies have indicated that judges are more likely to write or join separate opinions in politically salient cases (e.g., Hettinger, Lindquist, and Martinek 2006; Maltzman, Spriggs, and Wahlbeck 2000; Wahlbeck, Spriggs, and Maltzman 1999). In relatively unimportant cases, a justice might join the majority for the purposes of appearing consensual. However, in salient cases a justice might write or join a separate opinion in an attempt to etch his or her preferences into law for future cases. For example, in a memo to Justice Black, Chief Justice Burger (1971) discussed the importance of a case's broad salience as influencing his decision to forgo writing separately: "I do not really agree but the case is narrow and unimportant except to this one man. . . . I will join up with you in spite of my reservations." Moreover, since the justices must expend a sizeable amount of time in writing separate opinions, they might be more willing to disburse this scare resource in salient cases (Hettinger, Lindquist, and Martinek 2006: 58). As argued above, studies that use amicus briefs as a measure of a case's political salience ignore the informational role of the briefs, thus providing a questionable measure of a case's significance. Accordingly, an alternative measure is used here. Consistent with the previous chapter, I operationalize a measure of *Political Salience* that is scored 1 if the case appeared on the front page of the *New York Times* on the day after the Court's decision and 0 if it did not. While I recognize that this is an imperfect measure of salience, it is nonetheless an appropriate proxy for a case's importance because it is contemporaneous and does not suffer from content, recency, or temporal biases. The expected sign of this variable is positive, indicating that a justice is more likely to write or join a separate opinion in a politically salient case.

I also expect that a justice's decision to write or join a separate opinion will be influenced by the extent to which he or she has cooperated with the majority opinion author in the past. This captures the fact that Supreme Court justices are, in effect, participants in a repeated game (e.g., Murphy 1964: 38; Wahlbeck, Spriggs, and Maltzman 1999: 496). When two justices cooperate with one another by joining each other's opinions, norms of consensus have the potential to develop that might limit a justice's incentive to write or join a separate opinion because doing so can jeopardize the collegial nature of their relationship. To test this hypothesis, I adopt the measure of cooperation developed by Wahlbeck, Spriggs, and Maltzman (1999: 500) by calculating the percentage of cases in which each justice joined a separate opinion written by the majority opinion author during the previous term. To purge this variable of the ideological compatibility between the justices, I regressed the percentage of the time that the justice joined the majority opinion author's separate opinions on the measure of *Ideological Distance* and use the residuals as a proxy for *Cooperation*.[137] Because higher values indicate greater past cooperation after controlling for ideological compatibility, the expected sign of this variable is negative, indicating that a justice is less likely to author or join a separate opinion if he or she has cooperated with the majority opinion author in the past.

Finally, two variables are included in the model to capture the justices' institutional roles on the Court. First, I control for the possibility that chief justices will be less likely to write or join separate opinions (e.g., Brenner and Hagle 1996; Hettinger, Lindquist, and Martinek 2006; Wahlbeck, Spriggs, and Maltzman 1999). While the justices are functionally co-equal, in that their votes carry equal weight, chief justices also perform numerous administrative functions. These include circulating the initial discuss list of certiorari petitions, assigning opinions when they are part of the majority, and acting as head of the Judicial Conference of the United States, the administrative arm of the federal court system.

---

137 The *Cooperation* variable is scored zero for justices who did not serve on the Court during the previous term.

In addition to these time-consuming tasks that might decrease a chief justice's willingness to author or join a separate opinion, it has also been noted that chief justices may refrain from separate opinions to demonstrate norms of consensus. For example, Justice Ginsburg (1990: 150) observed that upon his elevation to chief justice, Rehnquist substantially reduced the number of separate opinions he authored or joined to restore norms of collegiality to the Court. Similarly, Chief Justice Roberts remarked that one of the goals of his leadership on the Court would be to reduce the number of separate opinions, presumably leading by example (Greenhouse 2007). To determine whether chief justices are less likely to engage in separate opinions, I include a *Chief Justice* variable scored 1 for Chief Justices Vinson, Warren, Burger, and Rehnquist, and 0 for all other justices (and Rehnquist prior to the 1986 term). I expect this variable will be positively signed, indicating that chief justices are less likely to author or join separate opinions.

I also expect that justices who are new to the bench will be less likely to write or join separate opinions for three reasons. First, justices who are new to the bench have been shown to experience acclimation effects that implicate time management (e.g., Hettinger, Lindquist, and Martinek 2006). Because the justices must expend valuable time in engaging in separate opinions, this might dissuade them from partaking in this form of dissensus. Second, freshman justices may refrain from authoring or joining separate opinions because their policy preferences are not yet well developed and, as such, they might be unwilling to challenge their more senior colleagues on the basis of underdeveloped policy preferences (e.g., Brenner 1983). Third, justices who are new to the bench may refrain from engaging in dissensus because they might be unaware of the circumstances that warrant such behavior (e.g., Hettinger, Lindquist, and Martinek 2006: 53). To test this hypothesis, I include a *Freshman* variable in the model, scored 1 if a justice has served less than two full terms on the Court and 0 otherwise. I expect this variable will be negatively signed, indicating that freshman justices are less likely to author or join separate opinions.

V. Empirical Results

Table 6.1 reports the results of the multinomial probit model predicting whether a justice authored or joined a regular concurring, special concurring,

Table 6.1. Multinomial Probit Model of a Justice's Decision to Write or Join a Separate Opinion, 1946-2001 Terms

Predictor	Dissenting Opinion		Regular Concurring Opinion		Special Concurring Opinion	
Total Amicus Briefs	.010***	[+0.4%]	.030***	[+0.7%]	.025***	[+0.7%]
	(.003)		(.004)		(.004)	
Ideological Distance	.232***	[+8.0%]	.110*	[+0.03%]	.295***	[+4.4%]
	(.031)		(.048)		(.039)	
Legal Complexity	.041**	[+0.6%]	.051**	[+0.2%]	.033	[n.s.]
	(.014)		(.021)		(.020)	
Legal Salience	.103**	[+0.2%]	.304***	[+0.5%]	.380***	[+0.8%]
	(.041)		(.058)		(.054)	
Political Salience	.435***	[+7.7%]	.507***	[+2.6%]	.439***	[+2.6%]
	(.033)		(.051)		(.047)	
Cooperation	−.046	[n.s.]	−.021	[n.s.]	−.157***	[−1.9%]
	(.031)		(.047)		(.039)	
Chief Justice	−.382***	[−6.1%]	−.361***	[−1.2%]	−.425***	[−2.1%]
	(.029)		(.045)		(.042)	
Freshman	−.251***	[−4.4%]	−.110**	[−0.2%]	−.210***	[−1.1%]
	(.034)		(.048)		(.046)	
Constant	−1.55***		−2.39***		−2.57***	
	(.065)		(.100)		(.082)	
N	51,244					
Wald χ^2	1,936.8***					
Percent Correctly Predicted	69.0					
Percent Reduction in Error	36.5					

The baseline category is joining the majority opinion. Numbers in parentheses indicate robust standard errors, clustered on case citation. * $p < .05$; ** $p < .01$; *** $p < .001$ (one-tailed). Numbers in brackets are marginal effects. n.s. = not significant.

or dissenting opinion. The model correctly predicts 69% of outcomes, for a percent reduction in error of 37%.[138] Of the 51,244 observations in the

138 Percent reduction in error is based on the tau statistic, which compares the percentage of correctly predicted outcomes to the null model of random assignment based on the underlying distribution of the dependent variable. Tau is appropriate since it accounts for the distribution of nonmodal cases (e.g., Goodman and Kruskal 1954; Reynolds 1984).

data, 2,105 (4.1%) involve justices authoring or joining regular concurring opinions, 2,933 (5.7%) involve justices authoring or joining special concurring opinions, and 10,892 (21.3%) involve justices authoring or joining dissenting opinions. To facilitate interpretation, I report the marginal effects of each variable in brackets, which are calculated holding all other variables at their mean or modal values.

As this table makes clear, the model provides strong support for the hypothesized effect of amici curiae on the likelihood of observing separate opinions, even after controlling for more conventional influences on the decision to write or join a separate opinion. In substantive terms, compared with a case in which two amicus briefs are filed, in a case with six amicus briefs, the likelihood of observing a justice author or join a regular or special concurring opinion increases by about 1%, while the chances of observing a justice write or sign onto a dissenting opinion increase by 0.4%. This confirms my central argument that amicus briefs increase the justices' uncertainty as the correct application of the law, at the same time providing them with a well researched basis to cultivate a separate opinion. Though these changes in predicted probability may appear somewhat minor, it is important to note the relative infrequency with which the justices engage in this type of separate opinion writing. Although the justices author or join regular concurring, special concurring, and dissenting opinions in a nontrivial number of cases, this nonconsensual behavior constitutes only a small percentage of their activity on the Court. For example, justices author or join regular concurring opinions in only 4% of cases. Keeping that in mind, a 1% change in the likelihood of authoring or joining a regular concurring opinion should appropriately be viewed as a relatively strong predictor of that behavior. Further, when compared with the predicted probabilities of the other variables in the model, it is clear that amicus briefs rank among the strongest influences on the decision to write or join a separate opinion. For dissenting opinions, amicus briefs are the sixth strongest influence; for regular concurring opinions, amicus briefs are the third strongest influence; and for special concurring opinions, amicus briefs are the seventh strongest influence. Thus, both statistically and substantively, amicus curiae briefs are a significant influence on the decision to engage in dissensus on the Supreme Court.

Moreover, the influence of amicus briefs on the decision to author or join a separate opinion is especially enhanced in cases attracting a large number of briefs. For example, compared with a case with no amicus briefs, in a case with 30 amicus briefs, a justice is 7% more likely to author or join a regular or special concurring opinion and 2% more likely to pen or sign onto a dissenting opinion. Because the Court is seeing more and more cases in which a large number of amicus briefs are filed, this suggests that separate opinions are likely to become a standard feature of the contemporary Roberts Court.

In addition to confirming the influence of amicus briefs, the results also indicate that a host of other factors contribute to a justice's decision to write or join a separate opinion. First, the results demonstrate that a justice's ideological distance from the majority opinion author has a profound effect on the decision to author or join dissenting and special concurring opinions, although its influence on regular concurring opinions is almost nonexistent. In substantive terms, a one standard deviation change in this variable, moving a justice further from the majority opinion author, corresponds to an 8% increase in the chances of dissenting and a 4% increase in the odds of specially concurring but has virtually no effect on the likelihood of authoring or joining a regular concurring opinion (0.03% increase). Because special concurring opinions and dissenting opinions are more direct expressions of discord with the majority opinion (Collins 2004b), this finding with respect to regular concurring opinions is not entirely surprising. Since justices who author or join regular concurring opinions merely expand on the reasoning behind the majority opinion, as opposed to disagreeing with that reasoning, it is sensible that the influence of the ideological distance between a regularly concurring justice and the majority opinion author is weak relative to other forms of dissensus.

Second, the results indicate that case specific factors shape the decision to write or join a separate opinion. A case's political salience has the most pronounced influence on the decision to engage in dissensus among the case-level attributes. In contrast with a nonsalient case, in a politically salient case a justice is 8% more likely to author or join a dissenting opinion and about 3% more likely to pen or sign onto a regular or special concurring opinion. In addition, a case's legal salience also matters. Compared with a case in which the Court's majority did not declare a law unconstitutional or overturn a precedent, a justice is 0.2% more likely to dissent, 0.5% more likely to regularly concur, and 0.8% more likely to specially concur in a legally salient case. Note also that a case's legal complexity plays a role in the decision to engage in separate opinion writing. For example, as compared with a case with only a single issue or legal provision, in the most legally complex cases in the data, with numerous issues and legal provisions, a justice is 8% more likely to dissent and 3% more likely to regularly concur.

The results also provide support for a strategic perspective of judicial decision making. That is, cooperation, which accounts for the interpersonal dynamics between two justices, reduces the likelihood of observing a justice write or join a special concurring opinion, although it does not appear to contribute to the decision to author or sign onto a dissenting or regular concurring opinion. To more clearly convey this influence, consider Justices Scalia, Stevens, and Thomas during the 2000 term. After controlling for the ideological compatibility between these justices, when Thomas authored the majority opinion, Scalia, who joined Thomas on eight separate opinions during the previous term, was likely to specially concur in only 4% of cases. More pronounced is Stevens, who joined Thomas on no separate opinions during the previous term: Stevens was 8% more likely to specially concur if Thomas wrote the majority opinion.

Finally, the results indicate that the institutional roles the justices occupy influence their decision to pen or join a separate opinion. Chief justices are 6% less likely to dissent, 1% less likely to regularly concur, and 2% less likely to specially concur. This corroborates the conventional wisdom that, seeking to restore norms of unanimity to an increasingly divided Court, chief justices lead by example by occasionally forgoing the option to write or join a separate opinion. In addition, freshman justices are 4% less likely to dissent, 1% less likely to specially concur, but only marginally unlikely to regularly concur (0.2%). This suggests that like other jurists in the federal system (e.g., Hettinger, Lindquist, and Martinek 2006), freshman justices on the Supreme Court undergo acclimation effects that limit the frequency with which they engage in separate opinion writing.

VI. Summary and Conclusions

The post–World War II Supreme Court has been marked by a rise in non-unanimous decisions as evidenced by the increase in separate opinions. At the same time, the number of amicus briefs filed at the Supreme Court has increased dramatically. Far from mere coincidence, the findings in this chapter illustrate that the rise in dissensus on the Court can be partially attributed to the surge of amicus filings. By raising new issues and expanding on issues that the litigants were only able to make in abbreviated form, amicus briefs create uncertainty as to the correct application of the law in the cases in which they are filed. In this mode, amicus briefs are able to light the fires of dissensus, motivating justices to express their displeasure with the majority's interpretation of the law. Moreover, by providing the justices with a well-researched basis on which they can cultivate a separate opinion, amicus briefs reduce the resource-costs implicated by the decision to author or join a separate opinion. Of course, this is not to say that amicus briefs are the only explanation for the rise in separate opinions. Indeed, a host of factors contribute to the decision to write or sign onto a separate opinion, including the justices' ideologies, institutional roles, past level of cooperation with the majority opinion author, as well as attributes of the cases, such as their legal and political salience. But, that amicus briefs play such a significant role in the decision to write or join a separate opinion illustrates the theoretical leverage gained in considering the informational role played by friends of the Court.

CHAPTER 7

Conclusions and Implications

In the spring of 2003, the conservative Rehnquist Court handed down two very controversial—and liberal—decisions. In *Lawrence v. Texas* (2003), a 6-3 majority of the Court struck down a Texas law that made it a crime for hom osexuals to participate in deviate sexual intercourse on the grounds that the law was inconsistent with the Fourteenth Amendment's Due Process Clause. In *Grutter v. Bollinger* (2003), a 5-4 majority of the Court upheld the University of Michigan Law School's use of racial preferences in its application process, despite the Fourteenth Amendment concerns implicated by the case.[139] That summer, an editorial cartoon by Pulitzer Prize winner Mike Luckovich was syndicated throughout the country's newspapers and on the Internet. The cartoon featured a reporter posing the justices a simple question: "After upholding affirmative action and striking down a ban on gay sex, where are you going now?? . . . " The justices, crammed into a 1960s-era Volkswagen microbus, simply answered: "To a 'Grateful Dead' concert dude!"[140]

---

139 However, the Court struck down the University of Michigan's undergraduate affirmative action policy in *Gratz v. Bollinger* (2003) for not providing the individualized review of each applicant that Justice Powell contemplated in *Regents of the University of California v. Bakke* (1978).

140 The Grateful Dead were a blues/country/folk/rock band from the San Francisco Bay Area commonly associated with liberal causes, such as environmentalism, social justice, and arts and cultural preservation.

Those decisions, and Luckovich's cartoon, highlight an important point: on occasion, even the conservative Rehnquist Court rendered liberal decisions on significant issues of public policy. Yet, from the standpoint of the attitudinal model, such occurrences are anomalies—the exceptions to the rule. The fact that the Rehnquist Court handed down those decisions suggests that the Court is more than a nine-member legislature. Indeed, it implies that factors other than attitudes shape the justices' decision making. One such factor is legal persuasion. Throughout this book, rigorous and systematic empirical support was provided for the contention that legal persuasion, submitted to the justices via amicus curiae briefs, offers additional insight into the choices justices make. Although the justices are free to ignore amicus briefs, they do not do so. Instead, the justices consider the arguments contained in these briefs and allow these briefs to shape their decision making. From the attitudinal perspective, the *Lawrence* and *Grutter* decisions are aberrations. From the legal persuasion perspective, these decisions are easily explained: rather than based solely on the justices' attitudinal predispositions, the justices likely considered legal arguments forwarded by the amici.

In *Lawrence*, the Court received 31 amicus briefs (15 liberal, 16 conservative) from an extremely diverse cross section of organizations. Amici included religious organizations (e.g., Agudath Israel of America), public interest law firms (e.g., Institute for Justice), medical societies (e.g., the American Public Health Association), public policy organizations (e.g., Center for Arizona Policy), academics, members of Congress, and U.S. states. In *Grutter*, 102 amicus briefs were submitted (83 liberal, 16 conservative) from a similarly diverse set of amici, including a television network (MTV), corporations (e.g., Exxon-Mobil), professional associations (e.g., the Society of American Law Teachers), labor unions (e.g., AFL-CIO), colleges and universities (e.g., Georgetown), academics, members of Congress, and U.S. states. Although I cannot definitively state what influence these amici had in those cases (nor is it my purpose to do so), the empirical evidence presented throughout this research, coupled with the justices' extensive citations to the amicus briefs,[141] suggests that the conservative Court's liberal decisions in *Lawrence* and *Grutter* were likely shaped, at least in part, by these amici. Returning to Schattschneider's analogy that opened this book, it appears that on occasion, interests

---

141 In *Lawrence*, the justices made reference to five separate amicus briefs in their opinions; in *Grutter*, they made 12 references.

groups are capable of doing "the kinds of things that determine the outcome of the fight" (1960: 2).

The purpose of this concluding chapter is to review the key findings of this research, paying particular attention to their normative and empirical implications. I begin with a summary of the results regarding interest group activity in the Court, followed by an exposition of interest group influence on the justices' decision making. I close with a discussion of the limitations of this analysis and offer suggestions for future research.

I. Amicus Participation: The Empirical Findings and Their Normative Implications

In *Federalist 10* and *51*, James Madison conceded that a nation committed to what would become the core freedoms of the First Amendment—assembly, petition, and speech—would inevitably have to confront the "mischiefs of faction." To Madison, interest groups would not act as occasional forces pressing on government sporadically, but instead would be perennial participants in the battle for public policy. Madison warned of the tyranny of the majority—the possibility that a single faction would rise to power and threaten the interests of smaller segments of society. For Madison, the mischiefs of faction could be controlled by setting the self interest of one faction against the egocentric tendencies of rival factions. Through this, Madison proposed that the tyranny of the majority could be kept in check, resulting in temperate public policy.

To control the selfish tendencies of organized interests, a diverse spectrum of groups must actively press to see their legal and policy preferences etched into law. This, of course, requires access to governmental actors. Without reasonably open admittance into policy making venues for all, particular types of organizations might be enabled to exert undue influence on policy makers, resulting in the tyranny of a privileged majority that enjoys unfettered ingress to government. This question of representation has long held a central position in the scholarly understanding of interest groups (e.g., Dahl 1961; Schattschneider 1960; Truman 1951). Chapters 2 and 3 added to this debate by investigating interest group access to, and participation in, the Supreme Court. The purpose of these chapters was to determine if, in the words of Schattschneider (1960: 34–35), "the heavenly chorus sings with a strong upper-class accent," as opposed to the pluralist ideal of a diverse array of interest groups finding a voice in the Court.

As it relates to access, the rules governing amicus curiae participation allow for essentially unhampered admittance into the Court, provided the potential amicus satisfies the Court's formal requirements for filing an amicus brief.[142] Thus, in terms of its institutional rules and norms, the Court is somewhat uniquely situated vis-à-vis the other branches of government. For example, the Court differs quite substantially from Congress, where geographical connections and campaign donations are the primary factors shaping interest group access to members (e.g., Wright 1989).[143] Similarly, the Court is distinct from the White House, where a group's ideological compatibility with the president governs access (e.g., Peterson 1992). While the Court's rules and norms with respect to amicus participation provide for the possibility that a wide array of organizations may file amicus briefs, this does not necessarily imply that groups are willing to take advantage of this state of affairs. Accordingly, it was necessary to evaluate the types of organizations that participate in the Court to determine if amicus activity is best explained through a pluralist or elitist lens.

To provide this information, Chapter 3 presented a typology of interest group participants during the Vinson, Warren, Burger, and Rehnquist Courts. The results indicated that an array of groups participate in the Court, evincing that interest group activity in the Court most closely comports with a pluralist view of representation. Elitist organizations, such as businesses and institutions, do not dominate amicus activity. Rather, a variety of interests use the Court in an attempt to imprint their legal and policy preferences into law. Moreover, both liberal and conservative organizations find a voice in the Court, filing amicus briefs in almost equal numbers. This again differs quite substantially from the legislative and executive branches, where the supremacy of businesses and institutions

---

142 Recall these rules require that the brief is filed by a member of the Supreme Court bar and the consent of both parties to litigation is obtained. If one or both of the parties decline consent to file, the potential amici can petition the Court for leave to file and the Court almost always grants such requests (e.g., Bradley and Gardner 1985; O'Connor and Epstein 1983a).

143 In addition, interest group participation in the Court is distinct from group participation in congressional committee hearings, which require that groups are either invited by the committee staff to give oral testimony or obtain the permission of the chair of the relevant committee prior to testifying (e.g., Wright 2003: 41). It is important to note that not all committee chairs are forthcoming with regard to extending invitations to testify. For example, the chairs of the Senate Judiciary Committee have varied dramatically with respect to authorizing interest groups to testify at judicial confirmation hearings and, currently, permission for interest groups to testify at lower court confirmation hearings is no longer granted (e.g., Bell 2002; Scherer 2005).

is well established (e.g., Golden 1988; Salisbury 1984; Schlozman and Tierney 1983, 1986; Yackee and Yackee 2006).

These findings clearly indicate that institutional rules and norms are of paramount importance in shaping organizational activity in government. Thus, the results corroborate the utility of institutional perspectives of the political and legal system, which focus on how attributes of institutions affect political behavior (e.g., March and Olsen 1984). In venues in which group access is relatively open, with few rules and norms preventing entrance to government, the diversity of interest group representation can flourish. Conversely, in institutions in which rules and norms create hurdles to participation, whether geographical, monetary, or ideological, the interest group choir will be biased toward those entities that are capable of overcoming these barriers to participation. From a normative standpoint, if the Madisonian ideal of counterbalancing the self interest of one faction against that of another is desirable, this suggests that institutional reformers should be especially attentive to rules and norms governing access to decision makers: fewer barriers to access appear to beget diverse representation.

While I have provided evidence of a pluralist society in terms of interest group representation in the Court, it is important to note that my analysis is limited by the fact that I cannot speak to the representation of the unorganized. Clearly, there are a number of latent interests in American society that have not yet mobilized themselves into active organizations as a result of collective action problems (Olson 1965). Most commonly, scholars have sought to explain barriers to the mobilization of the disadvantaged, particularly the poor (e.g., Hays 2001; Piven and Cloward 1977; Strolovitch 2006). Although to analyze the representation of the disadvantaged in the Court is beyond the scope of this book, a few comments are appropriate here. In the legal system, scholars have long noted that the criminally accused are particularly disadvantaged because, by definition, their adversary is an arm of the government, privy to extensive litigation resources (e.g., Galanter 1974; Lawrence 1989; Sheehan, Mishler, and Songer 1992). Since criminals have no formal organization to represent their interests (e.g., there is no National Association of Convicted Felons), a challenge to the pluralist perspective of interest group representation in the Court forwarded here can be mounted. However, it is important to note that although criminals have no lobby, their interests are represented by proxy organizations, such as the American Civil Liberties Union, the National Legal Aid and Defender Association, the National Association of

Criminal Defense Lawyers, and the like. In fact, during the 1946–2001 terms, an average of 12 amicus briefs were filed each term on behalf of the interests of the criminally accused, compared with 13 on behalf of prosecuting governments. While blunt, these numbers are telling in that the number of allies and enemies of an interest has the potential to play a clear role in the fate of litigation (Lowery and Gray 2004: 22). Thus, it is apparent that while disadvantaged members of society may be unable to overcome the collective action problems required for formal organization, the disadvantaged choir nonetheless finds a voice in the Court through various proxy organizations. This further corroborates the pluralist nature of interest group representation in the Supreme Court.

The results regarding interest group representation in the Court also speak to normative concerns about legal instrumentalism—using the language of the law to achieve economic, political, and social ends (e.g., Dewey 1916; Jhering 1913). Though instrumentalism undoubtedly has become a defining feature of American jurisprudence, critics of this state of affairs fear that using the law to achieve some ends threatens respect for the rule of law by hampering the perceived neutrality of judicial decision making. As Tamanaha (2006: 169) argues, interest group instrumentalism is problematic because it turns the legal system into yet another battleground for public policy. Because interest group advocacy efforts are marked by relaying their subjective versions of the public interest to judges, this can harm the neutrality of judicial decision making because groups have substantial incentives to present only those arguments that promote their agendas. In turn, this might cause judges to elevate the interests of particular organizations by rendering decisions in accord with what they (perhaps erroneously) understand to be the public interest.

A necessary condition for overcoming this troubling perspective of interest group instrumentalism is to enable judges to hear from a diverse spectrum of organizations who present conflicting views of the public interest. Through this, judges are better equipped to render decisions, not solely on the basis of a single perspective of the public interest but instead in accord with the ideal of the deliberative judge who takes many factors into consideration before rendering a decision, including varied perspectives of the public interest. This condition appears to have manifested itself in the Supreme Court through its open door policy regarding amicus briefs. Rather than hearing from only a small and homogenous set of interests, a diverse set of organizations regularly present the justices with a host of perspectives as to their subjective versions of the public interest through the legal language they marshal in amicus briefs. In this sense, critics who focus on the negative consequences of interest group litigation might find some peace of mind in the fact that by exploiting the adversarial system, interest groups enable the justices to take into consideration a host of interests and concerns in rendering their decisions. Indeed, Justice Ginsburg, who spent almost a decade of her pre-Court career as counsel for the liberal ACLU, adheres to this view of the benefits of interest group litigation in describing the role of conservative groups in the courts:

> Our system of justice works best when opposing positions are well represented and fully aired. I therefore greet the expansion of responsible public-interest lawyering on the "conservative" side as something good for the system, not a development to be deplored. (2001: 8)

As Tamanaha (2006: 169) notes, Ginsburg highlights two positive aspects of interest group litigation in this sentiment. First, she emphasizes that the quality of judicial decision making is enhanced when competing sides voice their opposing perspectives as to the legal merits of the case. This is consistent with the ideal of the deliberative judge who seeks to reach correct legal answers by thoroughly sifting through diverse perspectives on the law. Second, she elucidates how interest group activity can assist judicial decisions, "either through finding a compromise among competing ideas or by one or more ideas proving more persuasive than the others" (Tamanaha 2006: 169). This is in line with the pluralist view of interest groups, which asserts that through competition among groups, temperate public policies can be reached that most closely approximate the public interest (e.g., Truman 1951). This suggests that, notwithstanding other negative consequences of legal instrumentalism, some solace is offered by the fact that the Court's institutional rules promote the representation of a diverse set of interests, potentially improving the quality of judicial decision making.

II. Amicus Influence: The Empirical Findings and Their Normative Implications

For more than a century, a substantial debate has manifested itself with regard to the relationship between the role of law and the behavior of judicial decision makers. With regard to the U.S. Supreme Court, advocates of the attitudinal model argue that the justices are almost entirely motivated by their policy preferences and therefore the law is of little import in structuring judicial choice. Conversely, proponents of the legal model posit that while judicial ideology may play a role in shaping the choices justices make, legal considerations also influence judicial behavior. Near the heart of this debate is whether the very nature of the adversarial system of American jurisprudence—in which compelling argumentation is presented to jurists on both sides of a case—frees the justices to view information in a biased manner, reaching decisions not on the legal merits of a case, but instead in accord with what they are predisposed to believe (e.g., Baum 1997: 64–65; Segal and Spaeth 2002: 433; Wrightsman 2006: 119–120).

Just as there is an ongoing debate with respect to the role of law vis-à-vis attitudes, a similar controversy exists involving the influence of interest groups in the judicial arena. In particular, the point of contention centers on whether amicus curiae briefs filed by organized interests influence the choices U.S. Supreme Court justices make. On the one hand, numerous Supreme Court justices have publicly attested to the significance of amicus briefs in their decision making, as indicated by the quotations from Justices Breyer, Douglas, and O'Connor appearing in the introduction to this volume. On the other hand, despite the fact that more than 50 articles and books have examined this topic, scholars have reached the general consensus that interest group amicus briefs have little measurable influence on the justices' decision making. As Segal, Spaeth, and Benesh (2005: 329) recently explained "we have virtually no evidence to date that interest groups have an independent impact on the merits of Supreme Court decisions."

Chapter 4 married these two enduring debates by investigating whether amicus briefs influence the justices' decision making and, if so, whether the justices' responses to amicus briefs are most consistent with attitudinal or legal accounts of judicial decision making. I considered amicus briefs as sources of legal and political information and examined whether their influence is mediated by judicial ideology (i.e., dependent upon the congruence of the information in the briefs with the policy preferences of the justices), building on the cognitive response model developed in social psychology (e.g., Greenwald 1968; Kunda 1990; Petty, Ostrom, and Brock 1981). When subjected to rigorous empirical testing, the results demonstrated that not only do amicus briefs influence the justices' decision making, but also that for the overwhelming majority of the Court (95% of observations), ideology does not act as a mediating variable conditioning how the justices process the information contained in amicus filings. Thus, the results show that decision making on the Supreme Court is more than a function of the justices' attitudes and values.

In Chapter 5, I examined the influence of amicus briefs on the consistency of judicial decision making. Expanding on the notion that amicus briefs serve to attenuate the justices' reliance on their attitudes, I proposed that amicus briefs increase the ambiguity in the justices' already uncertain decision making, leading to more variable behavior. I argued that by raising new issues in the Court and persuading the justices to adopt positions that are attitudinally incongruent, amicus briefs confound the certainty surrounding the justices' perspectives as to the correct application of the law in a case. The findings indicated that amicus briefs are the single strongest predictor of increased variance in judicial decision making, thus providing substantial evidence that not all legal influences provide stability in the law.

Chapter 6 built on these previous chapters by investigating whether amicus curiae briefs contribute to a justice's decision to write or join a regular concurring, special concurring, or dissenting opinion. By providing the justices with diverse information regarding the potential legal and policy ramifications of a decision, amicus briefs create incertitude in the justices' already uncertain decision making while providing the justices with a well-researched basis for separate opinions. The results indicated that amicus briefs do indeed contribute to the decision to author or join a separate opinion, further supporting the informational role of amicus curiae in shaping the choices justices make.

In providing a systematic investigation into the influence of amicus curiae participation in the Supreme Court, I hope to contribute to the scholarly understanding of judicial decision making. Recall three postulates governing judicial choice that I have developed throughout this book. First, it is clear that judges make policy (e.g., Baum 1997; Dahl 1957; Holmes 1897; Miles and Sunstein 2006; Segal and Spaeth 1993, 2002). In the words of Chief Justice Marshall in *Marbury v. Madison* (1803), "It is emphatically the province and duty of the judicial department to say what the law is" (5 U.S. 137, at 177). While critics of judicial decision making might take issue with this role, this in no way changes the fact that in every case it disposes, the Court makes policy. This policy-making function ranges from the relatively mundane, such as redrawing the boundary between Georgia and South Carolina at the mouth of the Savannah River as a result of man-made avulsion (*Georgia v. South Carolina* 1990), to the highly significant, including desegregating the public schools (*Brown v. Board of Education* 1954) and effectively deciding the outcome of the 2000 presidential election (*Bush v. Gore* 2000).

The second postulate on which the proposed account of judicial decision making is based involves the indeterminacy of the law. Despite the fact that judicial opinions are written in a manner suggesting the law inescapably guides the judge toward a determinative outcome (Simon 1998), the law is incapable of providing objectively correct answers to questions facing courts (e.g., Cardozo 1921; Cohen 1935; Kelman 1987; Llewellyn 1931; Pound 1908; cf. Markovits 1998). Justice Cardozo explained the indeterminacy of the law as follows:

> I was much troubled in spirit, in my first years on the bench, to find how trackless was the ocean on which I had embarked. I sought for certainty. I was oppressed and disheartened when I found that the quest for it was futile. As the years have gone by, and as I have reflected more and more upon the nature of the judicial process, I have become reconciled to the uncertainty, because I have grown to see it as inevitable. (1921: 29)

Of course, this does not preclude the fact that some answers are more correct than others (Dworkin 1991). Indeed, I have advocated this premise throughout this research. Rather, the important point is that the indeterminacy of the law provides judges with the opportunity to use the language of the law to achieve various ends (Tamanaha 2006).

Finally, the perspective on judicial decision making forwarded here rests on the idea that judges pursue two primary operative goals that affect their decision making (e.g., Baum 1994, 1997; Klein 2002; Posner 1995; Pritchett 1969).[144] First, judges pursue policy goals. A core basis of the attitudinal model, the pursuit of policy goals means that judges attempt to shape the law in a manner consistent with their policy preferences.

---

144 Following Baum (1994), by operative goals, I am referring to goals that potentially influence judicial behavior. This differs from inherent goals, involving the ends that judges, as humans, strive to achieve. These latter goals include maximizing leisure time, maintaining their seats on the bench, and gaining respect among the legal community and citizenry more generally. In addition, because I am interested in developing a general theory of judging, I do not discuss idiosyncratic factors that might influence judicial behavior, such as what a judge ate for breakfast (e.g., Kozinski 2004).

While this is the predominant view espoused by political scientists (e.g., Rohde and Spaeth 1976; Segal and Spaeth 1993, 2002), I also propose that judges pursue legal goals (e.g., Dworkin 1978; Epstein and Kobylka 1992; Gillman 2001; Richards and Kritzer 2002). That is, in addition to seeking to etch their policy preferences into law, judges are concerned with making good law: attempting to determine the *most* legally appropriate answer to the controversy. Judges' motivations for pursing legal goals stem from the reality that judges are trained and cultured to be ultimately legal decision makers. As such, professional norms dictate that a judge's primary responsibility is to make good faith efforts to seek out reasonably accurate legal answers.

With this in mind, the results of this research suggest that judicial decision making follows a bottom-up, as opposed to a top-down, process (e.g., Kahneman, Slovic, and Tversky 1982; Kunda 1999; Park and Smith 1989; Wolfe, Butcher, Lee, and Hyle 2003). A top-down process involves goal-oriented decision making in which a justice approaches a decision with the goal of reaching a conclusion that is in line with the justice's policy preferences. In so doing, the justice seeks out directional goals and downplays or disregards argumentation that challenges the justice's pre-existing biases (Kunda 1999: 236). Conversely, in bottom-up processing, a justice carefully reviews all of the available evidence and argumentation for the purpose of reaching a sound legal decision. In this mode, a justice is motivated by an accuracy goal (Kruglanski 1980). Rather than deciding the case solely on the basis of the justice's preconceived attitudinal pro-clivities, the justice sometimes labors to suppress the influence of these preferences in an attempt to reach the most legally correct answer. The evidence presented in this book provides support for the bottom-up ver-sion of legal decision making. While justices are perfectly free to ignore the influence of attitudinally incongruent information presented to them in amicus briefs (top-down cognition), they resist this temptation. Instead, they respond to the persuasive communications presented to them in incongruent amicus briefs in an effort to reach accurate legal answers (bottom-up cognition).

This, of course, is not to say that the justices' policy preferences do not shape their decision making. I have no doubt that attitudes are likely the primary influence on judicial decision making, and the results of this research support this position. Nor is it my purpose to rule out the possibility that the justices engage in motivated reasoning. The evidence presented here can only speak to the justices' responses to persuasion attempts in amicus briefs. Nonetheless, there is good reason to believe that the bottom-up approach to judicial choice is generalizable beyond an investigation into amicus influence (e.g., Braman 2006; Braman and Nelson 2007). Because the justices are educated and socialized into a culture that advocates the pursuit of accuracy goals in terms of interpreting the law, this suggests that their training leads them to view bottom-up decision making as a normative good. Perhaps more important, research in management science and social psychology indicates that individuals who are required to justify their decisions to some audience are especially likely to be motivated by accuracy goals (e.g., Frink and Ferris 1999; Mero 2007; Tetlock and Kim 1987). By holding decision makers accountable, individuals are prompted to engage in more reasoned and complex deliberation, leading to more objective decisions. This research is obviously applicable to the Supreme Court in that the justices are required to justify their decisions through opinion writing. Justice Ginsburg corroborates the galvanizing force of opinions in noting that "Public accountability through the disclosure of votes and opinion authors puts the judge's conscience and reputation on the line" (1990: 140). In this sense, far from merely acting as *post hoc* justifications for decisions made on the sole basis of policy preferences (Segal and Spaeth 1993, 2002), the bottom-up approach to judicial decision suggests that opinions might well reveal factors that motivate judicial choice.

Two significant normative concerns arise from the bottom-up view of judicial decision making. One the one hand, the bottom-up approach to legal choice is normatively desirable because it meshes closely with the ideal of judges as neutral decision makers who engage in reasoned deliberation. In this mode, judges approach cases with the intent of arriving at an interpretation of the law that is best supported by the tools of legal reasoning. To do this, judges examine the relevant evidence and argumentation, evaluate the utility of this information, and weigh the evidence to determine which perspective is most consistent with the correct application of the law. In this sense, judges fit closely with Baumeister and Newman's conception of the intuitive scientist who is motivated by an accuracy goal and "ultimately wants to choose the alternative that has the most and strongest support" (1994: 14).

On the other hand, when judges engage in this type of reasoned deliberation, the available evidence can act to overwhelm their cognitive processes by creating uncertainty with respect to the correct application of the law, leading to information overload. When this type of overload occurs, judges behave inconsistently and are more likely to write or join separate opinions that can undermine the stability of the law. In this way, one must recognize the inherent tension that exists between the legalist judge vis-à-vis the overtly political judge. For the legalist judge, aspiring to reach the most correct legal answer is the guiding principle in deliberation. But, because the law is incapable of definitively providing that answer, the judge must pick between his or her conception of the best solution, which is not always evident. When the legalist judge receives myriad interpretations of the correct application of the law, uncertainty is enhanced, leading to inconsistent decision making, which is normatively undesirable. For the attitudinal judge, the guiding motivation in deliberation is the pursuit of his or her policy preferences. Because this judge can discount or altogether ignore information that obstructs this pursuit, he or she is unlikely to fall prey to information overload. Rather, the political judge will behave in a very predictable, and very consistent, fashion by voting in accord with his or her attitudes. Thus, the conundrum. If we value consistency, this can be achieved through the appointment of ideologically extreme judges who will regularly vote to etch their preferences into law and seldom deviate from this behavior. If we value reasoned and neutral deliberation, provided by legalist judges, we must recognize that their behavior will be marked by instability due to the inherent indeterminacy of the law. This is clearly a most unsettling tradeoff.

III. Future Research

While this book has aspired to provide one of the most theoretically rich and empirically rigorous treatments of amicus influence in the Supreme Court to date, it is important to recognize that it is nonetheless limited in a number of regards. In reviewing these limitations, I hope to motivate future researchers to pick up where I have left off. Most obviously, this analysis is limited in that it cannot definitely tell us the *exact* mechanism under which amicus briefs influence the justices' decision making. That is, although this research provides clear evidence that amicus briefs are influential and that an attitudinal explanation for the influence of amici generally fails to find empirical support, I cannot rule out alternative explanations that are consistent with the legal persuasion model. While I have endeavored to provide a convincing theory for the influence of amicus briefs based on legal persuasion, it is vital to recognize that to interpret the results through the lens of other theoretical perspectives is possible. Two candidates, related to strategic characterizations of the Court, stand out as potentially offering alternative explanations for the influence of amicus briefs that are generally consonant with the empirical results supporting the legal persuasion model.

First, one might interpret these results as evincing the influence of public opinion on Supreme Court decision making. Under a public-opinion based model of judicial decision making, the justices are said to render decisions that are in line with public sentiment to ensure the institutional legitimacy of the Court (e.g., Flemming and Wood 1997; Mishler and Sheehan 1993) and to avoid drawing the ire of the elected branches of government, which might respond to public pressure by overriding the Court's decisions or allowing decisions to go unenforced (e.g., McGuire and Stimson 2004; Stimson, MacKuen, and Erickson 1995). By disposing of cases in a manner that is consistent with public opinion, the justices are able to maintain the public's favorable view of the Court, while decreasing the incentives for Congress and the president, who are electorally accountable, to interfere with the Court's dispositions of particular disputes. Applying this reasoning to the current analysis, if amicus briefs provide a proxy for public opinion on an issue, we would expect the justices to render decisions in line with the position supported by the largest number of amicus briefs, which is akin to the empirical predictions derived from the legal persuasion framework.

Though this is a plausible interpretation of the results presented in this book, it is improbable for three reasons. First, from a theoretical standpoint, it is not entirely clear why the justices should care about public opinion, even when considering the justices' desire to maintain the Court's legitimacy. Unlike the elected branches of government, which are reliant on a favorable climate of public opinion to ensure reelection, justices on the Supreme Court enjoy life tenure. This, in effect, insulates them from the pressures of the public (e.g., Segal and Spaeth 2002). Moreover, empirical evidence indicates that the Court is able to maintain a reservoir of goodwill among the American citizenry, even in the face of highly controversial decisions, such as *Bush v. Gore* (Caldeira and Gibson 1992; Gibson 2007). Because the public views the Court in such a positive light, irrespective of it rendering decidedly contentious decisions, it is unclear why the justices would feel it necessary to dispose of cases in accord with public opinion.

Second, of the empirical research that demonstrates an influence of public opinion on Supreme Court decision making, no studies have been able to provide evidence for the effect of public opinion on a case-by-case basis. Rather, these studies indicate that public opinion shapes judicial decision making based on lags ranging from one (e.g., Flemming and Wood 1997; McGuire and Stimson 2004) to five years (e.g., Mishler and Sheehan 1993). Given that extant studies have failed to link public opinion to the Court's individual decisions and given that this research explicitly ties amicus briefs to the justices' decision making on a case-by-case basis, to rectify these findings to conclude that amicus influence is best explained through the lens of public opinion is difficult.

Finally, and perhaps most important, in earlier research I tested an explanation for the influence of amicus briefs based on a public opinion perspective and uncovered no evidence for this account of amicus influence (Collins 2004a). To do this, I examined whether the justices respond to the number of amicus briefs supporting a particular litigant or if the justices respond to the number of cosigners on the amicus briefs. Because amicus briefs are typically filed by a host of organizations, this provides a fairly straightforward test for a public opinion-based explanation for amicus influence. That is, if the influence of amicus briefs is best explained through a public opinion perspective, we would expect the justices to render decisions consistent with the position supported by the largest number of cosigners on the amicus briefs since this indicates strong public support for a particular position. If, however, the justices value the information content of the briefs, we would expect the justices to render decisions consistent with the position supported by the largest number of amicus briefs, irrespective of the number of cosigners on the briefs. Consider, for example, a hypothetical case in which there are 10 amicus briefs filed for the petitioner, each filed by a district organization (10 briefs, 10 amici). On the respondent side, there are 2 amicus briefs, each cosigned by 20 organizations (2 briefs, 40 amici). Holding all else equal, if the justices value the informational content of the amicus briefs as they relate to providing the justices with persuasive argumentation supporting a particular perspective, the petitioner should emerge victorious since the briefs overwhelmingly support that litigant's position (10 briefs compared with 2 briefs). If, however, the justices use amicus briefs as a barometer of public opinion, the respondent should emerge victorious since number of cosigners overwhelmingly support that litigant's position (40 amici compared with 10 amici). Upon subjecting this rather direct test for the influence of amicus briefs to empirical scrutiny, the results were unambiguous: the justices do not respond to the number of cosigners on amicus briefs but do respond to the number of amicus briefs. Thus, the public opinion-based explanation for amici influence failed to garner empirical support.

The second plausible alternative interpretation of the results presented in this book is based on the separation of powers model (e.g., Epstein and Knight 1999). Under this view of judicial behavior, the justices are argued to consider the likely actions of the president and Congress and endeavor to avoid disposing of cases in a manner that is out-of-step with the preferences of those actors. They do this in an effort to limit or altogether remove the incentive for the elected branches to override their decisions or to indifferently enforce those decisions. If the justices are motivated by the desire to avoid having their decisions interfered with by the elected branches of government, this requires that the justices obtain information regarding the preferences of Congress and the president. Epstein and Knight (1999) argue that the justices can obtain this information from amicus curiae briefs.

Compared with public opinion accounts of judicial decision making, it is somewhat less clear whether the results in this book can be interpreted to support the separation of powers model. First, although it is evident that amicus briefs do provide the justices with information regarding the preferences of other actors in government, this information is far less frequently presented by amici as compared to legal and policy argumentation. For example, recall that Table 3.5 reveals that of the 121 separate arguments presented by the amici in the cases under analysis, only 7% of arguments focused on the preferences of other actors in government, while 73% of arguments were legal in nature and 19% of arguments focused on the policy ramifications of the decision. Moreover, when the amici present separation of powers argumentation, they tend to do so in rather vague ways, focusing on, for example, the proper role of the Court in a separation of powers system, rather than necessarily delineating the preferences of the current Congress.[145]

---

145 Epstein and Knight (1999) reached a similar conclusion in their analysis of 58 amicus briefs filed during the 1983 term. They found that amici mentioned the preferences of the current Congress in only 22% of briefs (although they did not indicate the extent to which amici focused their attention on the preferences of Congress vis-à-vis other forms of argumentation). They did, however, find that amici mentioned the preferences of the current president or the Solicitor General in 50% of briefs. The large

Second, it is rather difficult to theoretically link the empirical findings presented in this book regarding the influence of amicus briefs to the separation of powers model. That is, the separation of powers model is incapable of explaining why the justices respond to the number of amicus briefs supporting the liberal and conservative positions. While there are alternative methods to evaluate a separation of powers explanation for amicus influence, such as determining whether the justices are particularly responsive to briefs that convey the preferences of current actors in the executive and legislative branches, evidence supporting such an account would not necessarily be in conflict with the results presented here. This is the case because it is not evident how responding to persuasion provides evidence of considering the preferences of other governmental institutions. As Whittington (2000: 625) succinctly concludes in his analysis of the separation of powers explanation for amicus briefs: "A much more straightforward reading of the briefs is that they employ material that is relevant for judges seeking to interpret the law," a position fully in line with the legal persuasion model.

Third, the application of the separation of powers model to amici is further confounded by the fact that members of Congress will occasionally file amicus briefs on opposing sides of the dispute, communicating to the justices opposing perspectives on legislative intent (McLauchlan 2005: 96). This is a particularly troubling fact for the separation of powers model in that it indicates that even members of Congress do not necessarily agree as to their own preferences in enacting legislation. Simply put, if members of Congress cannot reach some harmony as to legislative preferences, why would we expect the justices to view congressional preferences as a serious constraint on their decision making?

Fourth, past research with regard to the influence of amicus briefs filed by members of Congress casts serious doubt on a separation of powers account of amicus influence. For example, Heberlig and Spill (2000) found that the Court endorsed the position advocated in amicus

---

percentage of amicus briefs focused on the preferences of the executive is likely a function of the fact that the Solicitor General participates in approximately 60% of the Court's cases, either as counsel for the executive branch or as an amicus (Nicholson and Collins 2008), while members of Congress participate as amici far less frequently (Heberlig and Spill 2000). Because it is a relatively common occurrence for amici to directly refute the amicus briefs filed by their opponents and because the SG is the most frequent target of this form of direct discord (Collins and Solowiej 2007), it should not be entirely surprising that the preferences of the executive are frequently relayed to the justices via amicus briefs.

briefs filed by members of Congress only 48% of the time and reveled that congresspersons fair even worse in statutory cases—those very cases in which Congress can most easily override the Court's decisions (see also McLauchlan 2005). In evaluating this evidence, Heberlig and Spill (2000: 205) conclude that "the filing of amicus briefs by members of Congress is not a sufficiently credible threat to deter the Court based upon the justices' preferences."

Finally, it is imperative to note that there is at least one aspect of the evidence presented in this book that can be interpreted in a manner that is fully consistent with the separation of powers model. That is, the robust results supporting the Solicitor General's strong influence on the Court provides substantiation for the view that the justices might defer to the preferences of the executive branch. While the findings with respect to the SG's influence is in accord with the separation of powers model, it should be recognized there is some ambiguity in the extant literature whether this is entirely supportive of a separation of powers model or is more generally reflective of the SG's almost unparalleled advocacy experience as compared to other members of the Supreme Court bar. That is, some attribute the SG's influence on the Court to institutional deference (e.g., Epstein and Knight 1999; Yates 2002), while others argue that the quality of the SG's legal argumentation might be the best explanation for the SG's influence on the Court (e.g., Lindquist and Klein 2003; McGuire 1998; Merrill 2003).[146]

An additional limitation of this research centers on its focus on a single court. I encourage future researchers to investigate the influence of amicus briefs and other forms of interest group litigation in the federal courts of appeals and district courts, as well as state courts. Moreover, it is important to recognize that foreign and multinational courts have similar mechanisms for interest group participation. Because the core theories presented here are generalizable, I am confident that their application to these judicial bodies will prove particularly fruitful, keeping in mind that the institutional structures of these courts likely shape judicial choice.

Inasmuch as this research was motivated by the development of generalizable theories of amicus influence, it is limited by the fact that I did

---

146 Others attribute the SG's influence to strategic litigation decisions (e.g., Zorn 2002) and to the SG's ideological compatibility with the Court (e.g., Bailey, Kamoie, and Maltzman 2005; Nicholson and Collins 2008).

not address whether certain amici are more influential than others. A growing body of scholarship, predicated on Galanter's (1974) seminal study of repeat players, indicates that the quality of argumentation and the status of litigants (and perhaps amici) can shape judicial choice (e.g., Johnson, Wahlbeck, and Spriggs 2006; McAtee and McGuire 2007; McGuire 1998). As applied to amicus briefs, this implies that courts might be particularly attentive to the arguments advanced by highly experienced advocates, giving those briefs favorable attention (e.g., Samuels 2004). Justice Thomas, one of the most conservative members of the Court, corroborated this point in describing amicus briefs filed by the liberal American Civil Liberties Union: "You know, I'm not one who gloms on to the ACLU's arguments. [But,] They are pretty principled about the positions they take, and they're well-informed and pretty helpful" (quoted in McDonald 2006). If Thomas's sentiment is generalizable beyond the ACLU, this suggests that future research will benefit from a consideration of the status of amici. In pursuing this line of research, recognizing that the study of a single issue area is likely most appropriate is important. Such is the case because repeat player amici generally confine their amicus participation to a narrow range of cases. For example, the ACLU participates predominately in civil rights and liberties cases. Americans for Effective Law Enforcement and the National Association of Criminal Defense Lawyers file amicus briefs almost exclusively in criminal disputes. The American Newspaper Publishers Association focuses on free expression law, while the AFL-CIO and the U.S. Chamber of Commerce target their amicus briefs toward cases involving the interests of business and labor.

In considering whether the Court privileges certain interests over others, this line of research is capable of providing added insight into the pluralist or elitist nature of interest group influence in the Court. To be sure, pluralist accounts of organizational activity are about more than participation; they also speak to group impact on government (Schattschneider 1960). While I have provided evidence for a pluralist vision of interest group participation in the Court, I cannot speak to whether certain interests are more influential than others. Future research into this will no doubt benefit our understanding of possible bias in the administration of justice.

The evidence supporting a bottom-up model of amicus influence intimates that it is profitable to examine how amicus briefs shape the content of the justices' opinions (e.g., Epstein and Kobylka 1992; Samuels 2004), particularly with regard to the types of arguments that amici furnish in support of their positions. Rather than serving solely as rationalizations for decisions, the bottom-up approach illuminates the reality that opinions might very well reveal influences on judicial choice. As such, this research was a necessary first step for the future investigation of amicus influence on judicial opinions in that a prerequisite for establishing the influence of interest groups on the content of opinions is to determine whether the amicus briefs shape the justices' voting behavior. To be sure, the importance of judicial opinions cannot be overstated. As authorities for the entire judicial system, opinions guide both lower court decisions and the advocacy efforts of litigators. Understanding how interest groups shape this form of doctrinal development will surely aid scholars in better comprehending the important role of organized interests in the legal system. This research also has the potential to offer leverage over whether the justices are particularly susceptible to certain types of arguments. For example, since groups marshal a wide array of legal language in their persuasion attempts, incorporating legal, political, and social scientific argumentation, uncovering whether particular styles of persuasion are more effective than others will surely contribute to our knowledge of friends of the court.

In addition to providing directions for future research on interest group litigation, this research also speaks to the analysis of judicial decision making more broadly. By developing a theory for amicus briefs based on the legal model, I join the growing body of scholars seeking to, through rigorous empirical research, bring the "jurisprudence" back into Shapiro's (1964) notion of "political jurisprudence" as an organizing principle for the study of judicial decision making (e.g., Lindquist and Klein 2003; McAtee and McGuire 2007; Richards and Kritzer 2002; Vigilante, Hettinger, and Zorn 2001). Central to my contribution is that I believe a careful understanding of the goals of the justices is vital to designing tests for the influence of these legal variables. Just as it was necessary to ascertain the goals of the justices before setting up empirical tests to determine whether the influence of amicus briefs is best explained by the legal or attitudinal framework, so too is it important to apply this concept to evaluating the influence of other legal variables, such as precedent (e.g., Richards and Kritzer 2002) and litigant argumentation (e.g., McGuire 1998). In this sense, assuming that the justices are uniformly influenced by these legal variables without providing rigorous tests for the possible mediating role of ideology in shaping the justices' responses to these legal factors is not appropriate. Only after controls are in place for the possible mediating role of ideology can researchers definitively state that the law matters, and not judicial ideology.

This research also reinforces the utility of employing interdisciplinary approaches to better understand the behavior of judicial decision makers. By incorporating theories from legal studies, management, marketing, political science, social psychology, and related disciplines, I join a growing number of scholars who are attentive to the profitability of a multifaceted approach to judicial choice (e.g., Baum 2006; Posner 1973; Simon 1998; Wrightsman 2006). This stems from the recognition that the study of the law is inherently interdisciplinary. The researcher who seeks to understand the behavior of jurists from a single disciplinary perspective does so at his or her own peril. If the study of judicial choice is to move forward, we must be attentive to the fact that no single discipline has a monopoly on legal decision making.

Appendix: Data and Data Reliability

The data on amicus curiae filings used in this project were either obtained from the Kearney and Merrill (2000) amicus curiae dataset or collected by the author.[147] Kearney and Merrill were kind enough to provide their extensive and highly reliable data on amicus curiae submissions in the Supreme Court for the 1946–1995 terms. Supplementary data were collected, bringing the data current to the 2001 term. In addition, data were collected to permit: (1) the expansion of Kearney and Merrill's amicus dataset from the case citation to the docket number as the unit of analysis, and (2) the inclusion of the Court's original jurisdiction cases. Below, I discuss Kearney and Merrill's data collection procedures, the expansiveness and limitations of their database, and the results of reliability analyses of their data. Following this, I present the data collection procedures employed by the author and the methodology used to code the ideological directions of the amicus briefs. I close with a brief methodological note.

I. The Kearney and Merrill Database[148]

Kearney and Merrill's database includes information on the number of amicus curiae submissions for each orally argued case decided on the

---

147 As a preliminary note, the amicus curiae data used in this project include all amicus briefs filed during the 1946–2001 terms for all orally argued cases decided on the merits. Thus, no distinction was made between individual and nonindividual amicus activity, unlike the Gibson (1997) database which includes only nonindividual amicus activity (e.g., amicus participation by interest groups and governmental entities).

148 This discussion of the Kearney and Merrill database was adopted from Kearney and Merrill's own discussion of their database (see Kearney and Merrill 2000: 835–844),

merits during the 1946–1995 terms, using the case citation as the unit of analysis (with some exceptions discussed below), excluding most of the Court's original jurisdiction cases. Variables derived from their database and used in the current project include information, for each case, regarding the following: (1) the number of amicus briefs filed supporting the petitioner, respondent, and those failing to identify their desired result in the conclusion section of the briefs; and (2) whether the Office of Solicitor General (SG) filed an amicus brief in a case and, if so, whether the brief supported the petitioner, respondent, or failed to identify its desired result in the brief's conclusion section.

Kearney and Merrill determined the litigant each amicus brief supported by following the classification scheme used by the Reporter of Decisions in the *United States Reports*. The Reporter uses a very uniform classification scheme and has a renowned reputation for meticulousness (Stern, Gressman, Shapiro, and Geller 2002: 29–32; Wagner 2001). The Reporter classifies the litigant each amicus brief supported based on statements made in the briefs. Specifically, the Reporter categorizes amicus briefs as supporting the petitioner if they state in their conclusion section that they are "urging reversal." The Reporter classifies amicus briefs as supporting the respondent if they state in their conclusion section that they are "urging affirmance." Briefs that do not contain such statements are classified by the Reporter without connection to either litigant. This information appears in the "Counsel" section of each case.

For example, in *Swint v. Chambers County Commission* (1995) the Reporter includes the following information in the "Counsel" section of *U.S. Reports*:

COUNSEL: Robert B. McDuff argued the cause for petitioners. With him on the briefs were Carlos A. Williams, Bryan Stevenson, and Bernard Harcourt.

Paul R. Q. Wolfson argued the cause for the United States as amicus curiae in support of petitioners. On the brief were Solicitor General Days, Assistant Attorney General Patrick, Deputy Solicitor General Bender, Beth S. Brinkmann, Jessica Dunsay Silver, and Linda F. Thome.

---

as well as a series of email communications with Joseph Kearney over several months during 2003.

Paul M. Smith argued the cause for respondents. With him on the brief for respondent Chambers County Commission were Bruce J. Ennis, Donald B. Verrilli, Jr., James W. Webb, Kendrick E. Webb, and Bart Harmon.*

* J. Michael McGuinness filed a brief for the Southern States Police Benevolent Association as amicus curiae urging reversal.

Briefs of amici curiae urging affirmance were filed for Jefferson County, Alabama, by Charles S. Wagner; and for the National Association of Counties et al. by Richard Ruda.

Mitchell F. Dolin, T. Jeremy Gunn, Steven R. Shapiro, Michael A. Cooper, Herbert J. Hansell, Norman Redlich, Thomas J. Henderson, and Sharon R. Vinick filed a brief for the American Civil Liberties Union et al. as amici curiae.

This case is classified as having two briefs filed for the petitioner (the SG and the Southern States Police Benevolent Association), two briefs filed for the respondent (Jefferson County, Alabama, and the National Association of Counties et al.), and one brief that failed to identify, in its conclusion section, the party it supported (ACLU et al.).

While the Reporter's classification rubric is uniform (and logical), it has one drawback. Specifically, by relying solely on the conclusion sections of the briefs to determine the party supported by the amici, the Reporter classifies a nontrivial number of briefs as not urging a particular disposition, when, in fact, they do. For example, in *Swint*, the ACLU's amicus brief is classified as failing to advocate for a particular outcome since its conclusion section states the following:

> Alabama law provides that counties have law enforcement powers and it establishes county sheriffs as law enforcement policymakers for each county. The sheriffs are elected by the county and are paid by the county. Their offices are funded by the county treasury. They have jurisdiction only in their own counties and do not report to any official outside the county. In Alabama, county sheriffs are, as a matter of law, final law enforcement policymakers at the county level.

> For the same reason that Alabama cannot immunize its sheriffs from Section 1983 liability by broadly construing the state's sovereign immunity doctrine, Alabama cannot shield its counties from

Section 1983 liability by technically designating county sheriffs as state officials when such a designation does not correspond to the way in which sheriffs actually exercise their law enforcement authority.[149]

Clearly, the ACLU's amicus brief does not state that it urges a particular outcome in its conclusion section. But, on the brief's cover it states the following: "BRIEF AMICI CURIAE SUPPORTING PETITIONERS OF AMERICAN CIVIL LIBERTIES UNION, ACLU OF ALABAMA, AND LAWYERS' COMMITTEE FOR CIVIL RIGHTS UNDER LAW." Thus, although the ACLU does not reveal its preferred disposition in the brief's conclusion section, it does so on the brief's cover. The Reporter, nonetheless, classifies the brief as failing to urge a particular result.

Briefs failing to identify their preferred result in their conclusion section make up 18% of all amicus briefs in the Kearney and Merrill database. Because this is probably a larger percentage of briefs urging an "other" outcome than likely comports with reality, Kearney and Merrill analyzed a random sample of 256 of these briefs. They discovered that 240 of these briefs actually supported either the petitioner or respondent, but failed to indicate these preferences in their conclusion sections. Of these briefs, 127 supported the petitioner, 113 supported the respondent, and 16 actually supported neither party. Of the 240 briefs that were classified as failing to specify their preferred outcome in their conclusion section, 52.9% were filed for the petitioner and 47.1% were filed for the respondent, compared with 50.3% for the petitioner and 49.1% for the respondent in their universe of cases.[150] Based on these figures, Kearney and Merrill concluded that amicus briefs classified as "other" are evenly and randomly dispersed among their support of petitioner and respondents. To provide a more solid basis for this conclusion, I performed t-tests on this data. The results indicated that no statistically significant differences existed between the mean number of amicus briefs supporting the petitioner (respondent) in the random subsample as compared with the mean number of amicus briefs supporting the petitioner (respondent) the universe of cases.[151]

---

149 See amicus curiae brief of the ACLU et al., *Swint v. Chambers County Commission* (1995).

150 The figures for the universe of cases exclude the 18% of amicus briefs that are classified as "other."

151 In addition, I selected a random sample of 60 amicus briefs that the Reporter listed as failing to identify the preferred disposition in their conclusion section. Of these

To determine the validity of Kearney and Merrill's database, I performed an extensive reliability analysis. Specifically, I extracted a random sample of 155 (approximately 2.5%) cases from the whole dataset. Because it is unlikely that Kearney and Merrill's database reports amicus participation in a case where no such participation occurred, I oversampled cases with amicus participation. The random sample includes 117 cases (approximately 75%) where Kearney and Merrill indicated that amicus briefs were filed and 38 cases (approximately 25%) where Kearney and Merrill indicated that no amicus briefs were present. Upon checking Kearney and Merrill's data, no discrepancies were discovered between the data I collected and that data Kearney and Merrill reported for any of the variables used in this project.

II. The Original Data Collection

To update Kearney and Merrill's database to the 2001 term and augment its content, I supplemented their data with additional information on amicus filings. I first expanded Kearney and Merrill's database from using the case citation to the docket number as the unit of analysis.[152] Kearney and Merrill employ the case citation as the unit of analysis, with some exceptions. In other words, they primarily employ the lead case as their unit of analysis. For example, in *Kennedy v. Mendoza-Martinez* (1963), Kearney and Merrill collected amicus data on the lead case (*Kennedy*), indicating that the ACLU filed an amicus brief in support of the respondent. But, this case was decided in conjunction with *Rusk v. Cort* (1962), which is identified by a separate docket number (although both cases share the same case citation). In the latter case, the ACLU filed an amicus brief supporting the respondent, as did Angelika Schneider. Thus, in *Kennedy* a single amicus brief was filed, whereas in *Rusk* two such briefs were filed.

---

randomly sampled briefs, 30 were filed for the petitioner, 28 for the respondent, and 2 for neither party. I further analyzed the types of litigants supported, the issue areas and terms in which the briefs were filed, and the identity of the amici. No obvious patterns emerged. See also Collins (2004a, 2007).

152 The Court routinely combines several cases with similar factual circumstances under a case citation and disposes of each case with a single opinion. In such cases, when the case citation is employed as the unit of analysis, one record exists for the case (i.e., the opinion). When one uses the docket number as the unit of analysis, records exist for each case consolidated under the same opinion.

In the vast majority of cases in their database, Kearney and Merrill employ the case citation as the unit of analysis. However, in a small number of cases, they use the docket number as the unit of analysis. They do this in circumstances in which the lead case did not have any amicus participation, but a non-lead case decided under the same opinion (i.e., a case identified by its docket number) had such participation. While this was an appropriate means of data collection for their purposes, it presented a problem for this analysis. Specifically, because the amicus data collected for this project were merged with the Spaeth (2002, 2003) databases, which allow researchers to select their own units of analysis (e.g., case citation *or* docket number, case citation *and* docket number), I was forced to back check every case in which at least one amicus brief was filed and the Court's opinion disposed of more than one case.[153] In other words, I checked and/or recollected amicus data on every case, following the collection procedures discussed above, in which the docket number might be employed as the unit of analysis and where Kearney and Merrill indicated that at least one amicus brief was filed. It was unnecessary to back check cases in which the Kearney and Merrill database indicated that no amicus briefs were filed because such cases contained no amicus filings for any of the docket numbers disposed of under the case citation. After this re-collection effort, which resulted in a very small number of changes, I was left with a dataset that indicates the number of amicus briefs (if any) filed for each case (using the docket number as the unit of analysis), including information on the amicus activity of the SG, that the Court disposed of with oral arguments during the 1946–1995 terms. Thus, this "new" database uses the docket number as the unit of analysis.

Having expanded Kearney and Merrill's database to use the docket number as the unit of analysis, I next collected data on amicus filings for cases missing in the Kearney and Merrill database but appearing in the Spaeth data. This required collecting additional amicus data on roughly 200 cases, about 80% of which were original jurisdiction cases. Accordingly, I collected this data following the same procedures discussed above with regard to the Kearney and Merrill database. This left me with a dataset

---

153 I accomplished this by merging the Kearney and Merrill data with the Spaeth (2002, 2003) databases on case citation. I then checked each case citation that had more than one docket number and where Kearney and Merrill indicated that at least one amicus brief was filed.

that included information on amicus curiae filings for every orally argued case reported in the Spaeth datasets during the 1946–1995 terms.

The final data collection step was to update the amicus data to the 2001 term. This was done using Lexis-Nexis, an online legal database that follows the reporting procedures of the Reporter of Decisions. To update the amicus data to the 2001 term, I replicated the collection procedures used by Kearney and Merrill (discussed above). For each docket number, I examined the "Counsel" section of each case, calculating the number of amicus briefs filed for the petitioner, respondent, and those failing to identify their desired result in the conclusion section of the briefs. I then collected information regarding the amicus activity of the SG: specifically, whether he participated in a case and, if so, whether his briefs were filed in support of the petitioner, respondent, or failed to identify the desired result in the conclusion section of the briefs.

The final dataset includes information for every orally argued case decided by the Supreme Court during the 1946–2001 terms that is identified in the Spaeth databases on: (1) how many amicus briefs were filed in each case supporting the petitioner, respondent, and failed to identify the amici's desired result in the conclusion section of the brief; and (2) this same data on the Solicitor General.

III. Identifying the Liberal and Conservative Nature of the Amicus Curiae Briefs

Having collected complete data on amicus curiae submissions for the 1946–2001 terms, it was next necessary to code the conservative or liberal nature of the argumentation in these briefs. To do this, I followed standard practice (e.g., Bailey, Kamoie, and Maltzman 2005; Deen, Ignagni, and Meernick 2003; Johnson, Wahlbeck, and Spriggs 2006). I coded briefs that urged the Court to reverse a liberal lower court decision as advocating for the conservative position and briefs that urged the Court to reverse a conservative lower court decision as advocating for the liberal position. I coded briefs that urged the Court to affirm a liberal lower court decision as advocating for the liberal position and briefs that urged the Court to affirm a conservative lower court decision as advocating for the conservative position. The determinations as to whether the lower court decisions were liberal or conservative in nature was based on information in the Spaeth (2002, 2003) databases. By making these determinations based on the liberal or conservative nature of the lower court decisions, coupled with whether the amici supported the petitioner or respondent, I was able to avoid reading each individual amicus brief to uncover its ideological content. This would have been a monumental, if not impossible, task as there are more than 15,000 amicus briefs in the data. More important, by adopting this method, I am able to ensure that the liberal or conservative nature of the argumentation in the briefs is determined on the same basis as the liberal and conservative nature of the justice's votes. For example, if Spaeth identified the lower court decision as liberal in nature and the Supreme Court reversed the lower court, those justices who join the majority are categorized as having cast conservative votes, while those who dissented are categorized as having cast liberal votes. Identically, amicus briefs that urged the Court to reverse the lower court's liberal decision are coded as having advocated for the conservative outcome, while briefs that urged the Court to affirm the lower court's liberal decision are categorized as having advocated for the liberal outcome. Had I chose to read each amicus brief to determine the ideological nature of its argumentation, this would have, in all likelihood, been a much less reliable data collection procedure. I could not have definitively stated that my coding of the briefs was made on the exact same basis as those of the ideological nature of the justices' voting behavior made by Spaeth. By employing the procedure discussed above, I can affirmatively state that this is the case.

Finally, it is necessary to revisit the issue of the amicus briefs coded as "other" to determine if there is a systematic bias with regard to ideology in those "other" briefs that are treated as missing data in the empirical models. In other words, the fact that those "other" briefs are roughly equal in terms of advocating for reversals or affirmances does not necessarily mean that they are evenly distributed with regard to urging liberal or conservative outcomes. Accordingly, it was necessary to examine if systematic differences exist. To do this, I collected data on all amicus submissions during the 1996–2001 terms using Westlaw, a legal search engine that contains the actual briefs themselves.[154] Instead of relying on the information provided by the Reporter of Decisions with regard to whether the briefs advocated for reversals or affirmances, I examined the briefs myself and collected this data from the covers of the briefs.

---

154 Though it would be optimal to examine a larger period of time, at the time of this writing, Westlaw only contains full records of the briefs after the 1995 term.

After determining the liberal or conservative nature of the argumentation in these briefs (following the coding procedures discussed above), I compared the differences between the data collected on the basis of the Reporter's classifications with the data collected by examining the covers of the briefs with regard to the liberal or conservative nature of the argumentation in the briefs. To do this, I generated two variables. The first variable, *Liberal Difference*, was generated by subtracting the number of liberal amicus briefs identified on the basis of the Reporter's classifications from the "true" number of liberal briefs identified in Westlaw. The second variable, *Conservative Difference*, was generated by subtracting the number of conservative amicus briefs identified on the basis of the Reporter's classifications from the "true" number of conservative amicus briefs identified in Westlaw. If systematic bias exists with respect to the distribution of these variables, we would expect sharp distinctions between them. For example, if all of the "other" briefs did, in fact, advocate for the conservative outcome, then the *Liberal Difference* variable would equal 0 (indicating that no difference exists between the number of liberal briefs regardless of whether this information was obtained from the Reporter's classification method or by reading the briefs themselves), while the values for the *Conservative Difference* variable would be positive for all instances in which the Reporter misclassified a conservative brief as urging an "other" outcome. Using the case as the unit of analysis, the mean of the *Liberal Difference* variable is 0.128, while the mean of the *Conservative Difference* variable is 0.130. A *t* test reveals this difference of means is insignificant.[155] Thus, I can state with reasonable confidence that the exclusion of such "other" briefs does not bias the findings in this project.

IV. A Final Word on Methodology

As a final methodological note, I will add that I have performed alternative specifications of the statistical models appearing in Chapters 4, 5, and 6 by including dummy variables for each term in the data, save one (e.g., Beck, Katz, and Tucker 1998). The purpose of including these term-specific variables is to provide controls for any temporal dependence in the data,

---

155 The insignificant nature of this difference is confirmed when considering only those cases in which the number of liberal and conservative briefs differs depending on whether the briefs were identified by the Reporter's classification or through Westlaw (i.e., when *Liberal Difference* and/or *Conservative Difference* are not equal to zero).

which may be related to factors such as the increase in amicus participation over time, the composition of the executive and legislative branches (e.g., Epstein and Knight 1998; Eskridge 1991), and alterations to the Supreme Court's agenda (Baum 1988; Pacelle 1991). The results of those surrogate model specifications are consistent with the results reported in Chapters 4, 5, and 6, both statistically and substantively. I forgo reporting the results of those models since their substantive interpretation, through predicted probabilities, requires that I (somewhat arbitrarily) select a single Supreme Court term to hold constant in order to generate meaningful predications. That is to say, it requires me to report empirical results that only apply to a single Supreme Court term. Because the goal of this book is to provide a generalizable treatment of the influence of amicus curiae briefs that is not limited to a single term of the Court, and because the substantive findings remain effectively unchanged, I rely on the results derived from the more parsimonious models that exclude these term-specific dummy variables throughout the book.

REFERENCES

Abelson, Robert P., Elliot Aronson, William J. McGuire, Theodore M. Newcomb, Milton J. Rosenberg, and Percy H. Tannenbaum, eds. 1968. *Theories of Cognitive Consistency: A Sourcebook.* Chicago: Rand McNally.

Acker, James R. 1990. "Social Science in Supreme Court Criminal Cases and Briefs: The Actual and Potential Contribution of Social Scientists as Amici Curiae." *Law and Human Behavior* 14(1): 25–42.

Acker, James R. 1993. "Mortal Friends and Enemies: Amici Curiae in Supreme Court Death Penalty Cases." *New England Journal on Criminal and Civil Confinement* 19(1): 1–59.

Ackerman, Erin, and Joel B. Grossman. 2004. "Competing Constitutional Claims: *Boy Scouts of America v. Dale* (2000)." In *Creating Constitutional Change: Clashes over Power and Liberty in the Supreme Court,* ed. Gregg Ivers and Kevin T. McGuire. Charlottesville, VA: University of Virginia Press.

Ai, Chunrong, and Edward C. Norton. 2003. "Interaction Terms in Logit and Probit Models." *Economics Letters* 80(1): 123–129.

Alger, Jonathan, and Marvin Krislov. 2004. "You've Got to Have Friends: Lessons Learned from the Role of Amici in the University of Michigan Cases." *Journal of College and University Law* 30(3): 503–529.

Aldrich, John H., and Forrest D. Nelson. 1984. *Linear Probability, Logit, and Probit Models.* Newbury Park, CA: Sage Publications.

Alvarez, R. Michael, and John Brehm. 1995. "American Ambivalence Towards Abortion Policy: Development of a Heteroskedastic Probit Model of Competing Values." *American Journal of Political Science* 39(4): 1055–1082.

Alvarez, R. Michael, and John Brehm. 2002. *Hard Choices, Easy Answers: Values, Information, and American Public Opinion.* Princeton, NJ: Princeton University Press.

Bacon, Francis. [1620] 1994. *Novum Organum—With Other Parts of the Great Instauration,* ed. Peter Urbach and John Gibson. Chicago: Open Court Publishing Co.

Bailey, Michael A., Brian Kamoie, and Forrest Maltzman. 2005. "Signals from the Tenth Justice: The Political Role of the Solicitor General in Supreme Court Decision Making." *American Journal of Political Science* 49(1): 72–85.

Baker, Lynn A. 1996. "Interdisciplinary Due Diligence: The Case for Common Sense in the Search for the Swing Justice." *Southern California Law Review* 70(1): 187–217.

Banner, Stuart. 2003. "The Myth of the Neutral Amicus: American Courts and Their Friends, 1790-1890." *Constitutional Commentary* 20(1): 131–150.

Barker, Lucius J. 1967. "Third Parties in Litigation: A Systematic View of the Judicial Function." *Journal of Politics* 29(1): 41–69.

Bartels, Brandon L. 2005. "Heterogeneity in Supreme Court Decision-Making: How Case-Level Factors Alter Preference-Based Behavior." Paper Presented at the Annual Meeting of the Midwest Political Science Association, Chicago.

Baum, Lawrence. 1988. "Measuring Policy Change in the U.S. Supreme Court." *American Political Science Review* 82(3): 905–912.

Baum, Lawrence. 1994. "What Judges Want: Judges' Goals and Judicial Behavior." *Political Research Quarterly* 47(3): 749–768.

Baum, Lawrence. 1997. *The Puzzle of Judicial Behavior*. Ann Arbor, MI: The University of Michigan Press.

Baum, Lawrence. 2006. *Judges and Their Audiences: A Perspective on Judicial Behavior*. Princeton, NJ: Princeton University Press.

Baumeister, Roy F., and Leonard S. Newman. 1994. "Self-Regulation of Cognitive Inference and Decision Processes." *Personality and Social Psychology Bulletin* 20(1): 3–19.

Baumgartner, Frank R., and Beth L. Leech. 1998. *Basic Interests: The Importance of Groups in Politics and in Political Science*. Princeton, NJ: Princeton University Press.

Beck, Nathaniel, Jonathan N. Katz, and Richard Tucker. 1998. "Taking Time Seriously: Time-Series-Cross-Section Analysis with a Binary Dependent Variable." *American Journal of Political Science* 42 (4): 1260–1288.

Behuniak-Long, Susan. 1991. "Friendly Fire: Amici Curiae and *Webster v. Reproductive Health Services.*" *Judicature* 74(5): 261–270.

Bell, Lauren Cohen. 2002. *Warring Factions: Interest Groups, Money, and the New Politics of Senate Confirmation*. Columbus, OH: Ohio State University Press.

Bennett, Robert W. 2001. "Counter-Conversationalism and the Sense of Difficulty." *Northwestern University Law Review* 95(3): 845–906.

Benoit, William L. 1987. "Argumentation and Credibility Appeals in Persuasion." *Southern Speech Communication Journal* 52(Winter): 181–197.

Benoit, William L. 1989. "Attorney Argumentation and Supreme Court Opinions." *Argumentation and Advocacy* 26(Summer): 22–38.

Bentley, Arthur F. 1908. *The Process of Government: A Study of Social Pressures.* Chicago: University of Chicago Press.

Berry, Jeffrey M. 1997. *The Interest Group Society*. 3rd ed. New York: Longman.

Bersoff, Donald N., and David W. Ogden. 1991. "APA Amicus Curiae Briefs: Furthering Lesbian and Gay Male Civil Rights." *American Psychologist* 46(9): 950–956.

Bickel, Alexander M. 1962. *The Least Dangerous Branch: The Supreme Court at the Bar of Politics*. Indianapolis, IN: Bobbs-Merrill.

Birkby, Robert H., and Walter F. Murphy. 1964. "Interest Group Conflict in the Judicial Arena: The First Amendment and Group Access to the Courts." *Texas Law Review* 42(7): 1018–1048.

Blasecki, Janet L. 1990. "Justice Lewis F. Powell: Swing Voter or Staunch Conservative?" *Journal of Politics* 52(2): 530–547.

Bobbitt, Philip C. 1991. *Constitutional Interpretation*. Oxford, UK: Blackwell.

Bradley, Robert C., and Paul Gardner. 1985. "Underdogs, Upperdogs, and the Use of the Amicus Brief: Trends and Explanations." *Justice System Journal* 10(1): 78–96.

Braman, Eileen. 2006. "Reasoning on the Threshold: Testing the Separability of Preferences in Legal Decision Making." *Journal of Politics* 68(2): 308–321.

Braman, Eileen, and Thomas E. Nelson. 2007. "Mechanism of Motivated Reasoning? Analogical Perception in Discrimination Disputes." *American Journal of Political Science* 51(4): 940–956.

Brambor, Thomas, William Roberts Clark, and Matt Golder. 2006. "Understanding Interaction Models: Improving Empirical Analyses." *Political Analysis* 14(1): 63–82.

Brenner, Saul. 1980. "Fluidity on the United States Supreme Court: A Reexamination." *American Journal of Political Science* 24(3): 526–535.

Brenner, Saul. 1983. "Another Look at Freshman Indecisiveness on the United States Supreme Court." *Polity* 16(3): 320–328.

Brenner, Saul, and Theodore S. Arrington. 2002. "Measuring Salience on the Supreme Court: A Research Note." *Jurimetrics* 43(Fall): 99–113.

Brenner, Saul, and Timothy M. Hagle. 1996. "Opinion Writing and the Acclimation Effect." *Political Behavior* 18(3): 235–261.

Brenner, Saul, and Harold J. Spaeth. 1995. *Stare Indecisis: The Alteration of Precedent on the Supreme Court, 1946–1992*. Cambridge, UK: Cambridge University Press.

Brenner, Saul, Timothy M. Hagle, and Harold J. Spaeth. 1989. "The Defection of the Marginal Justice on the Warren Court." *Western Political Quarterly* 42(3): 409–425.

Breyer, Stephen. 1998. "The Interdependence of Science and Law." *Judicature* 82(1): 24–27.

Brodie, Ian. 2002. *Friends of the Court: The Privileging of Interest Group Litigants in Canada*. Albany, NY: State University of New York Press.

Burger, Warren E. 1971. Memorandum to Hugo L. Black, May 20. Papers of Justice William J. Brennan, Jr. Washington, DC: Library of Congress Manuscript Division.

Burton, Steven J. 1992. *Judging in Good Faith*. Cambridge, UK: Cambridge University Press.

Byrne, Jennifer R. 1998. "Toward a Colorblind Constitution: Justice O'Connor's Narrowing of Affirmative Action." *Saint Louis University Law Journal* 42(2): 619–675.

Cacioppo, John T., Stephen G. Harkins, and Richard E. Petty. 1981. "The Nature of Attitudes and Cognitive Responses and Their Relationships to Behavior." In *Cognitive Responses in Persuasion*, ed. Richard E. Petty, Thomas M. Ostrom, and Timothy C. Brock. Hillsdale, N.J.: Lawrence Erlbaum Associates.

Caldeira, Gregory A., and James L. Gibson. 1992. "The Etiology of Public Support for the Supreme Court." *American Journal of Political Science* 36(3): 635–664.

Caldeira, Gregory A., and John R. Wright. 1988. "Organized Interests and Agenda Setting in the U.S. Supreme Court." *American Political Science Review* 82(4): 1109–1127.

Caldeira, Gregory A., and John R. Wright. 1990. "Amici Curiae Before the Supreme Court: Who Participates, When, and How Much?" *Journal of Politics* 52(3): 782–806.

Caldeira, Gregory A., and John R. Wright. 1998. "Organized Interests Before the Supreme Court: Setting the Agenda." Paper Presented at the Annual Meeting of the American Political Science Association, Boston.

Caldeira, Gregory A., and Christopher J. W. Zorn. 1998. "Of Time and Consensual Norms in the Supreme Court." *American Journal of Political Science* 42(3): 874–902.

Caldeira, Gregory A., Marie Hojnacki, and John R. Wright. 2000. "The Lobbying Activities of Organized Interests in Federal Judicial Nominations." *Journal of Politics* 62(1): 51–69.

Calder, Bobby, Chester A. Insko, and Ben Yandell. 1974. "The Relation of Cognitive and Memorial Processes to Persuasion in a Simulated Jury Trial." *Journal of Applied Social Psychology* 4(1): 62–93.

Campbell, J. Louis, III. 1983. "The Spirit of Dissent." *Judicature* 66(7): 304–312.

Canon, Bradley C. 1973. "Reactions of State Supreme Courts to a U.S. Supreme Court Civil Liberties Decision." *Law and Society Review* 8(1): 109–134.

Caplan, Lincoln. 1987. *The Tenth Justice: The Solicitor General and the Rule of Law*. New York: Vintage Books.

Cardozo, Benjamin N. 1921. *The Nature of the Judicial Process*. New Haven, CT: Yale University Press.

Cardozo, Benjamin N. 1939. "Law and Literature." *Harvard Law Review* 52(3): 471–489.

Casagrande, David G. 1999. "Information as Verb: Re-conceptualizing Information for Cognitive and Ecological Models." *Georgia Journal of Ecological Anthropology* 3: 4–13.

Casper, Jonathan D. 1976. "The Supreme Court and National Policy Making." *American Political Science Review* 70(1): 50–63.

Chaiken, Shelly. 1980. "Heuristic Versus Systematic Information Processing and the Use of Source Versus Message Cues in Persuasion." *Journal of Personality and Social Psychology* 39(5): 752–766.

Chauncey, George. 2004. "'What Gay Studies Taught the Court': The Historians' Amicus Brief in *Lawrence v. Texas*." *GLQ: A Journal of Gay and Lesbian Studies* 10(3): 509–538.

Chen, Paul. 2007. "The Informational Role of Amici Curiae Briefs in *Gonzalez v. Raich*." *Southern Illinois University Law Journal* 31(2): 217–241.

Cigler, Allan J., and Burdett A. Loomis, eds. 2002. *Interest Group Politics*. 6th ed. Washington, DC: CQ Press.

Cohen, Felix. 1935. "Transcendental Nonsense and the Functional Approach." *Columbia Law Review* 35(6): 809–849.

Colker, Ruth. 2007. "Justice Sandra Day O'Connor's Friends." *Ohio State Law Journal* 68(2): 517–608.

Collins, Paul M., Jr. 2004a. "Friends of the Court: Examining the Influence of Amicus Curiae Participation in U.S. Supreme Court Litigation." *Law and Society Review* 38(4): 807–832.

Collins, Paul M., Jr. 2004b. "Variable Voting Behavior on the Supreme Court: A Preliminary Analysis and Research Framework." *Justice System Journal* 25(1): 57–74.

Collins, Paul M., Jr. 2007. "Lobbyists before the U.S. Supreme Court: Investigating the Influence of Amicus Curiae Briefs." *Political Research Quarterly* 60(1): 55–70.

Collins, Paul M., Jr., and Lisa A. Solowiej. 2007. "Interest Group Participation, Competition, and Conflict in the U.S. Supreme Court." *Law and Social Inquiry* 32(4): 955–984.

Comparato, Scott A. 2003. *Amici Curiae and Strategic Behavior in State Supreme Courts*. Westport, CT: Praeger Publishers.

Corley, Pamela C. 2005. "The Impact of Dissensus." Paper Presented at the Annual Meeting of the Southern Political Science Association, New Orleans.

Cortner, Richard C. 1968. "Strategies and Tactics of Litigants in Constitutional Cases." *Journal of Public Law* 17(2): 287–307.

Covey, Frank M. 1959. "Amicus Curiae: Friend of the Court." *DePaul Law Review* 9(1): 30–37.

Coyle, Marcia. 2008. "Amicus Briefs are Ammo for Gun Case." *National Law Journal* March 10: 1.

Cross, Frank B. 1997. "Political Science and the New Legal Realism: A Case of Unfortunate Interdisciplinary Ignorance." *Northwestern University Law Review* 92(1): 251–326.

Dahl, Robert A. 1957. "Decision-Making in a Democracy: The Supreme Court as a National Policy-Maker." *Journal of Public Law* 6(Fall): 279–295.

Dahl, Robert A. 1961. *Who Governs? Democracy and Power in an American City.* New Haven, CT: Yale University Press.

Davis, Sue. 1989. *Justice Rehnquist and the Constitution.* Princeton, NJ: Princeton University Press.

Day, Jack G. 2001. "Words that Counted—A Vignette." *Case Western Reserve Law Review* 52(2): 373–374.

Days, Drew S., III. 2001. "When the President Says 'No': A Few Thoughts on Executive Power and the Tradition of Solicitor General Independence." *Journal of Appellate Practice and Process* 3(2): 509–520.

Deen, Rebecca E., Joseph Ignagni, and James Meernik. 2003. "The Solicitor General as Amicus, 1953-2000: How Influential?" *Judicature* 87(2): 60–71.

Devins, Neal. 2003. "Explaining *Grutter v. Bollinger.*" *University of Pennsylvania Law Review* 152(1): 347–383.

Dewey, John. 1916. "Force and Coercion." *International Journal of Ethics* 26(3): 359–367.

Dickson, Del. ed. 2001. *The Supreme Court in Conference (1940–1985): The Private Discussions Behind Nearly 300 Supreme Court Decisions.* New York: Oxford University Press.

Douglas, William O. 1962. "Transcript of Conversations between Justice William O. Douglas and Professor Walter F. Murphy." Cassette Number 9: May 23, 1962. On File with the Seeley G. Mudd Manuscript Library, Princeton University.

Dworkin, Ronald. 1978. *Taking Rights Seriously.* Cambridge, MA: Harvard University Press.

Dworkin, Ronald. 1985. *A Matter of Principle.* Cambridge, MA: Harvard University Press.

Dworkin, Ronald. 1991. "Pragmatism, Right Answers, and True Banality." In *Pragmatism in Law and Society,* ed. Michael Brint and William Weaver. Boulder, CO: Westview Press.

Eagly, Alice H., and Shelly Chaiken. 1984. "Cognitive Theories of Persuasion." In *Advances in Experimental Social Psychology,* ed. Leonard Berkowitz. Orlando, FL: Academic Press.

Edelman, Paul H., and Jim Chen. 1996. "The Most Dangerous Justice: The Supreme Court at the Bar of Mathematics." *Southern California Law Review* 70(1): 63–111.

Edelman, Paul H., and Jim Chen. 2001. "The Most Dangerous Justice Rides Again: Revisiting the Power Pageant of the Justices." *Minnesota Law Review* 86(1): 131–226.

Ennis, Bruce L. 1984. "Effective Amicus Briefs." *Catholic University Law Review* 33(3): 603–609.

Eppler, Martin J., and Jeanne Mengis. 2004. "The Concept of Information Overload: A Review of Literature from Organization Science, Accounting, Marketing, MIS, and Related Disciplines." *The Information Society* 20(5): 325–344.

Epstein, Lee. 1985. *Conservatives in Court*. Knoxville: University of Tennessee Press.

Epstein, Lee. 1991. "Courts and Interest Groups." In *The American Courts: A Critical Assessment*, ed. John B. Gates and Charles A. Johnson. Washington, DC: CQ Press.

Epstein, Lee. 1993. "Interest Group Litigation During the Rehnquist Court Era." *Journal of Law and Politics* 9(4): 639–717.

Epstein, Lee. 1994. "Exploring the Participation of Organized Interests in State Court Litigation." *Political Research Quarterly* 47(2): 335–351.

Epstein, Lee, and Jack Knight. 1998. *The Choices Justices Make*. Washington, DC: CQ Press.

Epstein, Lee, and Jack Knight. 1999. "Mapping Out the Strategic Terrain: The Informational Role of Amici Curiae." In *Supreme Court Decision-Making: New Institutionalist Approaches*, ed. Cornell W. Clayton and Howard Gillman. Chicago: University of Chicago Press.

Epstein, Lee, and Joseph F. Kobylka. 1992. *The Supreme Court and Legal Change: Abortion and the Death Penalty*. Chapel Hill: The University of North Carolina Press.

Epstein, Lee, and C. K. Rowland. 1991. "Debunking the Myth of Interest Group Invincibility in the Courts." *American Political Science Review* 85(1): 205–217.

Epstein, Lee, and Jeffrey A. Segal. 2000. "Measuring Issue Salience." *American Journal of Political Science* 44(1): 66–83.

Epstein, Lee, and Jeffrey A. Segal. 2005. *Advice and Consent: The Political of Judicial Appointments*. New York: Oxford University Press.

Epstein, Lee, and Thomas G. Walker. 2004. *Constitutional Law for a Changing America: Rights, Liberties, and Justice*. 5th ed. Washington, DC: CQ Press.

Epstein, Lee, Jack Knight, and Andrew D. Martin. 2001. "The Supreme Court as a *Strategic* National Policymaker." *Emory Law Journal* 50(2): 583–611.

Epstein, Lee, Jeffrey A. Segal, and Timothy R. Johnson. 1996. "The Claim of Issue Creation on the U.S. Supreme Court." *American Political Science Review* 90(4): 845–852.

Epstein, Lee, Valerie Hoekstra, Jeffrey A. Segal, and Harold J. Spaeth. 1998. "Do Political Preferences Change? A Longitudinal Study of U.S. Supreme Court Justices." *Journal of Politics* 60(3): 801–818.

Epstein, Lee, Andrew D. Martin, Kevin M. Quinn, and Jeffrey A. Segal. 2007. "Ideological Drift Among Supreme Court Justices: Who, When, and How Important?" *Northwestern University Law Review* 101(4): 1483–1541.

Epstein, Lee, Jeffrey A. Segal, Harold J. Spaeth, and Thomas G. Walker. 1994. *The Supreme Court Compendium: Data, Decisions, and Developments*. Washington, D.C.: CQ Press.

Eskridge, William N., Jr. 1991. "Overriding Supreme Court Statutory Interpretation Decisions." *Yale Law Journal* 101(2): 331–455.

Eskridge, William N., Jr. 2002. "Some Effects of Identity-Based Social Movements on Constitutional Law in the Twentieth Century." *Michigan Law Review* 100(8): 2062–2407.

Evans, Michael, Wayne McIntosh, Jimmy Lin, and Cynthia Cates. 2007. "Recounting the Courts? Applying Automated Content Analysis to Enhance Empirical Legal Research." *Journal of Empirical Legal Studies* 4(4): 1007–1039.

Festinger, Leon. 1957. *A Theory of Cognitive Dissonance.* Evanston, Ill.: Row, Peterson and Company.

Flaherty, Francis J. 1983. "Amicus: A Friend or Foe?" *National Law Journal,* November 14: 1.

Flemming, Roy B., and B. Dan Wood. 1997. "The Public and the Supreme Court: Individual Justice Responsiveness to American Policy Moods." *American Journal of Political Science* 41(2): 468–498.

Forston, Robert F. 1975. "Communication Perspectives in the Legal Process." In *Speech Communication: A Basic Anthology,* ed. Ronald L. Applbaum, Owen O. Jenson, and Richard Carroll. New York: Macmillan.

Frank, Jerome. [1930] 1963. *Law and the Modern Mind.* New York: Anchor Books.

Frink, Dwight D., and Gerald R. Ferris. 1999. "The Moderating Effects of Accountability on the Conscientiousness-Performance Relationship." *Journal of Business and Psychology* 13(4): 515–524.

Galanter, Marc. 1974. "Why the 'Haves' Come Out Ahead: Speculations on the Limits of Legal Change." *Law and Society Review* 9(1): 95–160.

Gibson, James L. 1983. "From Simplicity to Complexity: The Development of Theory in the Study of Judicial Behavior." *Political Behavior* 5(1): 7–49.

Gibson, James L. 1997. *United States Supreme Court Judicial Database, Phase II: 1953–1993.* Houston: University of Houston [producer]. Ann Arbor, MI: Inter-University Consortium for Political and Social Research [distributor].

Gibson, James L. 2007. "The Legitimacy of the U.S. Supreme Court in a Polarized Polity." *Journal of Empirical Legal Studies* 4(3): 507–538.

Giles, Michael W., and Christopher Zorn. 2000. "Gibson Versus Case-Based Approaches: Concurring in Part, Dissenting in Part." *Law and Courts* 10(2): 10–16.

Gillman, Howard. 2001. "What's Law Got to Do with It? Judicial Behavioralists Test the 'Legal Model' of Judicial Decision Making." *Law and Social Inquiry* 26(2): 465–504.

Ginsburg, Ruth Bader. 1990. "Remarks on Writing Separately." *Washington Law Review* 65(1): 133–150.

Ginsburg, Ruth Bader. 2001. "In Pursuit of the Public Good: Access to Justice in the United States." *Washington University Journal of Law and Policy* 7(1): 1–15.

Goepp, Katharine. 2002. "Presumed Represented: Analyzing Intervention as of Right When the Government Is a Party." *Western New England Law Review* 24(1): 131–175.

Golden, Marissa Martino. 1998. "Interest Groups in the Rule-Making Process: Who Participates? Whose Voices Get Heard?" *Journal of Public Administration Research and Theory* 8(2): 245–270.

Goodman, Gail S., Murray Levine, Gary B. Melton, and David W. Ogden. 1991. "Child Witnesses and the Confrontation Clause: The American Psychological Association Brief in *Maryland v. Craig.*" *Law and Human Behavior* 15(1): 13–29.

Goodman, Leo A., and William H. Kruskal. 1954. "Measures of Association for Cross Classifications." *Journal of the American Statistical Association* 49(268): 732–764.

Gorsuch, Richard L. 1983. *Factor Analysis*. 2nd ed. Hillsdale, NJ: Lawrence Erlbaum.

Granger, Mark S. 2003. "Aiding in the Defense of Product Liability and Toxic Tort Litigation: Product Advisory Liability Council Celebrates its 20th Anniversary." *Environmental Law and Policy* July: 10.

Gray, Danielle C., and Travis LeBlanc. 2003. "Integrating Elite Law Schools and the Legal Profession: A View from the Black Law Students Associations of Harvard, Stanford, and Yale Law Schools." *Harvard Blackletter Law Journal* 19(Spring): 43–54.

Greene, William H. 2000. *Econometric Analysis*. 4th ed. Upper Saddle River, NJ: Prentice Hall.

Greenhouse, Linda. 2007. "As to the Direction of the Roberts Court: The Jury Is Still Out." *The New York Times*, March 6, Sec. A-15.

Greenwald, Anthony G. 1968. "Cognitive Learning, Cognitive Response to Persuasion, and Attitude Change." In *Psychological Foundations of Attitudes*, ed. Anthony G. Greenwald and Timothy C. Brock. New York: Academic Press.

Grether, David M., Alan Schwartz, and Louis L. Wilde. 1986. "The Irrelevance of Information Overload: An Analysis of Search and Disclosure." *Southern California Law Review* 59(2): 277–303.

Hagle, Timothy M. 1993. "'Freshman Effects' for Supreme Court Justices." *American Journal of Political Science* 37(4): 1142–1157.

Hagle, Timothy M., and Harold J. Spaeth. 1991. "Voting Fluidity and the Attitudinal Model of Supreme Court Decision Making." *Western Political Quarterly* 44(1): 119–128.

Hagle, Timothy M., and Harold J. Spaeth. 1993. "Ideological Patterns in the Justices' Voting in the Burger Court's Business Cases." *Journal of Politics* 55(2): 492–505.

Hakman, Nathan. 1966. "Lobbying the Supreme Court—An Appraisal of 'Political Science Folklore.'" *Fordham Law Review* 35(1): 15–50.

Hale, Sir Matthew. [1660–1676] 1971. *The History of the Common Law of England*, ed. Charles M. Gray. Chicago: University of Chicago Press.

Hall, Melinda Gann, and Paul Brace. 1996. "Justices' Responses to Case Facts: An Interactive Model." *American Politics Quarterly* 24(2): 237–261.

Halpern, Stephen C., and Kenneth N. Vines. 1977. "Institutional Disunity, the Judges' Bill and the Role of the U. S. Supreme Court." *Western Political Quarterly* 30(4): 471–483.

Hansford, Thomas G. 2004a. "Lobbying Strategies, Venue Selection, and Organized Interest Involvement at the U.S. Supreme Court." *American Politics Research* 32(2): 170–197.

Hansford, Thomas G. 2004b. "Information Provision, Organizational Constraints, and the Decision to Submit an Amicus Curiae Brief in a U.S. Supreme Court Case." *Political Research Quarterly* 57(2): 219–230.

Harper, Fowler V., and Edwin D. Etherington. 1953. "Lobbyists Before the Court." *University of Pennsylvania Law Review* 101(8): 1172–1177.

Harris, John F. 2004. "Despite Bush Flip-Flops, Kerry Gets Label," *The Washington Post*, September 23, Sec. A-1.

Harris, Michael J. 2000. "Amicus Curiae: Friend or Foe? The Limits of Friendship in American Jurisprudence." *Suffolk Journal of Trial and Appellate Advocacy* 5(1): 1–18.

Hassler, Gregory L., and Karen O'Connor. 1986. "Woodsy Witchdoctors Versus Judicial Guerrillas: The Role and Impact of Competing Interest Groups in Environmental Litigation." *Boston College Environmental Affairs Law Review* 13(4): 487–520.

Hays, R. Allen. 2001. *Who Speaks for the Poor? National Interest Groups and Social Policy*. New York: Routledge.

Heberlig, Eric, and Rorie Spill. 2000. "Congress at the Court: Members of Congress as Amici Curiae." *Southeastern Political Review* 28(2): 189–212.

Hedman, Susan. 1991. "Friends of the Earth and Friends of the Court: Assessing the Impact of Interest Group Amici Curiae in Environmental Cases Decided by the Supreme Court." *Virginia Environmental Law Journal* 10(2): 187–212.

Heider, Fritz. 1946. "Attitudes and Cognitive Organization." *Journal of Psychology* 21(1): 107–112.

Hettinger, Virginia A., Stefanie A. Lindquist, and Wendy L. Martinek. 2004. "Comparing Attitudinal and Strategic Accounts of Dissenting Behavior on the U.S. Courts of Appeals." *American Journal of Political Science* 48(1): 123–137.

Hettinger, Virginia A., Stefanie A. Lindquist, and Wendy L. Martinek. 2006. *Judging on a Collegial Court: Influences on Federal Appellate Decision Making*. Charlottesville, VA: University of Virginia Press.

Hilton, Seth. 1995. "Restraints on Homosexual Rights Legislation: Is There a Fundamental Right to Participate in the Political Process?" *University of California, Davis Law Review* 28(2): 445–473.

Holmes, Oliver Wendell. 1897. "The Path of the Law." *Harvard Law Review* 10(8): 457–478.

Howard, J. Woodford, Jr. 1968. "On the Fluidity of Judicial Choice." *American Political Science Review* 62(1): 43–56.

Howard, Robert M., and Jeffrey A. Segal. 2002. "An Original Look at Originalism." *Law and Society Review* 36(1): 113–138.

Imre, Christina J. 2001. "Friendly Persuasion: The Role of Amicus Briefs in Supreme Court Practice." *CEB Litigation Reporter* May: 80–82.

Insko, Chester A., E. Allan Lind, and Stephen LaTour. 1976. "Persuasion, Recall, and Thoughts." *Representative Research in Social Psychology* 7(1): 66–78.

Iselin, Errol R. 1993. "The Effects of the Information and Data Properties of Financial Ratios and Statements on Managerial Decision Quality." *Journal of Business Finance and Accounting* 20(2): 249–266.

Ivers, Gregg, and Karen O'Connor. 1987. "Friends as Foes: The Amicus Curiae Participation and Effectiveness of the American Civil Liberties Union and Americans for Effective Law Enforcement in Criminal Cases, 1969–1982." *Law and Policy* 9(2): 161–178.

Jervis, Robert. 1968. "Hypotheses on Misperception." *World Politics* 20(3): 454–479.

Jhering, Rudolph von. 1913. *Law as a Means to an End*. Boston: Boston Book Company.

Johnson, Timothy R. 2004. *Oral Arguments and Decision Making on the United States Supreme Court*. Albany, NY: State University of New York Press.

Johnson, Timothy R., and Matthew M. C. Roberts. 2003. "Oral Arguments, Amici Curiae, and the Attitudinal Model." Paper Presented at the Annual Meeting of the Midwest Political Science Association, Chicago.

Johnson, Timothy R., Paul J. Wahlbeck, and James F. Spriggs, II. 2006. "The Influence of Oral Arguments on the U.S. Supreme Court." *American Political Science Review* 100(1): 99–113.

Kagan, Robert A. 1991. "Adversarial Legalism and American Government." *Journal of Policy Analysis and Management* 10(3): 369–406.

Kagan, Robert A. 2002. *Adversarial Legalism: The American Way of Law*. Cambridge, MA: Harvard University Press.

Kaheny, Erin B., Susan B. Haire, and Sara C. Benesh. N.d. "Change over Tenure: Voting, Variance, and Decision Making on the U.S. Courts of Appeals." *American Journal of Political Science*: forthcoming.

Kahneman, Daniel, Paul Slovic, and Amos Tversky. 1982. *Judgment Under Uncertainty: Heuristics and Biases*. Cambridge, UK: Cambridge University Press.

Katz, Lewis R. 2001. "*Mapp* After Forty Years: Its Impact on Race in America." *Case Western Reserve Law Review* 52(2): 471–488.

Kearney, Joseph D., and Thomas W. Merrill. 2000. "The Influence of Amicus Curiae Briefs on the Supreme Court." *University of Pennsylvania Law Review* 148(3): 743–853.

Keck, Thomas M. 2004. *The Most Activist Supreme Court in History: The Road to Modern Judicial Conservatism*. Chicago: University of Chicago Press.

Keith, Linda Camp. 2007. "The United States Supreme Court and Judicial Review of Congress, 1803–2001." *Judicature* 90(4): 1–14.

Kelman, Mark. 1987. *A Guide to Critical Legal Studies*. Cambridge, MA: Harvard University Press.

Kelsh, John P. 1999. "The Opinion Delivery Practices of the United States Supreme Court, 1790–1945." *Washington University Law Quarterly* 77(1): 137–181.

Key, V. O., Jr. 1958. *Politics, Parties, and Pressure Groups*. New York: Thomas Y. Crowell Company.

Kirkpatrick, Samuel A., Dwight F. Davis, and Roby D. Robertson. 1976. "The Process of Political Decision-Making in Groups." *American Behavioral Scientist* 20(1): 33–64.

Klein, David E. 2002. *Making Law in the United States Courts of Appeals*. New York: Cambridge University Press.

Kobylka, Joseph F. 1987. "A Court Created Context for Group Litigation: Libertarian Groups and Obscenity." *Journal of Politics* 49(4): 1061–1078.

Kolbert, Kathryn. 1989. "The *Webster* Amicus Curiae Briefs: Perspectives on the Abortion Controversy and the Role of the Supreme Court." *American Journal of Law and Medicine* 15(2): 153–168.

Koshner, Andrew Jay. 1998. *Solving the Puzzle of Interest Group Litigation*. Westport, CT.: Praeger Press.

Kozinski, Alex. 2004. "What I Ate for Breakfast and Other Mysteries of Judicial Decision Making." In *Judges on Judging: Views from the Bench*, ed. David M. O'Brien. Washington, DC: CQ Press.

Krislov, Samuel. 1963. "The Amicus Curiae Brief: From Friendship to Advocacy." *Yale Law Journal* 72(4): 694–721.

Krosnick, Jon A., and Richard E. Petty. 1995. "Attitude Strength: An Overview." In *Attitude Strength: Antecedents and Consequences*, ed. Richard E. Petty and Jon A. Krosnick. Mahwah, NJ: Lawrence Erlbaum Associates.

Kruglanski, Arie W. 1980. "Lay Epistemo-Logic–Process and Contents: Another Look at Attribution Theory." *Psychological Review* 87(1): 70–87.

Kunda, Ziva. 1990. "The Case for Motivated Reasoning." *Psychological Bulletin* 108(3): 480–498.

Kunda, Ziva. 1999. *Social Cognition: Making Sense of People*. Cambridge, MA: MIT Press.

Lawrence, Susan E. 1989. "Legal Services Before the Supreme Court." *Judicature* 72(5): 266–273.

Leiter, Brian. 2005. "American Legal Realism." In *The Blackwell Guide to Philosophy of Law and Legal Theory*, ed. Martin Golding and William Edmundson. Oxford, UK: Blackwell.

Lewin, Kurt. 1951. *Field Theory in Social Science: Selected Theoretical Papers*. New York: Harper & Brothers Publishers.

Lindquist, Stefanie A., and David E. Klein. 2003. "The Influence of the Solicitor General: Evaluating Jurisprudential, Institutional and Attitudinal Effects in

Conflicts Cases." Paper Presented at the Annual Meeting of the American Political Science Association, Philadelphia.

Lindquist, Stefanie A., and David E. Klein. 2006. "The Influence of Jurisprudential Considerations on Supreme Court Decisionmaking: A Study of Conflict Cases." *Law and Society Review* 40(1): 135–161.

Llewellyn, Karl. 1931. "Some Realism About Realism—Responding to Dean Pound." *Harvard Law Review* 44(8): 1222–1264.

Long, Caroline. 2006. *Mapp v. Ohio: Guarding Against Unreasonable Searches and Seizures.* Lawrence, KS: University Press of Kansas.

Lord, Charles G., Mark R. Lepper, and Elizabeth Preston. 1984. "Considering the Opposite: A Corrective Strategy for Social Judgment." *Journal of Personality and Social Psychology* 47(6): 1231–1243.

Lord, Charles G., Lee Ross, and Mark R. Lepper. 1979. "Biased Assimilation and Attitude Polarization: The Effects of Prior Theories on Subsequently Considered Evidence." *Journal of Personality and Social Psychology* 37(11): 2098–2109.

Lowery, David. 2007. "Why Do Organized Interests Lobby? A Multi-Goal, Multi-Context Theory of Lobbying." *Polity* 39(1): 29–54.

Lowery, David, and Virginia Gray. 2004. "Bias in the Heavenly Chorus: Interests in Society and Before Government." *Journal of Theoretical Politics* 16(1): 5–29.

Lowman, Michael K. 1992. "The Litigating Amicus Curiae: When Does the Party Begin After the Friends Leave?" *American University Law Review* 41(4): 1243–1299.

Lynch, Kelly J. 2004. "Best Friends? Supreme Court Law Clerks on Effective Amicus Curiae Briefs." *Journal of Law and Politics* 20(1): 33–75.

MacIver, R. M. 1937. "Interests." In *Encyclopedia of the Social Sciences, Volume 7,* ed. Edwin R. A. Seligman. New York: Macmillan.

Madison, James. [1787–1788] 1982. *The Federalist 10 and 51,* ed. Garry Wills. New York: Bantam Books.

Malhotra, Naresh K. 1984. "Reflections on the Information Overload Paradigm in Consumer Decision Making." *Journal of Consumer Research* 10(4): 436–41.

Maltzman, Forrest, James F. Spriggs, II, and Paul J. Wahlbeck. 2000. *Crafting Law on the Supreme Court: The Collegial Game.* Cambridge, UK: Cambridge University Press.

Manz, William H. 2002. "Citations in Supreme Court Opinions and Briefs: A Comparative Study." *Law Library Journal* 94(2): 267–300.

March, James G., and Johan P. Olsen. 1984. "The New Institutionalism: Organizational Factors in Political Life." *American Political Science Review* 78(3): 734–749.

Markovits, Richard S. 1998. *Matters of Principle: Legitimate Legal Argument and Constitutional Interpretation.* New York: New York University Press.

Martin, Andrew D., and Kevin M. Quinn. 2002. "Dynamic Ideal Point Estimation via Markov Chain Monte Carlo for the U.S. Supreme Court, 1953–1999." *Political Analysis* 10(2):134–153.

Martin, Andrew D., Kevin M. Quinn, and Lee Epstein. 2005. "The Median Justice on the U.S. Supreme Court." *North Carolina Law Review* 83(5): 1275–1322.

Martinek, Wendy L. 2007. "Amici Curiae in the U.S. Courts of Appeals." *American Politics Research* 34(6): 803–824.

Mauro, Tony. 2007. "Business Community, ACLU Share Distaste for Higher Court Rule Changes." *Legal Times*, June 13.

McAtee, Andrea, and Kevin T. McGuire. 2007. "Lawyers, Justices, and Issue Salience: When and How Do Legal Arguments Affect the U.S. Supreme Court?" *Law and Society Review* 41(2): 259–278.

McDonald, R. Robin. 2006. "Justice Thomas Opens Up on 'Aggressive' Appellate Judges." *Fulton County Daily Report*, October 27. Available at: http://www.law.com/jsp/article.jsp?id=1161853523009&rss=newswire.

McGuire, Kevin T. 1990. "Obscenity, Libertarian Values and Decision Making in the Supreme Court." *American Politics Quarterly* 18(1): 47–67.

McGuire, Kevin T. 1995. "Repeat Players in the Supreme Court: The Role of Experienced Lawyers in Litigation Success." *Journal of Politics* 57(1): 187–196.

McGuire, Kevin T. 1998. "Explaining Executive Success in the U.S. Supreme Court." *Political Research Quarterly* 51(2): 505–526.

McGuire, Kevin T. 2002. *Understanding the U.S. Supreme Court: Cases and Controversies.* New York: McGraw-Hill.

McGuire, Kevin T., and James A. Stimson. 2004. "The Least Dangerous Branch Revisited: New Evidence on Supreme Court Responsiveness to Public Preferences." *Journal of Politics* 66(4): 1018–1035.

McLauchlan, Judithanne Scourfield. 2005. *Congressional Participation as* Amicus Curiae *Before the U.S. Supreme Court.* New York: LFB Scholarly Publishing.

Mendelson, Wallace. 1963. "The Neo-Behavioral Approach to the Judicial Process: A Critique." *American Political Science Review* 57(3): 593–603.

Mero, Neal P. 2007. "Accountability in a Performance Appraisal Context: The Effect of Audience and Form of Accounting on Rater Response and Behavior." *Journal of Management* 33(2): 223–252.

Merrill, Thomas W. 2003. "The Making of the Second Rehnquist Court: A Preliminary Analysis." *Saint Louis University Law Journal* 47(3): 569–658.

Miles, Thomas J., and Cass R. Sunstein. 2006. "Do Judges Make Regulatory Policy? An Empirical Investigation of *Chevron*." *University of Chicago Law Review* 73(3): 823–881.

Millburn, Thomas W., and Robert S. Billings. 1976. "Decision-Making Perspectives from Psychology: Dealing with Risk and Uncertainty." *American Behavioral Scientist* 20(1): 111–126.

Miller, Norman, and Debbra E. Colman. 1981. "Methodological Issues in Analyzing the Cognitive Mediation of Persuasion." In *Cognitive Responses in Persuasion*, ed. Richard E. Petty, Thomas M. Ostrom, and Timothy C. Brock. Hillsdale, NJ: Lawrence Erlbaum Associates.

Mishler, William, and Reginald S. Sheehan. 1993. "The Supreme Court as a Countermajoritarian Institution? The Impact of Public Opinion on Supreme Court Decisions." *American Political Science Review* 87(1): 87–101.

Moe, Terry M. 1980. *The Organization of Interests: Incentives and the Internal Dynamics of Political Interest Groups*. Chicago: University of Chicago Press.

Moorman, Anita M., and Lisa Pike Masteralexis. 2001. "Writing an Amicus Curiae Brief to the United States Supreme Court, *PGA Tour, Inc. v. Martin*: The Role of the Disability Sport Community in Interpreting the Americans with Disabilities Act." *Journal of Legal Aspects of Sport* 11(3): 285–315.

Morris, Thomas R. 1987. "States Before the U.S. Supreme Court: State Attorneys General as Amicus Curiae." *Judicature* 70(5): 298–306.

Morriss, Andrew P. 1999. "Private Amici Curiae and the Supreme Court's 1997–1998 Term Employment Law Jurisprudence." *William and Mary Bill of Rights Journal* 7(3): 823–911.

Murphy, Walter F. 1964. *Elements of Judicial Strategy*. Chicago: University of Chicago Press.

Nicholson, Chris, and Paul M. Collins, Jr. 2008 "The Solicitor General's Amicus Curiae Strategies in the Supreme Court." *American Politics Research* 36(3): 382–415.

Nicholson-Crotty, Sean. 2007. "State Merit Amicus Participation and Federalism Outcomes in the U.S. Supreme Court." *Publius: The Journal of Federalism* 37(4): 599–612.

O'Connor, Karen. 1980. *Women's Organizations' Use of the Courts*. Lexington, MA: Lexington Books.

O'Connor, Karen, and Lee Epstein. 1982a. "The Importance of Interest Group Involvement in Employment Discrimination Litigation." *Howard Law Journal* 25(4): 709–729.

O'Connor, Karen, and Lee Epstein. 1982b. "Amicus Participation in the U.S. Supreme Court: An Appraisal of Hackman's Folklore." *Law and Society Review* 16(2): 311–320.

O'Connor, Karen, and Lee Epstein. 1983a. "Court Rules and Workload: A Case Study of Rules Governing Amicus Curiae Participation." *Justice System Journal* 8(1): 35–45.

O'Connor, Karen, and Lee Epstein. 1983b. "The Rise of Conservative Interest Group Litigation." *Journal of Politics* 45(2): 479–489.

O'Connor, Sandra Day. 1996. "Henry Clay and the Supreme Court." Speech Delivered to the Henry Clay Memorial Foundation October 4. Available at: http://www.henryclay.org/sc.htm.

O'Connor, Sandra Day. 2003. *The Majesty of the Law: Reflections of a Supreme Court Justice*. New York: Random House.

Olson, Mancur. 1965. *The Logic of Collective Action: Public Goods and the Theory of Groups*. Cambridge, MA: Harvard University Press.

Olson, Susan M. 1990. "Interest-Group Litigation in Federal District Court: Beyond the Political Disadvantage Theory." *Journal of Politics* 52(3): 854–882.

O'Neill, Timothy J. 1985. *Bakke & the Politics of Equality: Friends and Foes in the Classroom of Litigation.* Middletown, CT: Wesleyan University Press.

Pacelle, Richard L., Jr. 1991. *The Transformation of the Supreme Court's Agenda: From the New Deal to the Reagan Administration.* Boulder, CO: Westview Press.

Pacelle, Richard, and Patricia Pauly. 1996. "The Freshman Effect Revisited: An Individual-Based Analysis." *American Review of Politics* 17(1): 1–22.

Pampel, Fred C. 2000. *Logistic Regression: A Primer.* Thousand Oaks, CA: Sage Publications.

Park, C. Whan, and Daniel C. Smith. 1989. "Product-Level Choice: A Top-Down or Bottom-Up Process?" *Journal of Consumer Research* 16(3): 289–299.

Parker, Frederick R., Jr. 1999. "*Washington v. Glucksberg* and *Vacco v. Quill*: An Analysis of the Amicus Curiae Briefs and the Supreme Court's Majority and Concurring Opinions." *Saint Louis University Law Journal* 43(2): 469–542.

Peltason, Jack W. 1955. *Federal Courts in the Political Process.* New York: Doubleday.

Perry, H. W., Jr. 1991. *Deciding to Decide: Agenda Setting in the United States Supreme Court.* Cambridge, MA: Harvard University Press.

Peterson, Mark A. 1992. "The Presidency and Organized Interests: White House Patterns of Interest Group Liaison." *American Political Science Review* 86(3): 612–625.

Petracca, Mark P. 1992. *The Politics of Interests: Interest Groups Transformed.* Boulder, CO: Westview Press.

Petty, Richard E., Thomas M. Ostrom, and Timothy C. Brock, eds. 1981. *Cognitive Responses in Persuasion.* Hillsdale, NJ: Lawrence Erlbaum Associates.

Pfeffer, Leo. 1981. "Amici in Church-State Litigation." *Law and Contemporary Problems* 44(2): 83–110.

Pinello, Daniel R. 2006. *America's Struggle for Same-Sex Marriage.* New York: Cambridge University Press.

Piven, Frances Fox, and Richard A. Cloward. 1977. *Poor People's Movements: Why They Succeed, How They Fail.* New York: Pantheon Books.

Posavac, Steven S., David M. Sanbonmatsu, and Russell H. Fazio. 1997. "Considering the Best Choice: Effects of the Salience and Accessibility of Alternatives on Attitude-Decision Consistency." *Journal of Personality and Social Psychology* 72(2): 253–261.

Posner, Richard A. 1973. *Economic Analysis of Law.* Boston: Little Brown.

Posner, Richard A. 1995. *Overcoming Law.* Cambridge, MA: Harvard University Press.

Pound, Roscoe. 1908. "Mechanical Jurisprudence." *Columbia Law Review* 8(8): 605–623.

Powell, Thomas R. 1917. "The Constitutional Issue in Minimum-Wage Legislation." *Minnesota Law Review* 2(1): 1–21.

Powell, Thomas R. 1924. "The Judiciality of Minimum-Wage Legislation." *Harvard Law Review* 37(5): 545–573.

Pritchett, C. Herman. 1948. *The Roosevelt Court: A Study in Judicial Politics and Values, 1937–1947*. New York: Macmillan.

Pritchett, C. Herman. 1969. "The Development of Judicial Research." In *Frontiers of Judicial Research*, ed. Joel B. Grossman and Joseph Tanenhaus. New York: John Wiley and Sons.

Puro, Steven. 1971. "The Role of Amicus Curiae in the United States Supreme Court: 1920–1966." Ph.D. Dissertation. Department of Political Science, State University of New York at Buffalo.

Ray, Laura Krugman. 1990. "The Justices Write Separately: Uses of the Concurrence by the Rehnquist Court." *University of California Davis Law Review* 23(4): 777–831.

Reynolds, Henry T. 1984. *Analysis of Nominal Data*. Newbury Park, CA: Sage Publications.

Richards, Mark J., and Herbert M. Kritzer. 2002. "Jurisprudential Regimes in Supreme Court Decision Making." *American Political Science Review* 96(2): 305–320.

Robertson, Roby D. 1980. "Small Group Decision Making: The Uncertain Role of Information in Reducing Uncertainty." *Political Behavior* 2(2): 163–188.

Roesch, Ronald, Stephen L. Golding, Valerie P. Hans, and N. Dickon Reppucci. 1991. "Social Science and the Courts: The Role of Amicus Curiae Briefs." *Law and Human Behavior* 15(1): 1–11.

Rohde, David W., and Harold J. Spaeth. 1976. *Supreme Court Decision Making*. San Francisco: W.H. Freeman & Co. Ltd.

Rosenberg, Gerald N. 2000. "Across the Great Divide (Between Law and Political Science)." *Green Bag* 3(Spring): 267–272.

Ross, Douglas, and Michael W. Catalano. 1988. "How State and Local Governments Fared in the United States Supreme Court for the Past Five Terms." *The Urban Lawyer* 20(2): 341–352.

Rumble, Wilfrid E., Jr. 1968. *American Legal Realism: Skepticism, Reform, and the Judicial Process*. Ithaca, NY: Cornell University Press.

Rushin, Robert, and Karen O'Connor. 1987. "Judicial Lobbying: Interest Groups, the Supreme Court and Issues of Freedom of Expression and Speech." *Southeastern Political Review* 15(1): 47–65.

Rustad, Michael, and Thomas Koenig. 1993. "The Supreme Court and Junk Social Science: Selective Distortion in Amicus Briefs." *North Carolina Law Review* 72(1): 91–162.

Salisbury, Robert H. 1984. "Interest Representation: The Dominance of Institutions." *American Political Science Review* 78(1): 64–76.

Salokar, Rebecca Mae. 1992. *The Solicitor General: The Politics of Law*. Philadelphia, PA: Temple University Press.

Samuels, Suzanne Uttaro. 1995. "Amici Curiae and the Supreme Court's Review of Fetal Protection Policies." *Judicature* 78(5): 236–241.

Samuels, Suzanne Uttaro. 2004. *First among Friends: Interest Groups, the U.S. Supreme Court, and the Right to Privacy.* Westport, CT: Praeger Publishers.

Sartori, Giovanni. 1970. "Concept Misformation in Comparative Politics." *American Political Science Review* 64(4): 1033–1053.

Scalia, Antonin. 1994. "The Dissenting Opinion." *Journal of Supreme Court History* 1994: 33–44.

Schattschneider, E. E. 1960. *The Semisovereign People: A Realist's View of Democracy in America.* New York: Holt, Rinehart, and Winston.

Scheppele, Kim Lane, and Jack L. Walker. 1991. "The Litigation Strategies of Interest Groups." In *Mobilizing Interest Groups in America: Patrons, Professions, and Social Movements,* ed. Jack L. Walker. Ann Arbor, MI: University of Michigan Press.

Scherer, Nancy. 2005. *Scoring Points: Politicians, Activists, and the Lower Federal Court Appointment Process.* Stanford, CA: Stanford University Press.

Schlozman, Kay Lehman, and John T. Tierney. 1983. "More of the Same: Washington Pressure Group Activity in a Decade of Change." *Journal of Politics* 45(2): 351–377.

Schlozman, Kay Lehman, and John T. Tierney. 1986. *Organized Interests and American Democracy.* New York: Harper and Row.

Schmidt, Patrick D., and David A. Yalof. 2004. "The 'Swing Voter' Revisited: Justice Anthony Kennedy and the First Amendment Right of Free Speech." *Political Research Quarterly* 57(2): 209–217.

Schubert, Glendon A. 1959. *Quantitative Analysis of Judicial Behavior.* Glencoe, IL: Free Press.

Schubert, Glendon A. 1965. *The Judicial Mind: The Attitudes and Ideologies of Supreme Court Justices, 1946–1963.* New York: Free Press.

Schubert, Glendon A. 1974. *The Judicial Mind Revisited.* New York: Oxford University Press.

Schubert, James N., Steven A. Peterson, Glendon A. Schubert, and Stephen Wasby. 1992. "Observing Supreme Court Oral Argument: A Biosocial Approach." *Politics and the Life Sciences* 11(February): 35–51.

Schwartz, Harold I., and Robert Boland. 1995. "Using Science to Influence the Supreme Court on the Right to Refuse Treatment: *Amicus Curiae* Briefs in *Washington v. Harper.*" *Bulletin of the American Academy of Psychiatry and the Law* 23(1): 135–146.

Sebok, Anthony J. 1998. *Legal Positivism in American Jurisprudence.* Cambridge, UK: Cambridge University Press.

Segal, Jeffrey A. 1986. "Supreme Court Justices as Human Decision Makers: An Individual-Level Analysis of the Search and Seizure Cases." *Journal of Politics* 48(4): 938–955.

Segal, Jeffrey A. 1988. "Amicus Curiae Briefs by the Solicitor General During the Warren and Burger Courts: A Research Note." *Western Political Quarterly* 41(1): 135–144.

Segal, Jeffrey A. 1997. "Separation-of-Powers Games in the Positive Theory of Congress and Courts." *American Political Science Review* 91(1): 28–44.

Segal, Jeffrey A., and Albert D. Cover. 1989. "Ideological Values and the Votes of U. S. Supreme Court Justices." *American Political Science Review* 83(2): 557–565.

Segal, Jeffrey A., Lee Epstein, Charles M. Cameron, and Harold J. Spaeth. 1995. "Ideological Values and the Votes of U.S. Supreme Court Justices Revisited." *Journal of Politics* 57(3): 812–823.

Segal, Jeffrey A., and Harold J. Spaeth. 1993. *The Supreme Court and the Attitudinal Model.* Cambridge, UK: Cambridge University Press.

Segal, Jeffrey A., and Harold J. Spaeth. 1994. "The Authors Respond." *Law and Courts* 4(1): 10–12.

Segal, Jeffrey A., and Harold J. Spaeth. 1996. "The Influence of Stare Decisis on the Votes of United States Supreme Court Justices." *American Journal of Political Science* 40(4): 971–1003.

Segal, Jeffrey A., and Harold J. Spaeth. 2002. *The Supreme Court and the Attitudinal Model Revisited.* Cambridge, UK: Cambridge University Press.

Segal, Jeffrey A., Harold J. Spaeth, and Sara C. Benesh. 2005. *The Supreme Court in the American Legal System.* New York: Cambridge University Press.

Severin, Werner J., and James W. Tankard. 1997. *Communication Theories: Origins, Methods, and Uses in the Mass Media.* New York: Longman.

Shapiro, Martin M. 1964. *Law and Politics in the Supreme Court: New Approaches to Political Jurisprudence.* London, NY: Free Press of Glencoe.

Shavell, Steven. 1995. "The Appeals Process as a Means of Error Correction." *Journal of Legal Studies* 24(2): 379–426.

Sheehan, Reginald S., William Mishler, and Donald R. Songer. 1992. "Ideology, Status and the Differential Success of Direct Parties Before the Supreme Court." *American Political Science Review* 86(2): 464–471.

Simon, Dan. 1998. "A Psychological Model of Judicial Decision Making." *Rutgers Law Journal* 30(1): 1–142.

Simon, Dan, Chadwick J. Snow, and Stephen J. Read. 2004. "The Redux of Cognitive Consistency Theories: Evidence Judgments by Constraint Satisfaction." *Journal of Personality and Social Psychology* 86(6): 814–837.

Simon, Herbert A. 1979. "Information Processing Models of Cognition." *Annual Review of Psychology* 1979(30): 363–396.

Smith, Gary F., and Beth E. Terrell. 1995. "The Amicus Curiae: A Powerful Friend for Poverty Law Advocates." *Clearinghouse Review* 29(November–December): 772–792.

Smyth, Russell, and Parish Kumar Narayan. 2006. "Multiple Regime Shifts in Concurring and Dissenting Opinions on the U.S. Supreme Court." *Journal of Empirical Legal Studies* 3(1): 79–98.

Snyder, Eloise C. 1958. "The Supreme Court as a Small Group." *Social Forces* 36(3): 232–238.

Snyder, Eloise C. 1959. "Uncertainty and the Supreme Court's Decisions." *American Journal of Sociology* 65(3): 241–245.

Solowiej, Lisa A., and Paul M. Collins, Jr. 2008. "Counteractive Lobbying in the U.S. Supreme Court." Paper Presented at the Annual Meeting of the Southern Political Science Association, New Orleans.

Songer, Donald R., and Susan Haire. 1992. "Integrating Alternative Approaches to the Study of Judicial Voting: Obscenity Cases in the U.S. Courts of Appeals." *American Journal of Political Science* 36(4): 963–982.

Songer, Donald R., Ashlyn Kuersten, and Erin Kaheny. 2000. "Why the Haves Don't Always Come Out Ahead: Repeat Players Meet Amici Curiae for the Disadvantaged." *Political Research Quarterly* 53(3): 537–556.

Songer, Donald R., and Reginald S. Sheehan. 1990. "Supreme Court Impact on Compliance and Outcomes: *Miranda* and *New York Times* in the United States Courts of Appeals." *Western Political Quarterly* 43(2): 297–316.

Songer, Donald R., and Reginald S. Sheehan. 1992. "Who Wins on Appeal? Upperdogs and Underdogs in the United States Courts of Appeals." *American Journal of Political Science* 36(1): 235–258.

Songer, Donald R., and Reginald S. Sheehan. 1993. "Interest Group Success in the Courts: Amicus Participation in the Supreme Court." *Political Research Quarterly* 46(2): 339–354.

Songer, Donald R., Jeffrey A. Segal, and Charles M. Cameron. 1994. "The Hierarchy of Justice: Testing a Principal-Agent Model of Supreme Court-Circuit Court Interactions." *American Journal of Political Science* 38(3): 673–696.

Spaeth, Harold J. 2002. *The Vinson-Warren Supreme Court Judicial Database, 1946–1968 Terms.* East Lansing, MI: Department of Political Science, Michigan State University. Available at: http://web.as.uky.edu/polisci/ulmerproject/sct-data.htm.

Spaeth, Harold J. 2003. *The Original United States Supreme Court Database, 1953–2004 Terms.* East Lansing, MI: Department of Political Science, Michigan State University. Available at: http://web.as.uky.edu/polisci/ulmer-project/sctdata.htm.

Spaeth, Harold J. 2005. "Chief Justice Rehnquist: 'Poster Child' for the Attitudinal Model." *Judicature* 89(3): 108–115.

Spaeth, Harold J. 2007. *The Original United States Supreme Court Database, 1953–2006 Terms.* East Lansing, MI: Department of Political Science, Michigan State University. Available at: http://web.as.uky.edu/polisci/ulmerproject/sct-data.htm.

Spaeth, Harold J., and Jeffrey A. Segal. 1999. *Majority Rule or Minority Will: Adherence to Precedent on the U.S. Supreme Court.* Cambridge, UK: Cambridge University Press.

Spriggs, James F., II. 1996. "The Supreme Court and Federal Administrative Agencies: A Resource-Based Theory and Analysis of Judicial Impact." *American Journal of Political Science* 40(4): 1122–1151.

Spriggs, James F., II. 2003. "The Attitudinal Model: An Explanation of Case Dispositions, Not Substantive Policy Outcomes." *Law and Courts* 13(3): 23–26.

Spriggs, James F., II, and Thomas G. Hansford. 2001. "Explaining the Overruling of U.S. Supreme Court Precedent." *Journal of Politics* 63(4): 1091–1111.

Spriggs, James F., II, and Paul J. Wahlbeck. 1997. "Amicus Curiae and the Role of Information at the Supreme Court." *Political Research Quarterly* 50(3): 365–386.

Stern, Robert L., Eugene Gressman, Stephen M. Shapiro, and Kenneth S. Geller. 2002. *Supreme Court Practice: For Practice in the Supreme Court of the United States*. 8th ed. Washington, DC: Bureau of National Affairs.

Stewart, Potter. 1983. "The Road to *Mapp v. Ohio* and Beyond: The Origins, Development and Future of the Exclusionary Rule in Search-and-Seizure Cases." *Columbia Law Review* 83(6): 1365–1404.

Stimson, James A., Michael B. MacKuen, and Robert S. Erikson. 1995. "Dynamic Representation." *American Political Science Review* 89(3): 543–565.

Strolovitch, Dara Z. 2006. "Do Interest Groups Represent the Disadvantaged? Advocacy at the Intersections of Race, Class, and Gender." *Journal of Politics* 68(4): 894–910.

Stumpf, Harry P. 1998. *American Judicial Politics*. 2nd ed. Upper Saddle River, NJ: Prentice Hall.

Sungaila, Mary-Christine. 1999. "Effective Amicus Practice Before the United States Supreme Court: A Case Study." *Southern California Review of Law and Women's Studies* 8(2): 187–196.

Sunstein, Cass R., David Schkade, Lisa M. Ellman, and Andres Sawicki. 2006. *Are Judges Political? An Empirical Analysis of the Federal Judiciary*. Washington, DC: Brookings Institution Press.

Tai, Stephanie. 2000. "Friendly Science: Medical, Scientific, and Technical Amici Before the Supreme Court." *Washington University Law Quarterly* 78(3): 789–930.

Tamanaha, Brian Z. 2006. *Law as a Means to an End: Threat to the Rule of Law*. Cambridge, UK: Cambridge University Press.

Tamanaha, Brian Z. 2007. "The Realism of the 'Formalist' Age." St. John's Legal Studies Research Paper No. 06-0073. Available at SSRN: http://ssrn.com/abstract=985083.

Tanenhaus, Joseph, Marvin Schick, Matthew Muraskin, and Daniel Rosen. 1963. "The Supreme Court's Certiorari Jurisdiction: Cue Theory." In *Judicial Decision-Making*, ed. Glendon A. Schubert. New York: Free Press.

Tetlock, Philip E., and Jae Il Kim. 1987. "Accountability and Judgment Process in a Personality Prediction Task." *Journal of Personality and Social Psychology* 52(4): 700–709.

Traut, Carol Ann, and Craig F. Emmert. 1998. "Expanding the Integrated Model of Judicial Decision Making: The California Justices and Capital Punishment." *Journal of Politics* 60(4): 1166–1180.

Tremper, Charles R. 1987. "Organized Psychology's Efforts to Influence Judicial Policy-Making." *American Psychologist* 42(5): 496–501.

Truman, David B. 1951. *The Governmental Process: Political Interests and Public Opinion.* New York: Knopf.

Ulmer, S. Sidney. 1984. "The Supreme Court's Certiorari Decisions: Conflict as a Predictive Variable." *American Political Science Review* 78(4): 901–911.

Unah, Isaac, and Ange-Marie Hancock. 2006. "U.S. Supreme Court Decision Making, Case Salience, and the Attitudinal Model." *Law and Policy* 28(3): 295–320.

Vigilante, Katherine O'Harra, Virginia Hettinger, and Christopher Zorn. 2001. "Legal Arguments and Supreme Court Decision Making: An Experimental Approach." Paper Presented at the Annual Meeting of the Midwest Political Science Association, Chicago.

Vose, Clement E. 1955. "NAACP Strategy in the Covenant Cases." *Case Western Reserve Law Review* 6(2): 101–145.

Vose, Clement E. 1958. "Litigation as a Form of Pressure Group Activity." *Annals of the American Academy of Political and Social Science* 319(September): 20–31.

Vose, Clement E. 1959. *Caucasians Only: The Supreme Court, the N.A.A.C.P., and the Restrictive Covenant Cases.* Berkeley, CA: University of California Press.

Wagner, Frank D. 2001. "The Role of the Supreme Court Reporter in History." *Journal of Supreme Court History* 29(1): 1–23.

Wahlbeck, Paul J., James F. Spriggs, II, and Forrest Maltzman. 1999. "The Politics of Dissents and Concurrences on the U.S. Supreme Court." *American Politics Quarterly* 27(4): 488–514.

Walker, Thomas G., and Lee Epstein. 1993. *The Supreme Court of the United States: An Introduction.* New York: St. Martin's Press.

Walker, Thomas G., Lee Epstein, and William J. Dixon. 1988. "On the Mysterious Demise of Consensual Norms in the United States Supreme Court." *Journal of Politics* 50(2): 361–389.

Ward, Stephanie Francis. 2007. "Friends of the Court Are Friends of Mine." *ABA Journal* November. Available at: http://www.abajournal.com/magazine/friends_of_the_court_are_friends_of_mine/.

Wasby, Stephen L. 1995. *Race Relations Litigation in an Age of Complexity.* Charlottesville, VA: University of Virginia Press.

Waxman, Seth P. 1998. "Presenting the Case of the United States as it Should Be: The Solicitor General in Historical Context." June 1, 1998. Address to the Supreme Court Historical Society. Available at: www.usdoj.gov/osg/aboutosg/sgarticle.html.

Wheeler, Stanton, Bliss Cartwright, Robert A. Kagan, and Lawrence M. Friedman. 1987. "Do the 'Haves' Come Out Ahead? Winning and Losing in State Supreme Courts, 1870–1970." *Law and Society Review* 21(3): 403–446.

Whittington, Keith E. 2000. "Once More Unto the Breach: Post Behavioralist Approaches to Judicial Politics." *Law and Social Inquiry* 25(2): 601–634.

Wicker, Allan W. 1969. "Attitudes versus Actions: The Relationship of Verbal and Overt Behavioral Responses to Attitude Objects." *Journal of Social Issues* 25(4): 41–78.

Wohl, Alexander. 1996. "Friends with Agendas: Amicus Curiae Briefs May be More Popular Than Persuasive." *American Bar Association Journal* 82 (November): 46–50.

Wolfe, Jeremy M., Serena J. Butcher, Carol Lee, and Megan Hyle. 2003. "Changing Your Mind: On the Contributions of Top-Down and Bottom-Up Guidance in Visual Search for Feature Singletons." *Journal of Experimental Psychology: Human Perception and Performance* 29(2): 483–502.

Woodward, Bob, and Scott Armstrong. 1979. *The Brethren: Inside the Supreme Court.* New York: Simon and Schuster.

Wright, John R. 1989. "PAC Contributions, Lobbying, and Representation." *Journal of Politics* 51(3): 713–729.

Wright, John R. 2003. *Interest Groups and Congress: Lobbying, Contributions, and Influence.* New York: Longman.

Wrightsman, Lawrence S. 1999. *Judicial Decision Making: Is Psychology Relevant?* New York: Kluwer Academic.

Wrightsman, Lawrence S. 2006. *The Psychology of the Supreme Court.* Oxford, UK: Oxford University Press.

Yackee, Jason Webb, and Susan Webb Yackee. 2006. "A Bias Towards Business? Assessing Interest Group Influence on the U.S. Bureaucracy." *Journal of Politics* 68(1): 128–139.

Yates, Jeff. 2002. *Popular Justice: Presidential Prestige and Executive Success in the Supreme Court.* Albany, NY: State University of New York Press.

Yntema, Hessel E. 1934. "Legal Science and Reform." *Columbia Law Review* 34(2): 207–229.

Zorn, Christopher. 2002. "U.S. Government Litigation Strategies in the Federal Appellate Courts." *Political Research Quarterly* 55(1): 145–166.

TABLE OF CASES

INDEX

Note to Index: An *f* following a page number indicates a figure on that page; an *n* after a page number indicates a note on that page; a *t* following a page number indicates a table on that page.